Taking Issue

COMPANION VOLUME

The companion volume in this series is:
Telling Tales: Perspectives on Guidance and Counselling in Learning
Edited by Richard Edwards, Roger Harrison and Alan Tait.

Both of these Readers are part of a course, Guidance and Counselling in Learning, that is itself part of The Open University MA Programme.

THE OPEN UNIVERSITY MA IN EDUCATION

The Open University MA in Education is now firmly established as the most popular post-graduate degree for education professionals in Europe, with over 3,500 students registering each year. The MA in Education is designed particularly for those with experience of teaching, the advisory service, educational administration or allied fields.

Structure of the MA

The MA is a modular degree, and students are therefore free to select from a range of options the programme which best fits in with their interests and professional goals. Specialist lines in management, primary education and lifelong learning are also available. Study in The Open University's Advanced Diploma can also be counted towards the MA, and successful study in the MA programme entitles students to apply for entry into The Open University Doctorate in Education programme.

COURSES CURRENTLY AVAILABLE:

- Management
- Child Development
- Primary Education
- Learning, Curriculum and Assessment
- Special Needs
- Language and Literacy
- Mentoring

- Education Training and Employment
- Gender
- Educational Research
- Science Education
- Adult Learners
- Maths Education
- Guidance and Counselling in Learning

OU supported open learning

The MA in Education programme provides great flexibility. Students study at their own pace, in their own time, anywhere in the European Union. They receive specially prepared study materials, supported by tutorials, thus offering the chance to work with other students.

The Doctorate in Education

The Doctorate in Education is a new part-time doctoral degree, combining taught courses, research methods and a dissertation designed to meet the needs of professionals in education and related areas who are seeking to extend and deepen their knowledge and understanding of contemporary educational issues. It should help them to:

- develop appropriate skills in educational research and enquiry
- carry out research in order to contribute to professional knowledge and practice.

The Doctorate in Education builds upon successful study within the Open University MA in Education programme.

How to apply

If you would like to register for this programme, or simply to find out more information, please write for the *Professional Development in Education* prospectus to the Course Reservations Centre, PO Box 724, The Open University, Walton Hall, Milton Keynes, MK7 6ZS, UK (Telephone 0 [0 44]1908 653231).

Taking Issue

Debates in guidance and
counselling in learning

Edited by
Megan Crawford,
Richard Edwards
and Lesley Kydd
at The Open University

London and New York
in association with
The Open University

First published 1998
by Routledge
11 New Fetter Lane, London EC4P 4EE

Simultaneously published in the USA and Canada
by Routledge
29 West 35th Street, New York, NY 10001

Typeset in Garamond by The Florence Group, Stoodleigh, Devon
Printed and bound in Great Britain by Page Brothers (Norwich) Ltd

British Library Cataloguing in Publication Data
A catalogue record for this book is available
from the British Library

Library of Congress Cataloging in Publication Data
Taking issue: debates in guidance and counselling in learning/
  [edited by] Megan Crawford, Richard Edwards, and Lesley Kydd.
  Includes bibliographical references and index.
  1. Educational counselling – Moral and ethical aspects –
  Great Britain. 2. Counseling – Moral and ethical aspects –
  Great Britain. 3. Students – Services for – Great Britain.
  I. Crawford, Megan, 1957– . II. Edwards, Richard, 1956– .
  III. Kydd, Lesley, 1950– ,
LB1027.5.T326 1998   98–17804 CIP

ISBN 0–415–19667–1

Contents

PART II
Modes of delivery   75

PART III
Accessibility, client-centredness and impartiality   153

Figures

Acknowledgements

While the publishers have made every effort to contact copyright holders of previously published material in this volume, they would be grateful to hear from any they were unable to contact.

Chapter 1 Bond, T. (1992) 'Ethical issues in counselling in education', in *British Journal of Guidance and Counselling*, 20, 1: 51–63.

Chapter 2 Carroll, M. (1996) 'Ethical issues in workplace counselling', in *Workplace Counselling*, Chapter 8, London: Sage.

Chapter 3 Bailey, D. (1993) 'Gender and educational guidance: questions of feminist practice', in *British Journal of Guidance and Counselling*, 21, 2: 161–74.

Chapter 4 Meijers, F. and Piggott, C. (1995) 'Careers guidance and ethnic minorities in Holland and Britain', in *British Journal of Guidance and Counselling*, 23, 1: 53–67.

Chapter 6 Earwaker, J. (1992) 'The tutorial relationship', in *Helping and Supporting Students*, Chapter 6, Buckingham: The Open University Press.

Chapter 7 Ratigan, B. (1997) 'Counselling in groups', in *The Handbook of Counselling*, Chapter 6, London: Routledge.

Chapter 10 Hunt, M. (1994) 'The present and future use of IT to support guidance', in *The Future Use of Information Technology in Guidance*, Coventry: NCET.

Chapter 15 Rogers, C. (1983) 'The interpersonal relationship in the facilitation of learning', in *Freedom to Learn for the 80s*, Merril.

Chapter 16 Upton, G. (1993) 'Putting problems in context – the family and the school', in *Counselling in Schools: a Reader*, London: David Fulton.

Taking issue

Introducing debates in guidance and counselling in learning

Megan Crawford, Richard Edwards and Lesley Kydd

Providing guidance and counselling in different learning settings inevitably raises a wide range of issues and differing views about them. This book offers insights into some of the issues and, in particular, focuses on the dilemmas and complexities involved in attempting to adhere to the principles of 'good practice' in guidance and counselling in learning. By drawing together a range of chapters on a number of key issues within diverse settings, we hope to illustrate how, while many of these issues are defined and bounded by their context in particular ways, nonetheless they can help us to extend our knowledge and understanding of the complexity of practices. The book is divided into three parts, each of which deals with a different set of issues. The first part deals with issues of ethics and equity. The second examines issues surrounding different ways of providing guidance and counselling in learning. The third part addresses issues of accessibility, client-centredness and impartiality.

The book is arranged in this order because issues of ethics underpin all of the activities of guidance and counselling in learning. We are all familiar with guidance and counselling situations which present difficult decisions for the practitioner to make. Although we tend to practise within our own personal ethical code, increasingly we have to take account of recommendations for good practice contained in institutional guidelines as well as the codes of a number of professional organisations. Each of you will bring to the book your own particular codes of practice and varied experiences. We hope your responses to each chapter will lead you to challenge some of your own assumptions and beliefs about guidance and counselling to help you to develop as a practitioner.

For anyone who engages in guidance and counselling in learning, some of the most crucial issues relate to the ethics of practice. These are complex areas to explore, and as you practise, you will need to engage with the various dilemmas and tensions that may arise. As such, issues are invariably not straightforward and the answers may be more a clarification of an ethical dilemma than a clear answer to all situations which may arise. The readings in Part I explore different aspects of ethics and explore them in relation both to context and ways of working.

In Chapter 1, Tim Bond discusses the two distinct systems of ethics and practice used by counsellors in education in the UK, the integrated and the differentiated models. Issues relating to referral, confidentiality, accountability for resources, and the outcomes of counselling are discussed. The diversity of practice within educational settings makes this discussion a useful initial starting point. This is then expanded to examine ethical issues in workplace counselling by Michael Carroll in Chapter 2. He looks at how counsellors in the workplace are faced with unique ethical dilemmas while, at the same time, having to deal with similar problems to those discussed by Bond. The daily eventuality of coming across problems which require reference to ethical decision-making is stressed, as is the need for ethical 'antennae' to help frame them. He argues for employee counsellors to have a code of ethics specifically for workplace counselling.

It is often suggested that central to ethical practice is equitable practice. Yet what constitutes equity in guidance and counselling is open to debate. Diane Bailey raises questions in Chapter 3 about gender in relation to guidance and counselling in education. She looks at the difficulties associated with discourse theory, research on curriculum construction and therapeutic counselling and teases out the implications and questions for those involved. Gender is seen as one of the key ways in which culture is shaped, and therefore, has a great deal to tell us in terms of extending our guidance and counselling practices. Frans Meijers and Carrie Piggott (Chapter 4) frame equity issues in terms of the development of equal opportunities for minority ethnic groups through career guidance. Drawing on work from Holland and the UK, they look at emotional barriers both in relation to face-to-face client work and in terms of service development. The concept of 'career negotiation' is presented to reflect the process of internal and external dialogue needed to 'empower' clients. In Chapter 5, Jo Wiggans develops these dilemmas in relation to mentoring in higher education in the UK. The mentee/mentor relationship requires careful consideration of principles and ethics. Wiggans suggests that it is the 'ability of enabling relationships' that helps cut through barriers to learning. She discusses this in relation to minority groups. The chapters suggest that there is a distinction between adherence to codes of practice and practising ethically, with the latter always involving interpretation and judgement. They also suggest that formal adherence to equal opportunities does not really come to terms with the complexities of power and inequality in the provision of different forms of guidance and counselling in learning.

Part II discusses different forms of interaction and different settings for guidance and counselling. For example, in a one-to-one relationship or in a group; on the telephone or through electronic media. Your own experience may span a number of these areas. We explore the increasing use of group and distance strategies and their implications for practice. As you read, you will become more aware both of the benefits and the drawbacks of different ways of working. You may already have a personal preference, of course. New developments in technology mean that there are many and varied possibilities in using information and communication technologies in guidance and counselling. Technology may sometimes be mediated by a guidance worker, or such interactions may not have a direct human face. Its implications for the substance and practices of guidance and counselling have yet to be fully understood. Developing ways in which these new methods can best support users are challenging in themselves.

John Earwaker examines the one-to-one, face-to-face student/tutor relationship in UK higher education in Chapter 6. He outlines the unequal status between the tutor and the students and proposes that the key issue is one that is fundamental to all helping – of providing 'objectivity' to the student in order that they are able to manage their own learning. This one-to-one relationship can be contrasted with Bernard Rattigan's overview of group counselling as a process in Chapter 7 which highlights the theoretical and clinical perspectives of group counselling, as well as factors that add to the development of groups over time. Purpose and settings are brought to the fore and examined to see how these link in with the goals of the group. Ratigan suggests developments in training that are needed if group counselling is used, something which is of equal importance for those involved in group guidance.

The diversification of forms of interaction has been increasing in recent years with the developing use of forms of technology. In Chapter 8 by Judith George, guidance and counselling is mediated by the telephone. This raises a number of interesting issues since many of the non-verbal communication cues which we all use in face-to-face contact are not available. This does not mean, however, that the telephone is not a rich and relatively cheap means of providing effective guidance and counselling services. It is also worth remembering, as George points out, that the telephone is often the initial point of contact in conventional services as well as for distance learning organisations. This chapter highlights recent research into the area and provides an overview of good practice in using the telephone both for teaching and counselling purposes. Alan Tait's Chapter 9 follows the developments in guidance and counselling within a distance learning institution, the UK Open University. He traces shifting practices and philosophies, in particular, the movement from educational counselling to guidance and customer care. This illustrates how different ways of providing guidance and counselling are as much to do with context and institutional culture as they are with the forms of interaction adopted.

The use of information and communication technologies is set to have an increasing influence on the nature and substance of guidance and counselling in learning. In Chapter 10 Malcolm Hunt identifies the potential of this technology to influence the practice of guidance in education, and emphasises the pace of innovation in this field at the present time. Chapter 11 by

Marcus Offer looks at the growth in the use of information and technology in the field of careers education and guidance. He considers a number of important issues surrounding not only the use of such systems, but also the quantity and quality of the information which is now available. The use of computer systems and the internet raise a number of questions for practitioners of guidance and counselling. Offer suggests that the need to know how to operate these systems often obscures the 'real' questions which centre around the challenging area of re-evaluating roles for professional practitioners. For example, 'what is the role of professional guidance services when so much of what they offer can effectively be obtained via information technology direct to guidance seekers, now even in their own homes?'. Such questions are highly challenging, but also raise questions about accessibility and the nature of the process to which users are subject.

Part III explores some of the principles underpinning the delivery of guidance and counselling in practice. These are the questions first of the access of guidance and counselling services to particular groups in particular settings and their role in contributing to the accessibility of learning opportunities. Second, there are the debates surrounding client-centredness and the increasingly complex issue of maintaining impartiality in an environment which often leads into dilemmas about student retention and accountability. Once again, examining these issues demonstrates the complexity of practice, bounded as it is by such issues as setting, resources and the need to recruit and retain students.

Amy Blair and Lyn Tett report in Chapter 12 on access to guidance services for adult students in higher education in Scotland. They outline some of the changes and dilemmas which these services face, with an increased student population within which there is an increasing number of older adults. They suggest that higher education institutions may wish to develop guidance policies through a collaborative approach to policy-making. Similarly, in Chapter 13, Chris Watkins looks at the establishment of a 'whole-school' guidance policy as part of the provision of effective schooling in the UK. This provides a clear rationale for such a policy and an analysis of how guidance is made available to pupils through the curriculum, through tutorial groups and individually. Veronica McGivney (Chapter 14) discusses the relationship between motivation and the quality of guidance available for mature students in further and higher education in the UK. Her research indicates that retention rates are increased where students have access to good quality pre-entry and on-course guidance. She discusses the links between funding arrangements, student numbers and the need to maintain students in the system. The chapter draws attention to one of the dilemmas faced by many institutions in that good quality services are expensive to provide, but failure to provide them results in increased student attrition rates and that, in turn, means a loss of funding.

Motivation is also implicit in Carl Rogers' (Chapter 15) discussion of the interpersonal in the facilitation of learning. Rogers' humanistic psychology has been central to the development of client-centred approaches to guidance and counselling, and learner-centred approaches to teaching. He sees the goal of education as being the facilitation of change and the development of learning relationships through a specific 'human' form of interaction and a focus on the individual. Graham Upton argues, in Chapter 16, that such facilitation requires an 'ecosystemic' approach to students taking in the context of classroom, school, family and society. He suggests that behaviour problems in schools should be understood in terms of the interactions of all those involved. In other words, the problem is not in the person, but in their relationship to others and to their environment. The ecosystemic approach challenges the more traditional ways of locating behaviour problems within the individual, asking us to reframe our perceptions of the problem. Such reframings will lead to changes in how we react to and deal with the behaviour.

A major issue to emerge in recent years has been that surrounding the impartiality of guidance. As the provision of guidance has become enmeshed in the development of markets in education and training, so concern has developed that guidance is becoming marketing and recruitment oriented, rather than concerned with the requirements of learners. In Chapter 17, Graham Connelly discusses the issue of impartiality in adult guidance in Scotland. The importance of giving impartial advice and help to users is highlighted as a basic principle of good practice by guidance workers. However, giving impartial guidance is a complex issue which may bring practitioners into conflict not only with their organisations but also with their other roles. He concludes that being impartial is more to do with the nature of the interactive process than with supplying clients with a large quantity of information, and that impartiality can be legitimately qualified to provide effective guidance. The dilemmas surrounding guidance in particular contexts are also explored by Roger Harrison in Chapter 18. He explores the provision of guidance within an Employee Development Scheme in a large company in the UK. In particular, he examines the question of which interests predominate in such a scheme; the employees or the employers. Once again, the recognition of the qualified impartiality of the guidance on offer seems not to affect significantly the value gained by both employees and employers. This is indicative of social partnership models of workplace organisation within which guidance workers and counsellors may have an ambivalent position at times.

The above are not all the issues we could have taken. Nor have we been able to illustrate the full range of debates about the issues under discussion. In introducing this book, therefore, we are aware that we are also introducing an introduction. The issues and debates we indicate will continue, as there are no simple solutions to them. New issues and debates will emerge. We hope these chapters start to chart some of the complexity faced in providing guidance and counselling in learning. As readers, you will no doubt take issue and debate with us both the choice of issues and the positions we have chosen to highlight. If so, we will have achieved at least one of our goals.

Part I

Ethics and equity

Chapter 1

Ethical issues in counselling in education

Tim Bond

An edited version of 'Ethical issues in counselling in education', in *British Journal of Guidance and Counselling* 20, 1: 51–63 (1992).

A debate with considerable ethical implications is taking place in education about the role of the counsellor. On the one hand, there are those who view the counsellor as so integrated into the educational organisation that the role requires guidelines on ethics and practice which are quite specific to this situation and distinct from the practice of counsellors in other settings. On the other hand, there are those who see the role of the counsellor as being sufficiently different that it requires ethical and practical guidelines which are distinct from teaching and administrative roles in the organisation: these ethics would match those used by counsellors in other settings. Clearly, this is in part a debate about the professionalisation of counselling, but it also contains within it the potential for the development of two quite different ethical systems, with consequences for the client, counsellor and the organisation.

Although parallel debates are taking place in other settings, the debate is particularly intense within education because the two systems for understanding counselling outlined above already exist and both are in use within education. This is made possible because educational services are so diverse, ranging from pre-school nurseries, through primary and secondary schooling, to further and higher education for young and increasing numbers of mature adults. There are also specialist provisions for people with disabilities and for young people in residential or secure units because of behavioural problems or criminal offences. This variety in educational setting means that counsellors who are working with young pupils in organisations acting *in loco parentis*, or with people placed 'in care' or secure units for their own safety or the safety of others, are working in quite a different environment from those working with young adults. This is reflected by their experience of the counselling-organisation and the counsellor–client relationship. Looking across a range of organisations, as the degree of dependency of clients on the organisation rises, consequently increasing an institution's accountability for work with its pupils/students, so expectations intensify that any counselling will be thoroughly integrated into the organisation.

In this integrated model, the counsellor is viewed as having the same relationship to the organisation as all other members of staff, although s/he may be performing a different function. The counsellor would therefore be accountable under basically the same procedures as all other people within the organisation. The counselling would be offered from an assumption that institutional goals are compatible with an individual student's goals. For instance, in an educational institution for young offenders, it would be assumed that the agency's goal of stopping or reducing offending behaviour is also in the best interests of its students, and that the counsellor would be working towards this. In general education, it would be assumed that the counsellor would be working towards helping the individual to make the best of the educational opportunities available within that particular organisation. In this view it follows that the counsellor's primary responsibility is to promote the well-being of the organisation through work with clients and contributing to its policy decisions.

Although many counsellors in other settings would find this re-definition of who constitutes the client too novel and potentially confusing, some recognise the underlying point that counsellors in education are integral to an organisational setting, and that any ethical framework for their work needs to start from this assumption. There is also an ethical basis to support this assumption because there has been a shift in the value base of education from the 1950s towards one which coincides to a high degree with the values of counselling. This has involved a substantial shift away from valuing the dissemination of learning and knowledge as an end in itself, towards giving priority to the development of the individual. Schools and colleges have attempted increasingly to cater for their pupils as whole persons with needs for knowledge, skills and emotional support, rather than simply as empty buckets to be filled with knowledge (Haigh, 1975). This has resulted in structural changes in the way education is provided, leading to the introduction of comprehensive secondary schooling, the increasing integration of pupils with special needs, and the widening of access to further and higher education. This shift has also had a considerable impact on the way in which education is delivered: greater emphasis on pastoral care, active tutorials, and social skills training, and a shift from passive learning to a greater involvement of pupils and students in their own learning.

Implicit within these changes are an increasing value placed both on respect for the integrity of the individual learner, and on impartiality in the relationship between teacher and students. These are the same values espoused by the British Psychological Society (1985) and the British Association for Counselling (1990) as the basis for their codes of ethics and practice. Although the teaching profession has no comparable statements of ethics, the increase in status of the remedial and pastoral roles in education offers circumstantial evidence of the adherence to these values. Where this occurs, it is evidence of the extent to which educators and counsellors share the same values, or at least have complementary values, as they work towards the same organisational goal of developing the individual pupil or student. A corollary of this point is that the debate is not between two contradictory value systems but is about the best way of applying those values to the provision of counselling in education.

The alternative analysis of counselling in education is the differentiated model, which distinguishes the relationship between the counsellors and their organisation from that of other staff within the same organisation. The basis of this distinction is that the primary ethical responsibility of the counsellor is to the individual client seeking counselling, and that this responsibility is discharged differently from the tutor–pupil/student relationship. The counsellors work on the assumption that they will meet institutional goals by counselling in ways which respect individual clients' autonomy and conform to the best standards of ethics and practice in use by other counsellors in similar settings. Therefore respect for individual clients and standards of practice form the basis of their ethic. This view is most strongly held, although not unanimously, by counsellors working in further and higher education, where the counselling is more likely to be concerned with problems of client individuation and the institution is more accepting of individual student autonomy.

This sense of the distinctive nature of their work means that counsellors working in this model are likely, over matters relating to standards of practice, to treat with great significance dialogue with their colleagues from other institutions in professional organisations such as Counselling in Education and the Association for Student Counselling, both of which are divisions of the British Association for Counselling. This has given considerable impetus to the development of an ethical framework comparable to counsellors working in settings ranging from private practice to other statutory, voluntary, ecclesiastical or commercial organisations. The relationship between counsellors working in further and higher education and those working in these other settings has been highly cooperative, with the former making substantial contributions to the creation of codes of ethics and practice and to the emerging sense of professional identity for counsellors on a national scale.

There is thus a need to explore the ethical implications of these two distinctive trends within counselling in education and to identify the major differences between the two systems of thought.

ETHICAL ISSUES IN SOURCES AND METHODS OF REFERRAL

The ethical issues for the voluntary client who is adequately informed about the terms on which the counselling is offered are probably the same in both models of counselling. So long as the client has prior knowledge of how the counselling relates to other aspects of his/her life in the institution, the client is in a position to make an informed choice both about whether to take up counselling, and about the material worked on within counselling.

The application of this principle of the client's freedom to make an informed choice about taking up counselling is more difficult when the client is involuntary. This may arise due to the client being *sent* for counselling because someone else, usually a member of staff, decides that the client has a problem. Or it may arise where the counselling is integrated into the general education programme, so that pupils feel a strong expectation, by peers and staff, that they will participate in counselling. In these circumstances, the counsellor has to work harder to ensure that the clients can exercise their own choice, and in clarifying the basis for informing that choice. The general perception of counselling within the differentiated model as 'set apart' makes the realisation of the principle of client freedom easier to achieve than from within the integrated model. But both models, especially the integrated model, require a strong sense of the voluntary nature of counselling being fundamental to its values of 'respect' and 'integrity', and the counsellor needs to be able to communicate this both to clients and to colleagues within the institution. Part of making that choice is a clear understanding of what material will remain private to the counsellor–client relationship and what will be communicated to others.

ETHICAL ISSUES IN MAINTAINING CONFIDENTIALITY

One of the main differences between the integrated and differentiated models is the extent to which the counsellor includes other tutorial and administrative staff within the confidential relationship. Either the practice of including others within the confidential relationship, or of maintaining a high degree of confidentiality between counsellor and client, can be advocated on the basis of ethical argument.

Counsellors working within the integrated model are likely to start from the assumption that the content of the counselling can be revealed to others within the organisation who share a direct responsibility for the well-being of the client. They can do so on the grounds that the moral and legal contract that exists is primarily between the pupil and the educational organisation, represented by the senior manager, rather than between the pupil and individual employees such as the counsellor within the organisation. If the educational establishment has responsibilities similar to those of parents, due to the age of the pupils, or granted to them by a court because a young person's natural family has broken down or the young person is considered 'at risk' for any reason, it is understandable that the management of the organisation is reluctant to have significant information withheld from them. Indeed, numerous enquiries following the deaths of young people subjected to physical or sexual abuse have emphasised the importance of professionals liaising with each other to ensure that they are not each individually aware of different aspects of a situation which, had these been communicated, could have been joined together like pieces in a jigsaw to provide a more complete picture of the young person's circumstances. Their argument for sacrificing this degree of confidentiality is based on the ethical decision that the well-being of the child or young person takes precedence over the need to convey respect for the child's integrity by restricting confidentiality to the client–counsellor relationship. Safeguards for the client's confidence are still made possible by restricting such communications to those directly responsible for that person's well-being. However, in some instances, this could be all the teaching staff who have contact with that pupil, especially in residential and secure institutions.

In contrast, the counsellor working within the differentiated model is likely to offer a much higher degree of confidentiality. This is also based on ideas about the well-being of the client, but on a different analysis of how to achieve this. It is argued that unless children and young people can have access to relationships in which they can trust an adult to respect their confidences and to refrain from intervening without their agreement, it seems most likely that they will continue to suffer in silence most of the things that are worrying them, including abuse – physical, sexual and emotional.

The difference between counsellors working within the integrated and the differentiated models is not that one offers a confidential relationship and the other does not: it is more a difference in the degree of confidentiality offered. The values of 'respect' and 'integrity' therefore require that counsellors are clear themselves about the limits of the confidentiality they offer and that this is clearly communicated to potential clients who thereby retain control of what to disclose, and with knowledge of the likely consequences. Surveys of advisers and counsellors working with young people in the statutory and voluntary sector (Children's Legal Centre, 1989a; 1989b) revealed that substantial numbers of respondents either had no clear policy or had declared policies which did not accurately reflect their practice. The most common one of these was publicly to offer a confidential service where in practice confidentiality might be broken when either the client or others were at risk of serious physical harm. This survey included the educational psychologists, but not counsellors in schools and colleges. Experience suggests, however, that counsellors in education are no clearer about this issue than their counterparts in other settings.

ETHICS AND RESOURCES

Accountability for resources and the quality of service provided can pose a counsellor in education with major ethical dilemmas, because the user of the counselling is not also the provider of the resources to make the counselling possible. Resource providers quite reasonably expect to be able to evaluate the results of resource provision. In education, the evaluation of resource utilisation by teachers and administrators usually takes the form of a combination of direct observation and examination of the work records of the employee. This scrutiny is usually conducted by managers or someone from the inspectorate of the appropriate government department.

For the counsellor working within the integrated model who has included colleagues within the umbrella of confidentiality, this is not so ethically problematic. But for the counsellor working within the differentiated model who has offered a higher degree of confidentiality, the problem is how to be properly accountable without compromising agreements entered into with clients. Confidential information is identified as:

> personal information about clients, whether obtained directly or indirectly or by inference. Such information includes name, address, biographical details, and other descriptions of the client's life and circumstances which might result in identification of the client.
>
> (British Association for Counselling, 1990)

This would prevent direct observation of counselling clients, access to the case notes or discussion of named cases unless the client had explicitly waived confidentiality. On the other hand, it would permit the use of sources of information which avoid revealing the identity of the client, including: sound/video tapes and case records which conceal the client's identity; anonymous client feedback about the service they have received; statistical returns about the numbers of people using the service or kinds of problems raised; oral/written examination of the counsellor; and reports from the counsellor's supervisor(s) or line manager(s).

Counsellors, unlike tutors and administrators, are required to have 'counselling supervision/consultative support' on a formal and ongoing basis (British Association for Counselling, 1990). I have explored the issues around this elsewhere (Bond, 1990). Counselling supervision is primarily to safeguard the work with the client by promoting good standards of practice, the development of the counsellor's knowledge and skills, and support for the effects on the counsellor of working with other people's distress. Effective supervision involves maintaining a balance between addressing each of these three tasks. Although a counsellor working within the integrated model is unlikely to have the problems of confidentiality to prevent a line manager from performing any of these tasks, it is problematic for the manager to offer effective support. This is because the power relationship between line manager and counsellor is likely to prevent the counsellor exploring issues of personal vulnerability or doubts about his/her own competence. For these reasons it has been argued that counsellors should have access to independent support even when the line manager has substantial oversight of the counsellor's work and is sufficiently trained/experienced in counselling to perform the first two tasks. Counsellors working within the differentiated model are more likely to have independent supervision as an accepted part of their professional practice; amongst counsellors working in the integrated model this practice appears less well developed, as they have to overcome the expectation that they should be working on the same basis as other teachers and administrators.

ETHICAL IMPLICATIONS OF ROLE DIFFUSION

So far this chapter has assumed that there is a clear distinction between the role of counsellor and teacher/tutor. In practice, the distinction has become blurred, because many counsellors may also have a teaching function and many tutors may use 'counselling' to assist students with emotional and inter-personal problems.

When counselling is offered within the integrated model, this blurring of roles is likely to persist. The ethical implications of this have not yet been adequately explored. Hughes (1989) observed that:

> These changes, on the whole, have been healthy ones and have led to a decrease in some of the fears and underlying defensive attitudes to counselling. On the negative side, however, this diffusion of the counsellor role has been associated with a conceptual confusion between teaching and counselling and with subsequent identity problems for counsellor-teachers, constantly required to switch between teacher–pupil and counsellor–client types of relationship.

If, however, counselling is offered within the differentiated model, the establishment of boundaries between the roles is much more important, as it has implications both for the client's expectations of what is being offered and for the ways in which the counsellor is accountable to the educational organisation. Within the British Association for Counselling, the distinction between 'counselling' and 'using counselling skills' has been developed to provide a conceptual and ethical distinction for this kind of situation. This provides the conceptual leverage for the tutor to use counselling skills whilst remaining clearly within the tutor role, and within the ethical framework of the organisation and teaching profession, and for the counsellor to establish role differentiation in order to clarify a distinctive ethical framework and set of practices.

ETHICS AND OUTCOMES

Counsellors in educational settings can sometimes find themselves in situations where they are confronted with the stark questions of who decides what is a successful outcome – the client or the organisation.

When working within the integrated model, one of the risks in minimising the distinction between the counselling and teaching roles is that the client will confuse the roles and thus expect of the counsellor 'the kind of relationship which actually exists between the teacher and pupil in most classrooms', which 'is clearly one of authority, dominance and externally imposed control' (Best *et al.*, 1983). Best *et al.* were writing about mainstream primary and secondary schooling, but this must be even more true within secure and special units if the integrated model is also in use. It requires deliberate and systematic work on the part of the counsellor to ensure that both the client and the institution understand the voluntary nature of counselling. Failure to achieve this may lead to unethically intrusive work which violates respect for the client's autonomy. Although the client may resist by withdrawing into silence in the counselling, others may defer to the perceived authority and comply with what is expected of them. Over the past few years I have received anecdotal evidence that some clients invent issues and concerns in order to be seen to comply with what is expected of them, especially if counselling is perceived as one of the 'hoops' they must 'jump through' to get out of residential or secure environments. When this happens, 'counselling' has become a futile ritual dance; but will the institution recognise this? It is in everybody's interests to emphasise the voluntary nature of counselling. This ensures that counselling is undertaken only with those who want it, and avoids wasting resources on giving it to those who do not.

For counsellors working in either model, the question of who evaluates the outcome is brought sharply into focus when it becomes clear that what clients perceive as best for them conflicts with the interests of the educational establishment. For instance, a student may wish to leave a course which could represent a substantial loss in income for the institution, or worse, the closure of a course because it has dropped below the threshold of viability. This is a successful outcome for the individual client but not for the students left with the closure of their course or probably for the institution. Most counsellors and their managers in higher and further education accept that this will happen occasionally and believe this is the most ethical way of proceeding.

CONCLUSION

Although both of the ethical systems described here are in use in educational establishments, their mere existence does not necessarily mean that they are defensible as adequate frameworks for the provision of counselling. Either one of the systems could exist and be seriously flawed. The integrated model is probably less well understood by counsellors inside and outside education. From this preliminary examination, however, it would appear that much of the credibility of it as a system will depend on the extent to which the voluntary nature of counselling can be asserted and the extent to which the educational organisation shares the values of counselling. Without both of these criteria, there is the potential for counselling being used against young clients in ways comparable to the worst excesses of compulsory therapy in psychiatric care, outlined most recently by Masson (1989). Although the differentiated model is better understood by counsellors and has the bonus of helping to clarify their professional identity, it is not without its drawbacks. By placing so much emphasis on respect for the client as an individual, it has created a system which is more complex to manage within educational settings, and one which is vulnerable to seeming less obviously accountable to the organisation for the resources it consumes and the quality of service it provides.

The unresolved question which has substantial implications for either model is: are the two ethical systems mutually compatible? If the answer appears to be 'yes', it becomes arguable that they share the same values, but that because they take different views on the client–counsellor and client–organisation relationship, they come to different but not mutually incompatible views about the ethics and practice of counselling in specific settings. It may be that the association of the 'integrated' model with educational establishments working with younger or more 'at risk' clients, and the 'differentiated' model with establishments for more mature clients, provides the basis for a possible reconciliation between the two systems. When deciding which is the best model for a specific organisation, a test may need to be developed to help identify the circumstances in which each model is most appropriate. This may involve a combination of consideration of the degree of responsibility an organisation has *in loco parentis*, or for the security or safety of its pupils/students, as well as to a client's capacity to make decisions (in accordance with the principles outlined by Lord Scarman (1985) in the Gillick case).

Although the existence of the two ethical systems makes the development of the ethics of counselling in education more complex, it could be argued that this is a better option than having substantial numbers of counsellors working without a clear understanding of an appropriate ethical framework, because the only one available to them is irrelevant to their circumstances. An alternative possibility arises if it is decided that they are incompatible: that work within the integrated model could be viewed as a form of using counselling skills. This would have at least three consequences. It would leave the work which might otherwise have been thought of as counselling to another profession's ethical system, usually that of teacher or social worker. Perhaps more seriously from an ethical point of view, it might foster an 'absolutist' understanding of counselling both in and outside education, which would misrepresent the ethical constraints under which most counsellors work. It is only when a client approaches a counsellor who works alone in private practice that the client has the simple contractual relationship of being both the client and provider of the resources for the counselling, in the form of fees: only in these circumstances is the person seeking counselling both the client and the 'manager' to whom the counsellor is accountable. In all other circumstances, to a greater or lesser extent the counsellor owes accountability to both the client and the organisation within which the counsellor works. It is in education that the consequences of this splitting of accountability are most visible, because of the potential dependency of young clients on the organisation and the wider community. If, on the other hand, because of these specific circumstances, the integrated model were to become universally accepted within education services, this could result in educational counsellors working within a model which is substantially different from counsellors in most other settings and could leave them ethically isolated within the wider world of counselling.

It is too early to predict whether the integrated or differentiated model will predominate in the provision of counselling in education, or whether they will continue to coexist but in a more clearly demarcated way. What does seem certain is that both ethical systems are capable of further articulation and that this debate about ethics between counsellors in education is stimulating the development of both models and an exploration of the relationship between the two.

BIBLIOGRAPHY

Best, R., Ribbins, P., Jarvis, C., and Oddy, D. (1983) *Education and Care*, London: Heinemann.
Bond, T. (1990) 'Counselling Supervision – Ethical Issues', *Counselling*, Volume 1 No. 2, May.
British Association for Counselling (1990) *Code of Ethics and Practice for Counsellors*, Rugby: BAC.
British Psychological Society (1985) *A Code of Conduct for Psychologists*, Leicester: BPS.
Children's Legal Centre (1989a) 'A Child's Right to Confidentiality – Part One', *Childright*, No. 57, June.
Children's Legal Centre (1989b) 'A Child's Right to Confidentiality – Part Two', *Childright*, No. 58, July/August.
Haigh, G. (1975) *Pastoral Care*, London: Pitman.
Hughes, P. (1989) 'Counselling in Education (Primary and Secondary)'. In Dryden, W., Charles-Edwards, D., and Woolfe, R. (eds) *Handbook of Counselling in Britain*, London: Routledge.
Masson, J. (1989) *Against Therapy*, London: Collins.
Scarman, Lord Justice (1985) *Gillick v. West Norfolk and Wisbech Area Health Authority*, 3 All ER 402.

Chapter 2

Ethical issues in workplace counselling

Michael Carroll

An edited version of 'Ethical Issues in workplace counselling', in *Workplace Counselling*, Chapter 8, London: Sage (1996).

TRAINING IN ETHICAL DECISION-MAKING

Carroll (1994) entitled her research on workplace counsellors 'Building bridges' and saw one major aspect of the counsellor's role as best summarized in the phrase 'sophisticated mediation'. Both 'building bridges' and 'sophisticated mediation' highlight the potential conflict between two worlds (counselling and business) and two sets of responsibilities (to the individual client and to the organization). Standing at crossroads such as these inevitably raises ethical issues and dilemmas for workplace counsellors. From my own experience of working with workplace counsellors, the issues that cause most problems are always ethical. Counsellors in the workplace are constantly faced with ethical and professional dilemmas unique to this setting, as well as the full range of ethical dilemmas faced by counsellors in general. Oberer and Lee (1986) compare workplace counselling with attempting to do family therapy with one's own family. Two examples illustrate the ethical dilemmas.

> *Case example*
> A manager phones the counselling service to tell the counsellor that a member of her department is about to be made redundant. Since she (the manager) knows that this member of her department is coming to the counsellor for personal counselling, she wonders if the counsellor will break the bad news to the client.

> *Case example*
> A client who has just had a very poor appraisal that affects both his pay and career prospects tells the counsellor that his manager (who did the appraisal) has 'had it in for him' for some time and has told him that even though he is doing very good work his appraisal will be poor because the manager does not want him in his department. What does the counsellor do?

Conflicting responsibilities create difficulties for the workplace counsellor and occasionally crystallize around loyalty to the individual client versus loyalty to the organization. Such issues, among a host of others, cause headaches to counsellors in workplace counselling and raise a number of issues for them:

1   When do they move outside counselling to involve themselves with the organization?
2   When do they see what is happening as an organizational issue and bring it into the organizational domain?
3   When do they break confidentiality with or without the permission of clients?
4   When do they 'tell on the organization' when unethical practices are taking place (e.g. health and safety rules)?

ETHICAL ISSUES

Counselling in the workplace not only contends with the full range of ethical issues emerging from counselling in general, but also must deal with a full set of ethical issues emerging from within the organization in which counselling takes place, and between the organization and the counsellor. Puder (1983: 96) suggests that the counsellor in such circumstances needs 'the rational and intuitive perceptiveness necessary for straddling the worlds of business and mental health'.

Several ethical dilemmas arising from workplace counselling have been raised in the literature: confidentiality; the incompatibility between the organization's aims and the aims of counselling; the loyalty of the counsellor; and managing different roles with the same client. Even though these have been viewed in depth, there is little written on how the counsellor reaches an ethical decision. Few authors enable the practitioner to manage ethical issues and even fewer offer outlines for how ethical decisions can be implemented. Like ethical codes, the advice on how to reach decisions on ethical issues contains general principles rather than answers to particular situations. And, indeed, this is as it should be. Guidelines are meant to be general and their application to particular instances needs to be worked out rather than given. It is this 'working through', isolating the process of ethical decision-making, that is an important skill for counsellors.

Several difficulties in making ethical decisions in the workplace have been raised. Bishop and D'Rozario (1990) have pointed out that psychologists, and here we can include workplace counsellors, have largely an individualistic bias when assessing and working with clients. What is easily missed is the organizational dimension of this work. Rather than, too easily, making individuals responsible for their own problems, it is necessary to review the role of the organization in producing these same problems. Newton (1995) has used this same argument in reviewing the concept of stress in the workplace. He shows how easily we make individuals responsible for managing their stress at the same time as exonerating organizations from the blame of overloading or overworking employees. As a result, workplace counselling individualizes problems rather than attempts to see them in their collective context. Another ethical dilemma for workplace counsellors centres around their loyalties and when they might take the stance of an employee against the organization. This could happen in the event of a counsellor being convinced that an employee client was being blamed, and being punished, for what his/her boss did.

From a review of the literature on ethical issues in counselling, and from a survey of the various approaches to ethical decision-making, including the educational packages available, several areas emerge that seem basic to the field:

1   Making ethical decisions by 'intuition' (Kitchener, 1984) is not sufficient. Counsellors need to have a strategy for reaching decisions in counselling even though many of those decisions will be on an 'intuitive' basis.
2   Counsellors need access to a number of areas that will help them in the process of decision-making. These include supervision, colleagues with whom they can discuss situations, knowledge and access to codes of ethics, and various references from the literature that help in making ethical decisions.
3   Counsellors appreciate the use of case material as a way of struggling with the complexities of ethical issues in counselling. Their own cases, as well as examples from the work of others, can be used to great affect provided 'students do not overly concentrate on the clinical details of the case at the expense of its ethical dimension' (Fine and Ulrich, 1988: 546).
4   Ethical issues and dilemmas from organizational contexts in which counselling is used have particular aspects that need to be considered. Reviewing ethical decision-making within a purely individualistic approach, which psychologists and counsellors often use, does a disservice to the complexities of ethical problems within organizations.

Practical ethical decisions are a daily event for most counsellors: should I reach out and touch this client? Ought I to continue seeing this client or should I refer? Am I competent to deal with this issue? Is it time to end counselling in this instance? Many similar decisions are made, it seems, more by intuition than by design. Research appears to indicate that ethical decisions are made, not by reference to the books, or the codes of practice,

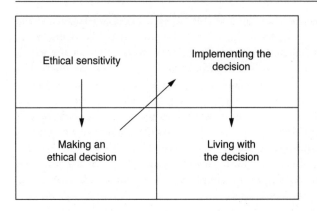

Figure 2.1 Four components of ethical decision-making (from Rest, 1984: 20)

but rather to 'unwritten, personal standards' (Patterson *et al.*, 1989). Ethical issues are perhaps even more solidly in-built into counselling in the workplace, where organizational concerns are sometimes in conflict with individual well-being. The workplace counsellor plies their trade at the interface between individual and organization, while themselves being members of the organization. Boundary problems can become a nightmare, loyalties a major concern. It seems unfair to allow the counsellor to face these either alone or without training in ethical decision-making. Providing the models to do so gives both confidence and competence.

MAKING ETHICAL DECISIONS IN THE WORKPLACE

Workplace counsellors need help in making ethical decisions that take into consideration both the individual client and the organization. Rest's (1984: 20) model of the four components involved in ethical decisions can be adapted by workplace counsellors to help them make sensitive decisions (see Figure 2.1).

Ethical sensitivity

The first component involves the ability to see and interpret behaviour and its effects on others. Pryor (1989) calls this 'ethical watchfulness' and recommends a number of ways of enhancing ethical sensitivity:

1   Being familiar with ethical codes and standards.
2   Making an effort to foresee ethically unclear possibilities before they actually occur.

3 Keeping an eye on the use of new techniques that may involve ethical dilemmas.
4 Examining the legal and organizational constraints of one's work in relation to one's ethical and professional allegiances.
5 Giving oneself time to think through ethically uncertain situations.

Ethical sensitivity implies a realization that virtually any action may have ethical implications. This highlights the need for careful forethought to prevent difficult situations arising for the counsellors. Many people do not see the implications of their behaviour on others. Rest (1984) has summarized research in this area which indicates that some individuals have difficulty in interpreting even the simplest situation as ethical, others need dramatic signs before they become aware that their behaviour is seriously affecting another, while a further group is over-sensitive to the implications of every action. Even when situations are seen as ethical/moral, individuals do not always act. Bernard and Jara (1986) show that even when psychologists were aware that ethical issues were involved, they often did nothing.

Besides the more obvious ethical violations, there are other ways in which counsellors and supervisors can exploit clients: excessive familiarity, non-clinical business matters, breaches of confidentiality, satisfaction of their own needs, impressing the client, asking favours of clients, being lax and being sadistic (Epstein and Simon, 1990: 451).

Creating ethical sensitivity means increasing awareness in counsellors that all situations are potentially ethical, and that the implications of behaviour can be far-reaching. There is certainly room for spontaneity in counselling but not for impulsivity. Carroll (1995) has suggested a number of ways in which ethical sensitivity can be enhanced in counsellors:

- case reviews
- identifying ethical issues arising from counselling work
- reading ethical codes and related literature
- case vignettes (what would you do?)
- exploring value issues arising from counselling work
- clarifying and confronting one's own values
- creating awareness around the 'power' issues involved in counselling
- reviewing critical incidents within counselling
- evaluating ethical frameworks and theories
- ascertaining levels of moral development and how this affects ethical decision-making.

With a higher level of ethical sensitivity, workplace counsellors are more able to pick up signs that will alert them to possible hazards. That awareness, in turn, will lead them to decide what to do in the circumstances.

Making an ethical decision

This entails judging what is the best course of action in *these* circumstances for *this* individual (client) within *this* organization. All these factors – the individual client, the particular organization, the specific situation – are relevant. Here counsellors weigh up the merits of various courses of action and decide on one. It is here that care is needed not to be too individualistic in making moral judgements: what is good for the client could be unhelpful for others, or for the organization. For instance, to make the decision not to break confidentiality may benefit the individual client but could be disastrous for the organization (where someone was embezzling or involved in insider dealing). Carroll (1995) has outlined a seven-stage methodology for ethical decision-making which is relevant to the workplace (see Figure 2.2). While time will not allow this lengthy procedure to be followed in all instances of an ethical dilemma, knowing and understanding the stages can help counsellors 'short-circuit' the process when needed. However, even when a decision to act has been made and a particular course of action seen as the most appropriate, it does not follow automatically that counsellors will take the next step, translating the decision to act into behaviours.

Implementing the decision

Implementing an ethical decision is not always easy. It can conflict with other interests, e.g. career, friendship, loyalty. Carroll (1995) has suggested steps to be taken when a moral decision has been made and needs to be implemented:

1   What steps need to be taken to implement the decision?
2   Which people are involved and who needs to be told what?
3   What restraints are there *not* to implement the ethical decision (e.g. politics of the situation, protection of a client, rationalization, etc.)?
4   What support is needed (by the counsellor, by the client, by others) to implement and to live with the results required.

It is relatively easy to underestimate the strength needed at times to implement ethical decisions, especially in the light of influence from colleagues, friends and, sometimes, parties with their own vested interests. Business settings are notorious for putting up with bad situations and doing nothing even when it is known what should be done.

Living with the decision

Unlike other decisions, an ethical decision can never be shown to be the correct and only course of action. Living with such a decision is about never knowing what was the right course of action to take. Even after a client

1 *Identify the ethical problem or dilemma*
   • What are the parameters of the situation?
   • What is the source of conflict for the client or for the counsellor?
   • Is the conflict with another person, group of people, or family member, or with the organization?
   • Is the conflict between the client and the counsellor?
   • Does the conflict involve legal, moral, ethical, religious, cultural, gender or value issues?
   • What are the counsellor's feelings about what is happening?
   • How may the problem be clearly defined, especially where terms are emotionally charged?

2 *Identify the potential issues involved*
   • What is the worst possible outcome?
   • What could happen if nothing is done?
   • What are the implications involved in this problem or dilemma?
   • What are the rights, responsibilities and welfare of all affected parties?

3 *Review the relevant ethical guidelines*
   • Do guidelines, principles or laws exist that are relevant to the dilemmas and may provide a possible solution?
   • Are the counsellor's values, ethics or morals in conflict with the relevant principles or guidelines?
   • Is the counsellor aware of the effect of values and does he or she have a rationale for the behaviour?
   • Are there relevant codes, sections, chapters of books etc. pertinent to this issue?
   • What further information is needed to help resolve the issue?

4 *Obtain consultation*
   • Bring the situation to supervision.
   • Talk with colleagues, where appropriate.
   • Consult line managers, if appropriate.
   • Talk to a lawyer (or an expert from another profession), again if appropriate.

5 *Consider possible and probable courses of action*
   • What are the alternatives (brainstorming without evaluating is helpful)?

6 *Enumerate the consequences of various decisions*
   • What are the implications for the client?
   • What are the implications for others?
   • What are the implications for the counsellor?

7 *Decide on what appears to be the best course of action*
   • Could you recommend this action to other counsellors in similar circumstances?
   • Would I condone this behaviour in another counsellor?
   • Can I defend this behaviour if it were made public?
   • Would I treat other clients in the same situation differently?

Figure 2.2 Seven-stage methodology for ethical decision-making

has been hospitalized, on the recommendation and action of the workplace counsellor, the doubts are not alleviated. Counsellors are still left with thoughts that they may have acted prematurely, especially if the client reacts negatively to their decision. Carroll (1995) has defined some of the issues involved:

1   Dealing with anxiety around the final decision.
2   Letting go of the situation and the dilemma.
3   Accepting the limitations involved.
4   Learning from the experience.
5   Using personal and professional support to live with the consequences of the decision.

In summary, there are no easy ways to make ethical decisions in the workplace. Counsellors will want to use supervision, colleagues, ethical codes and networks as methods of discussion and rehearsing for ethical demands of working in this setting. What is essential is the need to have clear and documented agreements on a number of areas:

1   Clarification of potentially conflictual relationships.
2   An understanding of the implications and limits of confidentiality in the workplace.
3   A clear formula by which employee counsellors are required to share information about clients with the organization.
4   The need to let clients know the limits of confidentiality if there are limits.

ETHICAL RESPONSIBILITIES FOR AND TO CLIENTS

Workplace counsellors provide the same ethical responsibilities to and for clients as do counsellors in other settings. Counsellors are recommended to acquaint themselves with these general ethical guidelines and to have read some of the dilemmas and issues emerging. Workplace counsellors are responsible for:

- setting up a safe environment for clients
- ensuring privacy
- safeguarding notes
- managing the counselling process
- negotiating confidentiality with clients
- ensuring clients understand what counselling means
- how they work with clients in other contexts (e.g. committees, canteen, sports facilities, etc.) so that confidentiality is safe

- clarity on what information, if any, counsellors would relay back to the organization with or without the consent of the client.

Confidentiality is a key issue in counselling with clients in workplace settings. Many clients do not use workplace counselling services because of their fear that word may get back to the organization, or notes made on their records, or it might affect their career prospects. Salt *et al.* (1992: 11) recommend clarity on the meaning of confidentiality in the workplace: 'Confidentiality as a concept is an all-or-nothing phenomenon. Something is either confidential or it is not. There is no room for shades of confidentiality. A clear policy stating *who needs to know what and why* is fundamental to providing an organisation with rules for maintaining confidentiality.' This policy needs to be carefully negotiated with clients. Even when confidentiality is clearly agreed, the counsellor can be put in a compromising situation by clients who exploit the counselling relationship for their own ends. Clients are not adverse to telling management that 'their counsellor told them' to take time off, that there was nothing wrong with them, that management style is to blame etc. Clients are not bound by confidentiality as are counsellors. In outlining the importance of confidentiality, Bond (1993) points out times when it can be broken:

- when clients give permission
- when information is already in the public domain
- when the public interest in preserving confidentiality is outweighed by the public interest in disclosure, e.g. when harm could result to the client or others
- for supervision/consultation purposes.

This raises several issues that need to be absolutely clear for workplace counsellors:

1   What is agreed with the employing organization in respect of client confidentiality? Are there contractual areas where counsellors must reveal information passed on to them by clients, with or without their (client's) permission?
2   Are potential clients aware of the limits governing confidentiality?
3   In contracting for counselling, counsellors will acquaint clients of the limits of confidentiality in this setting (i.e. counsellors will not offer a higher degree of confidentiality than that permitted by their contract).

A further issue of responsibility to clients is that of notes. Who should have access to these, both the official file and the personal notes of the counsellor? The *UK Standards of Practice and Professional Guidelines for Employee Assistance Programmes* (EAPA, 1995) makes several suggestions under the heading of keeping records: handle the destruction of individual client records in a confidential way; ensure the security of client files; be clear about who has access to these files; in so far as possible prevent their files being used in arbitration, employee litigations and disputes between the individual and the organization. Lee and Rosen (1984) offer three hints on protecting client privacy: minimize intrusiveness by controlling the amount of information gathered; maximize fairness in record keeping; and create legitimate expectations of the confidentiality of records, especially from organizations.

Workplace counsellors have a responsibility to employees about how they assess their 'problems'. Difficult and problematic employees are often so labelled because of their lack of conformity to the role expectations of the organization. Fairness to clients demands that employee counsellors bear in mind that the culture of the organization may be at variance with the client, and creating a problem between them. This awareness can save clients from being labelled as 'problems' when what is at issue is a mismatch between individual and organization. In other instances, employees can be viewed as problems when the organization is at fault, as in cases of sexual harassment or managers who are bullies.

ETHICAL RESPONSIBILITIES FOR AND TO THE ORGANIZATION

Workplace counsellors are employed by organizations and as such have responsibilities to those organizations. Clarity around the organization's demands is needed and clear contracts need to be drawn up so that roles and responsibilities are not in doubt. These include:

- maintaining the service
- agreeing to organizational policies
- a policy about the role of counselling in the organization
- when to involve the organization in counselling work
- feedback and statistics (reports)
- evaluating the service.

However, the workplace counsellor also has an ethical responsibility to help the organization review and change workplace practices and policies that are antagonistic to human welfare. These can range across physical conditions, mental wellness, stress levels, equal opportunities, sexual harassment, management practices, and a host of other areas. In a sense, employee counsellors are the 'conscience' of the organization, monitoring how people are treated and cared for and moving fast to build in safeguards where possible. Helping organizations to change to more ethically sound principles and practices for their employees is a key responsibility for workplace counsellors, and yet not a responsibility for which they are trained. How far are workplace counsellors responsible for the social and communal concerns of employees that arise from working within a particular organization? Some codes of practice would see this as a legitimate concern for the counselling practitioner. Others tend to side with the organization.

Lee and Rosen (1984) have outlined suggestions for maintaining ethical responsibility to the organization:

• develop an economical model to justify the counselling work
• negotiate a contract that specifies the interests of counsellors, consumers and organizations as well as the rights and responsibilities of each
• outline a framework for defining the problems appropriate for the counselling service
• develop guidelines for record keeping
• create and maintain professional relationships
• ascertain accreditation standards for programmes in industry.

Little has been written on the ethical responsibilities of workplace counsellors for and to the organization that employs them. Some authors see wide roles that the counsellor can legitimately play within the organization; others suggest narrowing tasks to those which deal directly with individual employees coming for counselling. What is clear, however, is that counsellors and, indeed, organizations ought to have an understanding of what those ethical responsibilities are before tasks are allocated.

EMPLOYEE COUNSELLORS' ETHICAL RESPONSIBILITIES FOR AND TO THEMSELVES

All counsellors, not just counsellors in the workplace, need to care for themselves. This is not just good advice but enters into the realm of an ethical responsibility; there are far too many examples of burn-out within the helping professions. This is partly due to good people working too hard, not recognizing the signs of stress in themselves even though they are good at recognizing them in others, and eventually having to rest because they 'break down' or become ill, physically and/or mentally.

Within organizational situations there are further elements to be considered; including how the culture and management of the organization may affect counsellors. There is some research to show that counsellors working in organizational/institutional settings suffer greater levels of stress than those working in private practice (Hellman and Morrison, 1987; Farber, 1990). Burn-out may be as much the result of organizational stress as it is the result of individuals not caring for themselves.

Brady *et al.* (1995) have reviewed the literature on stress among counsellors, and present seven steps of stress. Obviously, these stresses apply equally to counsellors in the workplace:

- patient (client) behaviours
- working conditions
- emotional depletion
- physical isolation
- psychic isolation
- therapeutic relationships
- personal disruptions.

Some of these factors will be more applicable to individual counsellors than others. And, of course, as House (1995: 87) remarks in the context of counselling in a medical setting, 'setting-specific stress will be experienced to the extent that the characteristics of the setting resonate unhelpfully or pathologically with the counsellor's personality dynamics'. Looking after self 'physically, emotionally, intellectually and spiritually' means having in place a number of support systems that will defray overstress and burn-out.

Managing the organization

Much has been written about stress in the workplace and it has become a commonplace to see stress as an everyday factor in modern organizational life rather than an exception. Many of the problems arriving at the door of the workplace counsellor will revolve around stress in the workplace. Not only does the employee counsellor have to deal with these problems and provide a place of 'containment' for them, but they will have to deal with their own stress and the stress emerging from working within particular organizations. The organization can stress counsellors in many ways.

Direct management style   The managerial style of the line manager of counsellors can be a very powerful source of stress. Looking after themselves and ensuring that they are working well sometimes means that counsellors in organizations have to 'manage their managers'. This can be educational. Not all organizational managers understand counselling, what it means, the boundaries involved, the stresses it puts on counsellors, and the emotional and psychological commitments necessary. Educating them to this can be time well spent and can result in an understanding that is supportive rather than a misrepresentation which can be stressful.

Organizational culture   We know enough about organizational culture to realize how influential it is on counselling provision, and how stressful that culture can be to counsellors. Within achievement cultures the counsellor will feel the stress of having to be an 'achiever', to show the effectiveness of counselling in the organization, to be alongside other achievers in a sometimes competitive and cut-throat market. Being able to manage the stresses of organizational culture will be extremely important if counsellors are not to collude with the very pathology of the organization.

Bureaucratic demands   Rarely are counsellors allowed to get on with counselling work alone. There are quite a number of time-consuming and emotionally draining requests from the organization. Brady *et al.* (1995: 6) put it well:

> virtually all healing contexts are dominated by a sense of damage, despair, and disease. And that's only the clients. Throw in bureaucratic nonsense, colleague misbehaviour, inadequate resources, onerous paperwork and assorted other organizational and peer problems and one begins to recognize the potential damage of working conditions in the helping professions.

There can be further commitments and demands from the organization: attending committees, managing budgets, helping devise policies, travel to other sites, sitting in on appraisals and interviews. Being alert to all these demands, knowing when to, and being able to, say 'no', as well as organizing self, are key issues in managing the organization.

Emergencies   Organizations are notorious for creating crisis-times: the report that should have been written by yesterday, the employee who has 'broken down' and must be seen immediately, the sexual harassment accusation which cannot be delayed, the fire-alarm that keeps going off. A workplace counsellor remarked that everyday life is dealing with chaos and that the opportunity of having a well-organized day that goes according to plan is a myth.

Negotiating terms and conditions

From the very beginning of working as a counsellor in an organization it is essential for counsellors to negotiate their tasks, roles and conditions of work. It is easy for boundaries to become unclear, and unless contracts are drawn up that allow counsellors to clarify their place in the organization, they will be in no position to negotiate when further demands are made.

Managing time

Crucial to the busy employee counsellor is his or her way of managing time. Within a few months of being employed, there will be huge demands on time. Managers will want them to see troubled employees, work with difficult members of staff, involve them in team development, and advise them on how to work with their people. The training department will want them to put on training in counselling and related areas, human resources will try to involve them in organizational change and development, and every employee with a grievance will attempt to enlist their help as an advocate against the organization. And this is not to look at the administrative side of their work: keeping statistics, publicizing the service, fielding the telephone calls, talking to outside individuals and groups who want to know about employee counselling, or are writing dissertations on counselling in the workplace and want access to information. Nor does it take into consideration the time spent in networking, in supervision, in continuing training and education. The demands are immense and, since most organizations are involved in some form of organizational change today, this will mean further individual demands from stressed clients.

A number of factors can help here:

- prioritizing activities will be essential
- maintaining a reasonable caseload
- time for emergencies
- time for administration
- time for reflecting on what is being done and what could be done
- assertiveness
- stress management techniques
- flexibility
- self-knowledge.

Knowing, recognizing and applying to self the signs of stress is equally important. Employee counsellors often do not recognize their own stress as effectively as they recognize it in others.

Managing self

Looking after oneself is crucial in counselling work, not only physically but emotionally and psychologically. Some factors here are:

1 How am I dealing with stress? Am I drinking alcohol above levels that are healthy?
2 How am I sleeping? Am I constantly tired? Sleep is often one of the first elements in life to be affected when stress becomes overwhelming. Too much sleep, too little sleep, early morning waking can all be signs of stress.
3 Am I exercising regularly? In the late 1960s, when R. Carkhuff was influential in counselling research and training, it was said that his

first question to those who would train with him concerned their physical fitness.

4   How rushed do I feel?
5   How do I fare on a stress inventory?
6   How am I emotionally, interpersonally?

Supervision

Several authors have attested to supervision as one way of helping contain some of the anxieties and emotions that arise in counselling work (Hawkins and Shohet, 1989; Inskipp and Proctor, 1993; Carroll, 1995). It is invaluable to workplace counsellors, offering a forum to think through what is happening to them as well as what is happening to their clients.

Networking

Besides supervision, making and maintaining contact with other employee counsellors is a very valuable way of creating a forum for individuals who may have the same issues for discussion, for hearing how others in similar circumstances are dealing with their problems, and for sharing ideas and strategies for managing stress. Talking is undoubtedly one of the main ways in which people deal with stress (Hope, 1985) and networking is a great forum for conversation. Realizing that other counsellors face similar difficulties can itself be a source of hope besides providing a safe environment in which to look at possible ways ahead.

Continuing training

Time needs to be left aside in a busy schedule for continuing training and education in counselling and the dimensions of workplace counselling. Training needs can be discussed within supervision and within networking where others can share training they have done and its effects on their work.

Not only is time on training time-out from a hectic schedule, but it is also the way to gain new skills, build up confidence, and be creative with new ways of working. All these can bring enthusiasm and creativity to work. We know that one way in which stress affects people is to stunt their enthusiasm and creativity: they go onto 'remote control' and do not have the mental or physical energy to think about new ways of doing old things.

Personal and social support

Paramount in people's well-being is the social support system they have. Pearson (1990) is very clear about the connections between social support and effectiveness as a human being. 'As we have seen', he writes, 'social support is a process basic to the development of humanness itself. Its presence or absence bears heavily on the development and maintenance of personal effectiveness. Therefore, we should expect to find support-related issues and events surfacing in almost any area of human endeavour' (1990: 201).

While personal support systems will differ from person to person, what is necessary is that employee counsellors know and be able to set up, within their personal lives, the support they need. Hawkins and Shohet (1989: 17) suggest a method for 'mapping your support system' that could be very helpful for employee counsellors. Briefly, they suggest using a large piece of paper to draw a map of your support system. In the centre draw a symbol to represent yourself and around it draw or represent all the elements of your support system (using symbols, diagrams, words, pictures, etc.). These will include individuals, teams, learning, courses, personal and professional relationships, places you go, meetings you attend, holidays – anything and everything in your life that sustains, supports, energizes, nurtures, enthuses, excites and challenges you positively. Next, show the connections between each representation and yourself: strong/weak, close/far away. Follow this by showing how you use that support system or not as the case may be, what blocks you from using it more. Draw in areas of support you would like but do not have at the moment. Hawkins and Shohet (1989) suggest sharing this with another person and looking in some detail at the following questions:

- Is this the kind of support you want?
- Is it enough? What sort of support is missing? How could you go about getting such support?
- What support is really positive for you to the extent that you must ensure that you nurture and maintain it?
- What blocks could you do something about reducing?

An action plan on building the support systems needed can be outlined from this discussion.

Workplace counsellors also use their own personal counselling as a source of support and self-assessment. Orme (1994) has argued that personal counselling may be more necessary for workplace counsellors than for counsellors in general because of the extra roles and responsibilities entailed in the job.

In summary, employee counsellors have a responsibility to care for themselves so that they can be effective within an organization and with their clients. Obviously, this entails monitoring closely what is happening to them and being able to take steps to offset dangers to their personal and professional lives.

THE ORGANIZATION'S ETHICAL
RESPONSIBILITIES FOR COUNSELLING PROVISION

In setting up counselling within its ambit, organizations have a responsibility to make it work effectively. Organizations have the responsibility of serving counsellors as they work with clients. Some of these responsibilities involve:

- providing administrative support
- providing secretarial support
- providing professional leadership and management
- listening to statistics and reports
- offering realistic budgets
- supporting counsellors as they publicize the service
- working out policies on counselling and confidentiality
- allowing counselling to influence corporate culture
- supporting counsellors' continuing development, training and support (especially in supervision)
- support from top levels of management
- working out clear contracts that cover confidentiality and what it means; the roles and responsibilities of counsellors.

Counsellors will want to consider whether they should work with organizations who refuse some or all of the above. Major problems emerge when organizations do not take their responsibilities to counselling and counsellors seriously, either because they do not understand what is involved, or have not thought through the implications enough, or simply do not resource the service sufficiently.

CONCLUSION

Ethical decision-making is a daily event for workplace counsellors. Great sensitivity, not to mention diplomacy, is needed to cope with what is potentially a minefield of problems. Counsellors need ethical antennae, as well as support, to help make key decisions that affect individual and organizational lives, and strength to live with the implications of those decisions. The sooner employee counsellors have a code of ethics for workplace counselling the better it will be for them: guidelines are not the final answer but they are valuable signposts along the way.

BIBLIOGRAPHY

Bernard, J. and Jara, C.S. (1986) 'The failure of clinical psychology graduate students to apply understood ethical principles', *Professional Psychology: Research and Practice*, 17(4): 313–15.

Bishop, B. and D'Rozario, P. (1990) 'A matter of ethics? A comment on Pryor "Conflicting responsibilities" (1989)', *Australian Psychologist*, 25(2): 215–19.

Bond, T. (1993) *Standards and Ethics for Counselling in Action*. London: Sage.

Brady, J.L., Healy, F.C., Norcross, J.C. and Guy, J.D. (1995) 'Stress in counsellors: an integrative research review', in W. Dryden (ed.), *The Stresses of Counselling in Action*. London: Sage. pp. 1–27.

Carroll, C. (1994) 'Building bridges: a study of employee counsellors in the private sector', unpublished MSc dissertation, City University, London.

Carroll, M. (1995) *Counselling Supervision: Theory, Skills and Practice*. London: Cassell.

Employee Assistance Programmes Association (1995) *UK Standards of Practice and Professional Guidelines for Employee Assistance Programmes*. London: EAP Association.

Epstein, R.S. and Simon, R.I. (1990) 'The exploitation index: an early warning indicator of boundary violations in psychotherapy', *Bulletin of the Menninger Clinic*, 54(4): 450–65.

Farber, B.A. (1990) 'Burnout in psychotherapists: incidence, types, and trends', *Psychotherapy in Private Practice*, 8: 35–44.

Fine, M. and Ulrich, L. (1988) 'Integrating psychology and philosophy in teaching a graduate course in ethics', *Professional Psychology: Research and Practice*, 19: 542–6.

Hawkins, P. and Shohet, R. (1989) *Supervision in the Helping Professions*. Milton Keynes: The Open University Press.

Hellman, I.D. and Morrison, T.L. (1987) 'Practice setting and type of caseload as factors in psychotherapist stress', *Psychotherapy*, 24: 427–33.

Hope, D. (1985) 'Counsellor stress and burnout', unpublished MA thesis, University of Reading.

House, R. (1995) 'The stresses of working in a general practice setting', in W. Dryden (ed.), *The Stresses of Counselling in Action*. London: Sage. pp. 87–107.

Inskipp, F. and Proctor, B. (1993) *Making the Most of Supervision*. Twickenham: Cascade Publications.

Kelloway, E.K. and Barling, J. (1991) 'Job characteristics, role stress and mental health', *Journal of Occupational Psychology*, 64: 291–304.

Kitchener, K.S. (1984) 'Intuition, critical evaluation and ethical principles: the foundation for ethical decisions in counseling psychology'. *The Counseling Psychologist*, 12(3): 43–55.

Lee, S.S. and Rosen, E.A. (1984) 'Employee counselling services: ethical dilemmas', *Personnel and Guidance Journal*, January, 276–80.

Newton, T. (1995) *Managing Stress: Emotion and Power at Work*. London: Sage.

Oberer, D. and Lee, S. (1986) 'The counselling psychologist in business and industry: ethical concerns', *Journal of Business and Psychology*, 1(2): 148–62.

Orme, G. (1994) 'The role of personal therapy in the training of workplace counsellors', unpublished diploma in Counselling at Work, TDA.

Patterson, J.B., Buckley, J. and Smull, M. (1989) 'Ethics in supported employment', *Journal of Applied Rehabilitation Counseling*, 20(3): 12–20.

Pearson, R.E. (1990) *Counseling and Social Support*. Newbury Park, CA: Sage.

Pryor, R.G.L. (1989) 'Conflicting responsibilities: a case study of an ethical dilemma for psychologists working in organisations', *Australian Psychologist*, 24: 293–305.

Puder, M. (1983) 'Credibility, confidentiality, and ethical issues in employee counselling programming', in James Manuso (ed.), *Occupational Clinical Psychology*. New York: Praeger, pp. 95–103.

Rest, J. (1984) 'Research on moral development: implications for training counseling psychologists', *The Counseling Psychologist*, 12(3): 19–29.

Salt, H., Callow, S. and Bor, R. (1992) 'Confidentiality about health problems at work', *Employee Counselling Today*, 4(4): 10–14.

Chapter 3

Gender and educational guidance
Questions of feminist practice

Diane Bailey

An edited version of 'Gender and educational guidance', in *British Journal of Guidance and Counselling*, 21, 2: 161–74 (1993).

A GENDERED MODEL OF EDUCATIONAL GUIDANCE?

This chapter asks how a feminist perspective might contribute a more thoroughly gendered approach to that family of practices which make up educational guidance. It seems that while feminists in the arts, in the natural and human sciences and in applied knowledges such as therapy and social work have made substantial progress in re-reading, if not reconstructing, their work through the lens of gender, educational guidance and counselling remain relatively untouched by such revisions. As a feminist and an educational counsellor, this concerns me.

The specific focus on gender is not because this is a superordinate category of social organisation, over class, ethnicity or age. The debate about the ontological, economic or biological bases for a hierarchy of social difference is too complex to enter here. In one helpful conceptualisation, race is the modality in which class is lived (Hall *et al.*, 1982) – and the same seems true of gender. We all live at the intersections of categories and it would be difficult to agree on a taxonomy of disadvantage. Any social position is potentially oppressive because any person can be a member of both target and non-target groups, as Green (1987) argues in respect of white female racism. Similarly, being female, black or working-class are not problems. But sexism, racism and elitism *are* profound problems because they are not contingent features but forms of oppression structured by social difference. The focus on gender is helpful in exploring a specific set of power relations, whilst recognising their continuing interpenetration with other forms of difference.

GUIDANCE, COUNSELLING AND THE LIBERAL TRADITION

One difficulty in developing a feminist perspective on guidance and counselling is that these are more like an extended family of practices than a discrete, securely theorised discipline. There is no single model. A summary of current practice indicates the broad terrain (see Figure 3.1). Guidance 'undertaken at all stages of learning' includes both pre-entry and post-entry services. *The Challenge of Change* (UDACE, 1986) provided a rationale and a definitional framework as a basis for subsequent excellent work (e.g. Rivis, 1989; Ames, 1987). The focus has been on structures of provision; on developmental and technical processes (learning competencies, structured interviewing); and on barriers to access and target groups (older learners). The thrust of this work has been empirical, rather than theoretical, with the underlying model of the person remaining largely implicit.

UDACE has concentrated on pre-entry services. Also within the extended family is educational counselling – the preferred term in The Open University, UK and in much of adult and distance education (that the definitions and terminology here are still contested does not affect the argument). Both guidance and counselling, as helping processes, are rooted in the liberal humanist tradition. In this tradition, forms of social difference tend to be individualised. Thus, in research, gender becomes a power-neutral variable; in practice, it becomes a personal attribute, usually of the client rather than of the practitioner. A cornerstone of the tradition is the autonomous, stable and unified individual – central to guidance concepts such as Rogerian person-centredness and Egan-inspired skilled helping (see, for example, Hawthorn and Wood, 1988; Bailey *et al.*, 1990).

A project examining differences between guidance, counselling, advice and other forms of helping, noted, in relation to forms of cultural difference, 'that the principles and philosophies of the activities will remain valid

---

Educational Guidance is:
• a helping process which overlaps with personal and vocational guidance
• a process of clarifying options
• the seven activities of guidance
  — informing
  — advising
  — counselling
  — assessing
  — enabling
  — advocating
  — feeding back
• informed by five values
  — client-centred
  — confidential
  — open and accessible
  — independent
  — freely available
• undertaken at all stages of learning

Figure 3.1 What is Educational Guidance? (from Brown, 1991)

and are applicable to the nature of the enterprise regardless of the group who operationalises it or of the specific need of the client group', though how activities are expressed will vary (Russell *et al.*, 1992: 2). This exemplifies well the belief that the guidance enterprise itself is, self-evidently, neutral or culture-fair.

From a different stable, though within the liberal tradition, is the account of careers education developed by Law and Watts (1977). Counselling objectives are defined as the development by the client of:

- self-awareness (including capacities, aptitudes, abilities, skills, values, goals and interests)
- opportunity awareness (including the identification and evaluation of available options)
- decision learning (including the processes and skills of reviewing options and making realistic action plans)
- transition learning (identifying and practising the multiple skills needed to implement decisions).

Developed specifically in relation to vocational guidance, this conceptualisation has equal validity for educational guidance, since career and learning trajectories for adults are often interrelated (Bailey, 1989), and for access work, given its comprehensive mapping of key elements in life transitions.

Nevertheless, it is difficult to read gender and other social differences into this map other than as contextual features in shaping opportunities or as attributes of the individual. The four-strand menu for effective counselling leaves its elements unconnected.

POSSIBLE CONTRIBUTIONS TOWARDS A GENDERED MODEL

Feminist questions concern how the making of the self and the making of opportunities correlate, how both self and social institutions are gendered to the core, and how gender is not only psychologically formative but politically structural in reproducing power. These questions seem like a small rehearsal of the major 1980s debate between the psychologists of occupational choice and the sociologists of opportunity structuring (Daws, 1981; Roberts, 1981). That (male) debate might be rerun with gender instead of class as its dominant paradigm, with women protagonists and with ethnographic studies of how women learn to labour (paraphrasing Willis, 1977) or labour to learn. However, there are difficulties in seeing gender as an issue of women's absence. Instead, some feminists identify a need for a radical remaking of disciplines and methodologies. For example, Smith explores the problems of 'writing women's experience into social science' so as to 'create a discipline that discloses society as we know it' (1991: 156). This means developing 'consciously non-positivist methods of inquiry' (ibid.: 166) and asking how women can become subjects as well as objects of inquiry.

Three fields of study seem to be potentially useful in considering educational guidance and counselling in relation to gender: theories of discourse: research on curricula and the construction of knowledge; and feminist practice in therapy and psychology.

THEORIES OF DISCOURSE AND GENDER

Discourse theories are, potentially, the most illuminating of the three, but the most difficult to bring into focus. Uncomfortably, they draw on many disciplines. Work in linguistics, psychology and philosophy suggests that the category 'the individual' as a unitary being is neither valid, nor for many purposes useful. It is a historically produced category with its ideological basis in Western culture arising specifically in the eighteenth-century Enlightenment, reinforced through nineteenth-century capitalism and – notoriously – sanctioned in entrepreneurial Thatcherite Britain. In discourse theories the idea of the autonomous and unified individual is replaced by that of the subject.

Lacan (1977) argues that the subject is always the site of contradiction. Our entry into language, the symbolic order, allows us to become human. It is through the acquisition of language that we become social beings. Only by adopting the position of the subject within language can the person produce meaning and make the world intelligible. However, the entry to language can be accomplished only with a profound split between the conscious self, the self which appears as 'I' in its own discourse, and the self which speaks, which is only partly represented there. The unconscious comes into being in the gap created by this division. The unconscious is the repository of repressed and pre-linguistic signifiers, a constant source of disruption to the symbolic order. The displacement of subjectivity across a range of discourses implies a range of positions from which the subject grasps itself and its relations to the real. These positions may be inconsistent so that pressure is created for the subject to seek new and non-contradictory subject positions.

Language is thus crucial to the formation of consciousness and the access to power. Access to language is sexually differentiated and is the means by which we become gendered and by which femininity and masculinity are defined. It is argued that women are both produced and inhibited by contradictory discourses. They participate both in the liberal discourse of freedom, self-determination and rationality, and at the same time in the specifically feminine discourse offered by society of submission, relative inadequacy and irrational intuition (Belsey and Moore, 1989). Attempts to locate a single coherent subject position within a nexus of subjectivities can create pressures which are – at worst – disabling (Walkerdine, 1981).

In linguistics there is interesting work on gender of more detailed empirical kinds (Cameron, 1985). In all known speech communities, male and female are primary categories. In writing, male is privileged over female. Sexual and other inequalities are encoded in language in multiple ways. For example, in the hierarchies of speech in English, women are less powerful than men. It is not that there is a women's language and a men's language, but that there are dominant and subordinate modes and women, as speaking subjects, make more use of the latter. It seems that in most speech communities women exhibit more of the characteristics of subordination than men: turn taking, minimal supporting responses, and continuity of subject from the previous speaker.

The work of Basil Bernstein on class, codes and control offers analyses at every level of how language, as a primary mode of social control, distributes and legitimates power. The work is focused on class, but intersects with gender. There are language-rich and language-poor groups not because the disadvantaged lack speech but because their speech is relatively undervalued. Bernstein's volume, *The Structuring of Pedagogic Discourse*, is a detailed, multi-layered examination of how class and other social relations 'penetrate the assumptions, principles and practices of schools so as to legitimize the few and invalidate the many' (Bernstein, 1990: 98–9). This work on language within pedagogy indicates how much we still have to find out about the power relations of all learning situations, whether face-to-face or dispersed in distance and open learning, and about how subject positions, including gender, are produced and reproduced. Ethnographic studies in further education are showing how masculinity is institutionalised through the internal discourses of education. Skeggs describes how female college students may resist masculine hegemony by subversively 'taking up masculine subject positions' in sexual banter and humour (1991: 127). Research is well developed on how distance education through its highly concrete and 'authoritative' materials can reinforce transmission models of teaching, despite interactive features and consumer choice of modules (Harris, 1988).

Implications for educational guidance include:

1   If gender difference is inscribed in all forms of textuality (written, graphic, spoken, electronic), and learners are both sited as subjects by educational practices and materials and also bring to them their own meanings, we need to reconceptualise the person within guidance theory.
2   Since guidance practice is never value-free and guidance practitioners, like clients and learners, are sited as subjects, greater reflexivity is needed in thinking about guidance interventions. This includes the gender/power issues between practitioners and clients/learners. These are potentially fruitful areas for staff development.

3   An informed understanding of language is important both in staff development and in contributing to clients'/learners' self and opportunity awareness. This could include:
   •   monitoring male/female designations, representations in text and imagery, and semantics
   •   awareness of language behaviours in learning situations
   •   discussion of language dynamics in group situations.

CURRICULUM DESIGN AND GENDER

Curriculum design raises questions both of epistemology (how knowledge is validated) and of political control (who has access and how hierarchies of knowledge are structured). Curriculum development can be a process whereby existing knowledge boundaries are reproduced and people are accommodated to existing social roles. This has key relevance to both pre-entry and post-entry guidance. Bernstein's work shows how contests over what counts as English or science or history within the English National Curriculum are arguments about the whole basis of social order. The curriculum, he argues, involves both visible and invisible pedagogies. Visible pedagogy is the transmission of authoritatively defined bodies of knowledge, with firm rules of sequencing and with assessment according to explicit external criteria. Invisible pedagogy involves the discursive, inexplicit rules of how things are done, including acquiring specific discourses.

Deconstructionists are now researching established disciplines to trace their ideological roles: for example, how medical science has persistently located women as the object of study rather than as the scientist (Jordanova, 1989), and how 'national curricula' of the past have contributed to notions of citizenship or Englishness. Matthew Arnold saw curriculum design as a matter of cultural selection, the purpose of which was moral regeneration. Raymond Williams, following Arnold, argued for a public curriculum to create the values of an educated democracy and a common culture (Williams, 1961). Foucault (1972) sees within curricula sets of regulatory practices and techniques which have corresponding forms of subjectivity and which thus internalise authority.

Present debates about a curriculum for higher education include two opposed perspectives. First, there is the traditionalist emphasis on academic knowledge as autonomous, hierarchical and informed by pure research. A university as cultural custodian should teach philosophy because that is an established area of human enquiry, conducted at a certain level. Secondly, there is the vocationalism of the new Right. Academia should respond to the market place in both its production of graduates and its research. Both views are conservative and both are male-dominated.

Counter-approaches to curriculum design informed by gender can be clustered into three types: reconstruction, incrementalism and transformation.

The *reconstruction of existing disciplines* aims to make them more inclusive of women. Feminist research has made considerable gains in recovering women's past contributions to knowledge and in showing how women have been systematically excluded from the construction of – say – biology, theology and art. History is probably the best-documented example, with women being made more visible, through detailed painstaking research, as both the subjects and the producers of history (Stanley, 1990). The feminisation of history is involving some realignment of discipline boundaries, and analysis of how history has functioned as a male discourse, with a key role in Foucault's sense in the creation of national identity.

The *incremental approach* involves 'adding on' women's studies as a discrete area. The conservative criticism of this development is that women's studies is an academic hybrid, lacking intellectual rigour and politically tendentious. The radical criticism of it is that it makes less likely any comprehensive review of the remaining curriculum. The ghetto of women's studies leaves unchallenged the edifice of men's studies that has stood from Plato onwards. However, the rationale for the incremental approach is that women's studies provide learning that is distinctive in both content and pedagogy. Blundell (1992), analysing the curriculum of adult education in the UK from the perspectives of four feminist discourses (liberal, radical, marxist and socialist), locates the 'adding women on' approach within the liberal tradition. She concludes that this approach, though ultimately ineffective in realigning power relationships, can successfully challenge sex-role stereotyping.

Transformation is the most radical approach since it questions all elements of the curriculum: content, process, pedagogies, assessment and validation. 'Feminism has to analyse how design of the curriculum reinforces attitudes to gender experienced as oppressive' (Parsons, 1990). The basis of this analysis is that all curricula are experienced differentially. Adults have acquired preferences for subjects and for learning styles through their socialisation, especially in previous schooling, with gender a key determinant. There is interesting research into women's preference for 'connected' learning and for links between cognitive and experiential domains (Belenky *et al.*, 1986). Women, relative to men, not only prefer shared and interactive learning, but may be more active in using local support systems to access this (Kirkup and von Prümmer, 1990). Such a preference for affiliation should not be read as deficient or as evidence of lacking 'independence'. The cultural association of masculinity with objective, rational, abstract forms of knowledge is being challenged (Gilligan, 1982). This correlation relegates all elements supposedly irrational to the opposite pole of femininity. 'Objectivity is male subjectivity' has become a feminist truism. If the curriculum is not gender-fair but actually functions to reproduce women's subordination, to devalue their learning preferences and to deny them role models, then transformation is desirable.

If the curriculum is structured by social difference, then it can eventually be transformed to comprehend a wider spectrum of knowledges, to be more inclusive of difference. One role of educational guidance might be to contribute to this permeability.

Implications for educational guidance include:

1   Those in independent, front-end guidance services need an understanding of the role of gender in shaping vocational self-images and development, their own as well as their clients'.
2   Educational counsellors might accept a responsibility to explore assumptions about curriculum design, discipline boundaries and forms of knowing. Those involved in the assessment of prior learning will necessarily confront some of the contradictions inherent in how knowledge is differentially construed and legitimised.
3   Theorists and practitioners could debate more widely the ideological bases of guidance: how far is it involved in accommodating learners to what exists; how substantial is its feedback role and how does it assemble relevant data for this; how oppositional or challenging should practitioners be in working with clients who seem constrained by sex-role stereotyping?
4   Those with guidance responsibilities in both pre-entry and post-entry services at present have marginal inputs to curriculum design. Enhancements might include:
    •   monitoring of existing curricula from the learners' perspectives, including both visible and invisible pedagogies
    •   lobbying for consideration of gender issues in the planning of new courses
    •   more women and more counsellors in academic planning
    •   the collection of qualitative as well as quantitative data on gender to feed back to providers.

FEMINIST THERAPY AND PSYCHOLOGY

Personal or therapeutic counselling and educational counselling in the UK relate to different theoretical traditions, although, increasingly, educationalists are undertaking counselling training and there is a commonality of skills. Personal counselling is largely concerned with people in distress, with dysfunction; educational and vocational counselling are concerned with people in transition, involving both cognitive and affective processes, but not necessarily dysfunction. Nevertheless, recent work on therapy and gender is relevant to educational practice. Three aspects could be singled out:

research on gender and psychological life; the analysis of counselling itself as a social practice; and work on single-sex groups.

Gender and psychology is now widely researched by academic psychologists and by counsellors. This includes work on subjectivity and methodology (Hollway, 1989); on how psychology contributes to popular conceptions of masculinity and femininity (Squire, 1989); and on the role of developmental psychology in maintaining and regulating gendered social relationships (Burman, 1991). In experimental psychology, Gilligan (1982) has argued that interpretations of data by male theorists have resulted in male experiences being established as the norm, with female characteristics appearing deviant. Read 'in a different voice', through female perspectives, the same data can support different theories. Of direct relevance to guidance theory is Hollway's (1991) research on gender within workplace power relations and the implications of this for training occupational psychologists. It is precisely work of this kind which could contribute to a more coherent understanding of self and opportunity awareness and the learning needed to manage transitions. A focus of research within therapy has been how the individual internalises the power relations, sex roles and psychodynamics of the family (Chaplin, 1989). Orthodox therapy has tended to see mental health as coterminous with a satisfactory nuclear family life – now a dissolving mirage. Feminist therapy starts from the premise that patriarchy is formative of the internal life of both women and men. The self is created divisively and gender is at its core (Eichenbaum and Orbach, 1987).

Feminist counselling draws more systematically on sociology than do most orthodox therapies. For example, Oakley's (1974) work on housework as repetitive, isolated and perpetually unachieved can inform counsellors' work with women. Similarly, work on mothering as not just an individual relationship (which in any case not all women have), but as a primary social institution which is simultaneously idealised and accorded low status, can illuminate the emotional and psychological states of both women and men. The vast majority of unpaid caring is done by women. At the same time, 45 per cent of the workforce is female. This diversity of role can exact a cost – in depression, stress, under-achievement or under-recognition. Within the right framework it can also strengthen women as learners, already skilled at time and task juggling, coping with discontinuity and regarding the home as a workplace. Whilst personal counsellors deal with the psychological costs, educational counsellors can help women realise the benefits.

The *examination of counselling itself as social practice* suggests how helping agencies of all complexions – psychiatry, therapy, counselling and guidance – partake of the dominant culture and may reflect cultural stereotypes. The interrogation of counselling as monocultural is well advanced (Saleh, 1989). The majority of counsellors in higher education services are women, though more services are headed by men. More women than men use the services and, significantly, women academics give more time and attention to personal problems presented by students and by colleagues than do men academics (Wheeler, 1989).

Single-sex groups, the third feature which is transferable from therapy to education, is the most directly practical. All-women groups are used occasionally in access work and women's studies courses. However, the law restricts the advertising of single-sex courses to those aimed at women who have been absent from full-time education because of domestic responsibilities or those providing training in areas where one sex is under-represented. It is counselling psychology which is substantially providing the rationale and the empirical research on single-sex group work. In therapy, more women than men form such groups and the groups achieve cohesiveness quicker than do mixed groups (Price, 1988). Women are temporarily released from the need to care for men; they take more risks; and they engage in interactions which might prove disruptive or threatening in the family or elsewhere. Opportunities for transference and counter-transference are significantly different within an all-female environment. In summary, such groups meet a need not met elsewhere in society and their very abnormality makes them valuable. These benefits seem so clearly transferable to educational contexts as to make single-sex groups for some purposes worth considering by counsellors, tutors and planners.

Implications for educational guidance include:

1   Group counselling with skilled management can provide 'virtual' experiences for participants in that it models processes in a relatively safe context and allows participants to try unfamiliar roles. This is particularly useful for decision learning and transition learning, as well as for the more usually invoked group support. The benefits are apparent, but in distance education the logistics of creating groups may be difficult or expensive.

2   Single-sex groups can provide good counter-cultural experiences for both sexes. The argument against such separatism is that for women it reinforces their dual status and creates the illusion of power that is not affirmed elsewhere. The learning environment is distorted and unreal. However, for some counselling purposes (especially the exploration of self and opportunity awareness) and for some learners, the advantages seem considerable, including:
    • trust may be more easily established because the group does not reproduce the dominant culture
    • self-disclosure (e.g. about past learning experiences) may be easier
    • an all-female micro-culture may avoid problematising women
    • opportunities for trying out roles (e.g. group leader, presenter) are created, in a potentially supportive environment.

3   Counselling services at both pre- and post-entry stages should monitor

cultural stereotyping in both structures and individual practice. Unlearning sexism is a problematic and continuing task for all of us – clients, practitioners and managers – and should be part of both staff development and of work with learners.

CONCLUSION

I have tried to indicate some of the implications and questions for guidance arising from three very extensive and volatile fields of knowledge. In each of these areas, feminists are making a substantial and specific contribution – readings and research which, amongst other things, are dissolving discipline boundaries. Of course, there is not one feminism, just as there is not one version of guidance. This makes any gendered model of guidance, synthesising current work even provisionally, very difficult to formulate.

It is, though, possible to suggest ways forward.

One is a continuation of the debates already developed by practitioners. Though unquantified by research, it is probable that women predominate in guidance roles (broadly defined) and also comprise the largest constituencies of clients. This enables a reflexive approach as well as providing the context for research. This means not only debating and lobbying on women-related issues (already keenly undertaken by agencies and individuals), but also exploring how the politics of gender shape the behaviours, meanings and institutions of guidance and counselling.

Second, we can draw on work discussed above to interrogate the most durable guidance approaches. For example, the elements of self-awareness and opportunity awareness in the Law and Watts configuration might be correlated, with gender as a formative modality. In structuring social relationships and meanings, difference produces both self and opportunities (or, in the vocabulary of post-modernism, subjectivity and power). What is needed, in Bernstein's terms, is a more dialectical account of how the outside becomes the inside and how the inside shapes the outside (Bernstein, 1990: 94). This is difficult, but I have tried to suggest how a great deal of exciting work on gender, as one of the binaries which powerfully organise our cultures, could help us in the task.

BIBLIOGRAPHY

Ames, E. (1987) *Financial Barriers to Access*. Leicester: Unit for the Development of Adult Continuing Education.

Bailey, D. (1989) 'Careers Counselling and Guidance'. In Dryden, W., Charles-Edwards, D., and Woolfe, R. (eds) *Handbook of Counselling in Britain*. London: Routledge/Tavistock.

Bailey, D., Docherty, A., Hawthorn, R., Opie, L., Hodgen, L., and Mares, P. (1990) *Counselling in Educational Guidance*. Cambridge: National Extension College.

Belenky, M.F., Clinchy, B.M., Goldberger, N.R., and Tarnle, J.M. (1986) *Women's Ways of Knowing: the Development of Self, Voice and Mind*. New York: Basic Books.

Belsey, C., and Moore, J. (1989) 'Introduction: the Story so Far'. In Belsey, C., and Moore, J. (eds): *The Feminist Reader: Essays in Gender and the Politics of Literary Criticism*. London: Macmillan.

Bernstein, B. (1990) *Class, Codes and Control, Volume IV: The Structuring of Pedagogic Discourse*. London: Routledge.

Blundell, S. (1992) 'Gender and the Curriculum of Adult Education'. *International Journal of Lifelong Learning*, Volume 11 No. 3, July-September.

Brown, J. (1991) 'What is Educational Guidance?', *Adults Learning*, Volume 2 No. 10, June.

Burman, E. (1991) 'Power, Gender and Developmental Psychology'. *Feminism and Psychology*, Volume 1 No. 1.

Cameron, D. (1985) *Feminism and Linguistic Theory*. London: Macmillan.

Chaplin, J. (1989) 'Counselling and Gender'. In Dryden, W., Charles-Edwards, D., and Woolfe, R. (eds): *Handbook of Counselling in Britain*. London: Routledge/Tavistock.

Daws, P.P. (1981) 'The Socialisation/Opportunity-Structure Theory of the Occupational Location of School Leavers: a Critical Approach'. In Watts, A.G., Super, D.E., and Kidd, J.M. (eds): *Career Development in Britain*. Cambridge: CRAC/Hobsons.

Eichenbaum, L., and Orbach, S. (1987) 'Separation and Intimacy: Crucial Practice Issues in Working with Women in Therapy'. In Ernst, S., and Maguire, M. (eds): *Living with the Sphinx*. London: Women's Press.

Foucault, M. (1972) *The Archaeology of Knowledge*. London: Pantheon/Tavistock.

Gilligan, C. (1982) *In a Different Voice*. Cambridge, Mass.: Harvard University Press.

Green, M. (1987) 'Women in the Oppressor Role: White Racism'. In Ernst, S., and Maguire, M. (eds): *Living with the Sphinx*. London: Women's Press.

Hall, S., Critcher, C., Jefferson, T., Clarke, J., and Roberts, B. (1982) *Policing the Crisis*. London: Macmillan.

Harris, D. (1988) *Openness and Closure in Distance Education*. London: Falmer.

Hawthorn, R., and Wood, R. (1988) *Training Issues in Educational Guidance*. Leicester: Unit for the Development of Adult Continuing Education.

Hollway, W. (1989) *Subjectivity and Method in Psychology: Gender, Meaning and Science*. London: Sage.

Hollway, W. (1991) 'The Psychologization of Feminism or the Feminization of Psychology'. *Feminism and Psychology*, Volume 1 No. 1.

Jordanova, L. (1989) *Sexual Visions: Images of Gender in Science and Medicine between the Eighteenth and Twentieth Centuries*. Hemel Hempstead: Harvester Wheatsheaf.

Kirkup, G., and von Prümmer, C. (1990) 'Support and Connectedness: the Needs of Women Distance Education Students', *Journal of Distance Education*, Volume V No. 2, Autumn.

Lacan, J. (1977) *Écrits* (translated by Alan Sheridan). London: Tavistock.

Law, B., and Watts, A.G. (1977) *Schools, Careers and Community*. London: Church Information Office.

Oakley, A. (1974) *The Sociology of Housework*. London: Martin Robertson.

Parsons, S.F. (1990) 'Feminist Challenges to Curriculum Design'. *Studies in the Education of Adults*, Volume 22 No. 1, April.

Price, J. (1988) 'Single-Sex Therapy Groups'. In Dryden, W., and Aveline, M. (eds): *Group Therapy in Britain*. Milton Keynes: The Open University Press.

Rivis, V. (1989) *Delivering Educational Guidance for Adults*. Leicester: Unit for the Development of Adult Continuing Education.

Roberts, K. (1981) 'The Sociology of Work Entry and Occupational Choice'. In Watts, A.G., Super, D.E., and Kidd, J.M. (eds): *Career Development in Britain*. Cambridge: CRAC/Hobsons.

Russell, J., Dexter, G., and Bond, T. (1992) *Differentiation Between Advice, Guidance, Befriending, Counselling Skills and Counselling: Summary Report*. Welwyn: Advice, Guidance and Counselling Lead Body Secretariat, August.

Saleh, M.A. (1989) 'Mono-Cultural Counselling'. *International Journal for the Advancement of Counselling*, Volume 12 No. 1, January.

Skeggs, B. (1991) 'Challenging Masculinity and Using Sexuality'. *British Journal of Sociology of Education*, Volume 12 No. 2.

Smith, D. (1991) 'Writing Women's Experience into Social Science'. *Feminism and Psychology*, Volume 1 No. 1.

Squire, C. (1989) *Significant Differences: Feminism in Psychology*. London: Routledge.

Stanley, L. (1990) 'Recovering Women in History from Feminist Deconstructionism'. *Women's Studies International Forum*, Volume 13 Nos. 1–2.

Unit for the Development of Adult Continuing Education (1986) *The Challenge of Change*. Leicester: UDACE.

Walkerdine, V. (1981) 'Sex, Power and Pedagogy'. *Screen Education*, No. 38, Spring.

Wheeler, S. (1989) 'Counselling Women'. *AUT Woman* (Newsletter of the Association of University Teachers), No. 18, Autumn.

Williams, R. (1961) *The Long Revolution*. London: Chatto & Windus.

Willis, P. (1977) *Learning to Labour: How Working Class Kids Get Working Class Jobs*. Farnborough: Saxon House.

Chapter 4

Careers guidance and ethnic minorities in Holland and Britain

Confronting fear and anger

Frans Meijers and Carrie Piggott

An edited version of 'Careers guidance and ethnic minorities in Holland and Britain', *in British Journal of Guidance and Counselling* 23, 1: 53–67 (1995).

INTRODUCTION

There has been much debate in the UK on the philosophies underpinning the work of those involved in developing equality of opportunity (e.g. Swann, 1985; Gewirtz, 1991; Forbes and Mead, 1992). A distinction has been made (ILEA, 1983) between three key perspectives:

- The *assimilation perspective*, in which it is expected that ethnic minorities should be enabled to fit in to society. Organisations which set out to treat all individuals as the same, or are 'colour-blind' in their philosophy, could be said to impose a form of cultural lobotomy on their clients, in denying the additional skills, knowledge and experience that they have as members of a minority culture. Where help is provided, it is informed by a notion of 'deficit', as defined by the providers.
- The *cultural diversity or multi-cultural perspective*, which seeks to recognise and validate the cultural beliefs, practices etc. of ethnic minorities, e.g. food, music, rituals. While beginning to affirm cultural differences as valuable assets in the community, this perspective has been seen as tokenistic, in paying insufficient attention to inequalities in employment, housing, education and training, and to the direct experience of racial discrimination.
- The *equality perspective*, which recognises institutional racism as evidence of unequal power and seeks to redress this through, for example, wider consultation and power-sharing, educational and training programmes that tackle issues of inequality and challenge a mono-cultural supremacy, and the development of policies and procedures to address discriminatory practices directly, including systems to monitor effectiveness.

This chapter sets out to explore the question of what a careers guidance service would look like, if it were operating from an equality perspective, and the problem of the barriers to the development of such services. We will first outline the national contexts of guidance services in Holland and the UK, and will explore the theoretical models underpinning practice, and the extent to which they provide an adequate foundation for work with ethnic minority clients. Then, we will draw out some conclusions about the scope for action in the present political and economic climates.

THE NATIONAL CONTEXTS

Britain and Holland have the highest proportion of 'visible ethnic minorities' – people 'likely to be discriminated against on the basis of colour' (Forbes and Mead, 1992: 1) – and the most extensive legislation covering racial discrimination in the European Community (*ibid.*). Both countries have well-established minority populations, although their composition is very different, with the main groups in Britain coming from the Caribbean and the Indian sub-continent, whilst the largest groups in Holland are Surinamese, Turkish and Moroccan.

In *Holland*, ethnic minority communities – however well-established – are nonetheless typically referred to as 'immigrants', reflecting the white majority's assumption that their stay is temporary and that eventually they will return to their countries of origin. People from Turkey and Morocco started to arrive in Holland in the early 1960s, and most have retained their own nationality, as have many of their children. The third generation though is predominantly Dutch. The Surinamese arrived in the mid-1970s, when Surinam gained its independence, and were Dutch citizens.

Forbes and Mead (1992) provide figures for 1988, when it was estimated that nearly three-quarters of a million people (4.9 per cent of the population) were from ethnic minorities. Recent statistics (Het Amsterdams Bureau voor Onderzoek en Statistiek, 1992) give a figure of 6 per cent of the total Dutch population, and predict that this will double in the next 25 years. The proportion among young people between 16–24 is approximately 12 per cent (Werdmölder, 1990: 4).

The Dutch Ministry of Internal Affairs (1992), in a Memorandum on Minorities, recognised that these communities could no longer be regarded as temporary residents, and raised questions of how to improve opportunities for those who had been marginalised in terms of the labour market, education, training, and society as a whole. The ineffectiveness of programmes to develop equality is evidenced by relatively high levels of unemployment: 40–50 per cent of the main minority groups, compared with 14 per cent of white people, and an even higher rate – 50–66 per cent – of ethnic minority young people, are unemployed (Roelandt and

Veenman, 1990: 17; Verweij, 1991: 11). This disparity has been attributed in part to lower educational levels and in part to racial discrimination in personnel practices (see, for example, Hooghiemstra *et al.*, 1990). It can be seen that careers practitioners, who might be expected to be closely involved with racial inequality in the labour market, have had relatively little impact, and until recently, little encouragement to seek more effective strategies.

Migration into *Britain* started somewhat earlier, with a larger influx in the 1960s. Forbes and Mead (1992) estimate that by 1989 the visible ethnic minority population numbered over 2.5 million (about 4.7 per cent of the total population). In contrast with Holland, 70 per cent were British citizens and 40 per cent had been born in Britain (*ibid*); about 8 per cent of under-16-year-olds were from ethnic minorities. Forbes and Mead conclude that minority groups are systematically disadvantaged in the labour market, although the nature and degree of disadvantage varies according to country of origin. They also point out that 'the position of visible minorities in the British labour market has improved in the last decade, in contrast to all other member states' (1992: 20). This has largely come about through the political pressure brought to bear by these groups, particularly in the metropolitan areas, and especially in relation to those services which have been under local democratic control, including education and careers guidance.

MODELS OF CAREERS GUIDANCE UNDERPINNING PRACTICE

(a) Holland

Training for Dutch practitioners of careers guidance draws heavily on the work of psychologists, with emphasis on the individual and the development of the self-concept. Two main models are apparent in practice, alongside an *ad hoc*, trial-and-error approach to delivery.

The first working model resembles an economic benefit approach, in which it is assumed that young people will put effort into programmes that will help them to get the jobs they want (Schultz, 1961). It is assumed that they will calculate the relationship between means and goals in a rational way.

The second working model draws on theories of occupational choice and career development, and again assumes a form of rationality, in presuming that the young person will be aware of the need for an early commitment, and will seek information and make plans to obtain outcomes that satisfy personal needs, make the best of individual talents and lead to long-term goals. The individual is seen as striving to achieve internal consistency, and the process is one of convergence on a limited range of possibilities.

Dutch research shows little evidence of this rationality in practice, except to some extent among middle-class white adolescents (Verijdt and Diederen,

1987: 11). More commonly, there is a closer relationship between factors like the level and type of education on the one hand and the duration of unemployment and actual work entered on the other, with the former factors operating in a limiting rather than a motivational way (Bullens, 1987: 30ff). In other words, disadvantaged young people, whether white or black, frequently abandon their ambitions when they realise that these are not realistic. Other research has shown that young adults are guided by traditional role expectations, combined with 'accidental' opportunities, i.e. jobs that are available locally and job ideas which they happen to encounter (Projektgruppe Weiterbildung, 1990). As long as young adults see themselves as youngsters, they are willing to prolong their stay in education. As soon as they consider themselves as adults, this willingness decreases very rapidly (Meijers, 1992). From then on, they demand a paid job in order to lead an adult life.

Few studies have been made of occupational choice processes among ethnic minority populations. Studies of educational and training projects designed to improve the market position of ethnic minority youngsters have explored the reasons why these young people have failed to develop effective plans to find paid employment when leaving these schemes, or are unwilling to participate in such programmes (Bom, 1989; Eising et al., 1990; Vlaming, 1991). These writers suggest that ethnic minority young people have been unable to develop a 'work identity' because of the discontinuity between their own aspirations, the training they are offered and their knowledge of the reality of the labour market. The youngsters realise that as older applicants they will be less attractive to employers, and that they can still expect to encounter discrimination in employment.

To conclude, Dutch practice is built on assumptions about individuals and the processes in which they are engaged, which are not supported by research on either white or ethnic minority youngsters. The Dutch word for guidance (*voorlichting*) – which translates literally as 'lighting the way ahead' – conveys an image of guidance practice in which professional expertise is used to throw light on the individual and his or her immediate path ahead, without penetrating the surrounding darkness.

(b) Britain

In Britain, practice has been dominated by two main strands of thinking: 'talent-matching', drawing on the principles and practices of early occupational psychologists (e.g. Rodger, 1952); and the developmental model, which has roots in counselling theory (e.g. Rogers, 1961; Super, 1981). The former was important in developing systematic techniques for interviewing and assessing client's abilities, interests, needs, personal circumstances and a similar technology for gathering information about opportunities, so that informed advice could be given to clients on which opportunities were most appropriate to them, or at best, so that clients could be enabled to see themselves in relation to the world of employment. The developmental model has been important in inspiring programmes of careers education and guidance: most practitioners have a strong commitment to concepts of an on-going process, with the individual as the primary focus. It is interesting nonetheless that the influential DOTS model (Decision Learning, Opportunity Awareness, Transition Learning and Self-Awareness) (Law and Watts, 1977), which informs much careers education in schools and colleges, draws heavily on talent-matching.

Many British practitioners while relying on talent-matching and developmental concepts and techniques in practice, have also been influenced by the work of sociologists (e.g. Roberts, 1974), which highlights the importance of opportunity structure in determining the actual development of an individual's career or work history. Structural factors such as educational level and type, family background and geographical location have been found to have greater predictive power than personal factors such as preferences and ambitions. Recent work (e.g. Banks *et al.*, 1992; Bynner and Roberts, 1991) shows how opportunities are patterned as 'trajectories' for key sub-groups within the youth cohort, and shows comparable patterning in Germany.

The possibility of a reconciliation between psychological and sociological factors emerged with the publication of Law's community interaction model (Law, 1981). This model recognises that the individual is neither entirely independent in seeking career goals nor entirely passive in pursuing his or her structural destiny, but is exposed to a variety of potential influences which may be influential in a variety of ways. Law's model directs the practitioner's attention to the client's immediate geographical area and to the networks within that area. This approach allows for the possibility of viewing the individual as a participant in the guidance process, rather than a peg, plant or pawn.

To conclude, the British practitioner can draw on a richer field of theory but practice tends to reflect a developmental orientation. There are, in addition, administrative pressures on practitioners to encourage clients to arrive at firm conclusions about their next steps, required by, for example, computer-based recording systems and training credit programmes. There is also less theoretical work available on the career development of ethnic minorities, and consideration of their unique position raises profound questions about the assumptions on which careers guidance is based.

KEY ISSUES IN THE PROCESS OF CAREERS GUIDANCE WITH ETHNIC MINORITIES

Before we outline the delivery of services in the Netherlands and the UK, we believe it would be useful to develop some key ideas about careers guidance as a process for developing equality in practice.

First, the role of the client as an equal partner needs recognition. A helping relationship has an implicit power dimension, in that the helper has certain resources which the client lacks. Ethnic minority clients may also invest their helpers with the impersonal power of their role, i.e. they may see them as agents of white authority or as representatives of the structures to which they are denied access. To empower clients, practitioners may first need to explore the relationship itself. They may have to recognise that their assumptions about choice processes may be inappropriate. Where a common culture cannot be assumed, techniques to draw out information from the client may be less relevant than autobiographical discussion to establish the client's frame of reference. The notion of the 'self' as a dynamic structure with many dimensions of facets – a 'family of selves' – has been developed by such writers as Rosenberg and Gara (1985), Markus and Wurf (1987) and Cantor and Kihlstrom (1987). A distinction has been drawn between 'contextual selves', e.g. the subidentities associated with a work role or a leisure role, and 'temporal selves', reflecting past, present and possible future identities. We cannot assume that the individual will have, or indeed want, an integrated self-concept, given that she or he may have access to at least two cultures and may as a result have multiple possibilities that are not necessarily in harmony (see, for example, Hermans, 1992). So the first task of an empowering guidance process will be to work with the client on his/her *'internal dialogue'*, in order to encourage the client to explore relevant selves and their implications.

Second, the importance of structural inequality and racism needs to inform the development of opportunity awareness. The client may need support in developing knowledge about the implications in developmental terms of different types and levels of work, the role of qualifications and of gender, the way in which work tends to be allocated, and the barriers that may be encountered by a black person. This knowledge is one part of an emerging *'external dialogue'*, by which the client can explore a wider range of opportunities in relation to the issues arising from the 'internal dialogue' and can start to chart a personal course within the minority and majority culture.

We would characterise the Dutch approach to careers work as vocational guidance, in its traditional sense, and the British approach as career development, or possibly careers guidance and counselling. Both approaches view the client as a rational actor, who will use the guidance process to seek help in pursuing occupational goals. The approach outlined here, based on the central concept of empowerment, could be described as *'career negotiation'*. In this conception of the guidance process, the individual would have the opportunity to discuss his/her selves with someone outside his/her frame of reference, who can recognise the 'bounded rationality' (Simon, 1983) of the individual's perceptions and help the individual to explore within and across cultural boundaries, including those that exist in the occupational sphere.

CAREERS WORK WITH ETHNIC MINORITIES IN PRACTICE

(a) Holland: client–adviser interaction

In the climate in which it was assumed that ethnic minorities would be temporary residents in Holland, services have tended to grapple with the 'presenting problems' of ethnic minority clients rather than tackle structural issues. Practice can be characterised as focusing on the client–adviser interaction. It is commonly supposed that because ethnic minority clients appear to be less realistic than their white peers in terms of their ambitions, they are in need of information about education, training and employment (Meijers, 1991). Gosselink (1989) found that much of the process of guidance involved information-giving, with less concern for individual interests and abilities or how they could be related to opportunities.

Since the 1980s there has also been the development of a recognisable multi-cultural perspective, in which descriptions of the supposed 'home culture' of different groups are identified, and in which practitioners are trained in the skills of intercultural communication. Meijers *et al.* (1993) showed that the majority of ethnic minority adolescents questioned had found the information and guidance received to be of little or no use. Their parents similarly felt that their concerns for their children's futures were not being taken seriously and that the information and guidance available did not help them to support their children in transition into either further education or the labour market.

Meijers (1993a) explores the reasons why careers professionals continue to invest in approaches that manifestly do not and cannot bring about structural change. First, he points to the lack of a structural critique within the psychology of vocational choice. Secondly, he identifies the fear of direct contact with minorities as a major barrier to service development.

In discussion with careers professionals, who were mainly teachers, Meijers (1993b) explored the nature of this fear and found that it had a number of aspects. First, there is the fear of listening: the fear that if clients talk about their hopes and fears for the future, the practitioner may be faced with issues with which they have no direct experience and which they cannot resolve. From a structural standpoint it is evident that the practitioner will not be able to 'solve the individual's problem', nor indeed would they see this as their goal. The fear of failure, albeit an imagined failure, is for many a powerful disincentive to engage in direct dialogue. Second, there is the fear of reinforcing discrimination. For example, one teacher saw dangers in developing materials on the lifestyles of Turkish and Moroccan youngsters, from a fear that anything written down would be seen as fact and applied stereotypically. Another aspect of this fear is the concern that special attention paid to minorities might be at the expense of white groups, and might provoke a backlash reaction. Third, there is the fear of direct contact with ethnic minorities themselves, fear of the anger that may be directed at them as 'front line' staff, fear for their own safety (in the psychological sense, but possible also in the physical sense).

Meijers concludes that guidance workers feel ill-prepared and powerless in their dealings with ethnic minorities, and seek to reduce the fear that this provokes by becoming experts on information and the best methods of communicating it. Far from empowering their clients, however, this leads to a one-way process in which individuals from ethnic minority groups are treated as lacking the competences of indigenous people. The usefulness of these competences remains unclear, nor is the possibility explored that other competences may be more useful.

A final point about guidance practitioners in the Netherlands: they are almost 100 per cent white. Although statistical information on this point is lacking, it is significant that as recently as 1992 the Labour Exchange Organisation, which then had a staff of 6,200, appointed 51 individuals from ethnic minority groups to supply a long-recognised need for advisers to provide guidance for the long-term unemployed from ethnic minority groups. The new advisers were appointed on temporary contracts that have to be renewed annually. In consequence, they are likely to be marginalised within the organisation and less likely to be in a position to influence policy with regard to ethnic minorities. In addition, working solely with ethnic minorities, they are isolated from mainstream guidance work and could be seen to have a 'token' function.

Turning to the staffing of careers guidance in education, a recent study made no distinction between indigenous and ethnic minority school counsellors, although the composition of the total group was analysed on many other variables (Mellink et al., 1992). This suggests that non-white school counsellors are an invisible minority.

(b) Britain: service development

Although progress towards equality has been slow in the UK, careers guidance services in some areas have developed a more complex approach than as yet has emerged in Holland. This approach can be characterised as focusing on service development. All services working with young people are expected to have an equal opportunities policy, backed by procedures to tackle specific instances of discrimination in practice. Some services, particularly in the metropolitan areas, have built up a major commitment to racial equality, have invested in staff training and have developed community links. There are several examples of local projects designed to develop services for specific ethnic minority groups, although these are often small-scale and with limited funding.

There is nevertheless evidence of dissatisfaction with careers advice (Wrench, 1992; Mirza, 1992) and of wide differences between careers officers in terms of their awareness of, understanding of, and response to equality issues within services in the nine main areas of large ethnic minority populations.

Unlike the situation in Holland, ethnic minority clients in the UK are increasingly well-qualified. Swann (1985) identified the 'paradox' of Asian performance in academic work, which was at least comparable to that of white students. Since then, growing numbers of students from a range of ethnic minority backgrounds have entered higher education and proceeded to professional and managerial careers. There is a developing body of research on the distress that ethnic minority students encounter in higher education (e.g. Singh, 1990; Siraj-Blatchford, 1991), and many professional groups are monitoring their ethnic minority composition and addressing issues of discrimination. A recent survey (LGMB/ICG, 1993) showed that 3.7 per cent of qualified careers officers, 11 per cent of all trainees and 21.6 per cent of employment assistants were from ethnic minority backgrounds. The numbers in management positions are not given, but are believed to be in single figures.

This growing body of evidence brings home the issue of structural inequality in a very immediate way. Apart from providing a basis from which to develop a socio-economic account of opportunities, it shows clearly that ethnic minorities are not lacking in abilities, nor in the determination to achieve, but that these qualities are still not fully recognised in the labour market.

It also raises the issue of equality within the Careers Service itself, as a set of organisational and interpersonal concerns. From the work cited and the authors' own experience, a number of patterns emerge: frustration with the limited opportunities for advancement from non-professional to professional to managerial roles, alienation from Euro-centric theory and professional practice, stress and high wastage rates in training and employment through marginalisation in study and work teams, plus the stress of 'biculturalism' (Thomas and Alderfer, 1989).

CONCLUSIONS: SOME IMPLICATIONS FOR FUTURE ACTION

Finally, we will consider some implications of the preceding sections in terms of four perspectives: the client, the practitioner, the guidance service, and the national perspective.

The client

Evidence is now emerging about, for example, the expectations, achievements and destinations of ethnic minority clients. More information, both quantitative and qualitative, is needed so that specific guidance needs and barriers to progression can be identified and addressed. In the case of young people, the expectations of parents may also be important. This information may be gathered directly from clients in interview or group sessions, by contact with community groups, or by more formal research methods. Farleigh (1990) provides an interesting example of a project based in a local Council for Voluntary Service, designed to raise the profile of the 'invisible communities' in the area and to develop voluntary and statutory provision as required.

The practitioners

We see real benefits in practitioners being educated and trained in multi-ethnic groups, and see a strong case for monitoring recruitment and, where necessary, targeting funding to ensure that this happens.

The discussion has highlighted some limitations of the core curriculum for learner-practitioners, and suggested the need to develop theoretical models which are informed by structural analysis and recognise the importance of empowerment. More work is now needed on the concepts of 'career negotiation', and the 'internal' and 'external' dialogue, as tools in the development of intercultural guidance practice.

In recognising that ethnic minority clients may draw on different frames of reference and face structural barriers, it also becomes apparent that practitioners will need a range of guidance skills that go beyond talent-matching, in particular those associated with personal counselling, outreach and advocacy. They will also need the opportunity in training to work on the feelings relating to fear and anger that have been discussed.

The guidance services

Services that are new to the issues raised above will need to consider developing an institutional framework, including, for example, developing a policy on equality, monitoring their own staffing and the destinations and achievements of their ethnic minority clients, identifying priorities for action and a senior person responsible for progressing work in this area, as well as arrangements for in-service training, procedures for handling incidents, and support for staff involved.

We hope that this chapter will also stimulate discussion on the issue of organisational development, in particular in recognising that the path to equality at the organisational level is not an easy one and is deserving of greater study and support, if cultural diversity is to be achieved.

The national level

Several points have been made that could have implications at a national level. The need for information, for instance, could be supported through project funding, while recruitment into careers service training and employment could be monitored nationally, with some consideration for designated funding to support ethnic minority entrants into mainstream work. Similarly, issues around service development could be facilitated by central support. More use could perhaps be encouraged of the European Social Fund to address issues relating to the exclusion of ethnic minorities from economic activity.

Meijers (1993c) argues for a strong role for central agencies, particularly the Dutch Ministry of Education and Science and the Central Commission for Employment, in ensuring the quality of guidance. While he welcomes the move to a decentralised structure for guidance services in Holland, in terms of their increased potential to innovate and tailor services to local requirements, he is particularly concerned that without central enforcement of criteria for the quality as well as the outputs of guidance, and without centrally developed plans for implementing and evaluating new developments, the quality of service will be eroded by market pressures.

A final, key concern is that the concentration of ethnic minorities in cities will obscure the fact that equality is a national issue, at least for guidance services. The exclusion or invisibility of minorities in other parts of the country acts as a barrier to mobility and sends messages to practitioners that are as clear as 'Keep Out' signs. Services of the future may need encouragement to remember that they recruit from a national pool, which is increasingly multi-ethnic.

BIBLIOGRAPHY

Banks, M., Bates, I., Breakwell, G., Bynner, B., Emler, N., Jamieson, L. and Roberts, K. (1992) *Career and Identities* (Milton Keynes: Open University Press).

Bom, W. (1989) *Van Klapstoel naar Fauteuil: Methodiek Banen-en Beroepenorientatie Herintredende Vrouwen (From Folding Chair to Easy Chair: a Methodology for Job and Career Orientation for Women Returners)* (Utrecht, Landelijk Steunpunt Vrouw en Werk).

Bullens, R. (1987) *Beroepskeuze in Lager Beroeps Onderwijs en Individueel Beroeps Onderwijs: Over de Ontwikkeling van een Beroepenkeuzeinteressetest (Occupational Choice in Secondary Vocational Education: On the Development of an Interest Guide for Occupational Choice)* (Lisse: Swets and Zeitlinger).

Bynner, J. and Roberts, K. (1991) *Youth and Work: Transition to Employment in England and Germany* (London: Anglo-German Foundation).

Cantor, N. and Kihlstrom, J.F. (1987) *Personality and Social Intelligence* (Englewood Cliffs: Prentice Hall).

Eising, H.T., Dierikx, M.M. and Zondervan, I. (1990) *Evaluatieonderzoek Vrouw en Werkwinkel: Eindrapport (Evaluation of 'Women and Work' Courses: Final Report)* ('s-Gravenhage, SZW) (Ministry for Social Affairs).

Farleigh, A. (1990) Invisible communities, *Community Care*, 22, March, pp. 30–31.

Forbes, I. and Mead, G. (1992) *Measure for Measure: a Comparative Analysis of Measures to Combat Racial Discrimination in the Member Countries of the European Community* Research Series No. 1. (Sheffield: Employment Department).

Gewirtz, D. (1991) Analysis of racism and sexism in education and strategies for change, *British Journal of Sociology of Education*, 12, pp. 183–201.

Gosselink, I. (1989) *Studie- en Beroepskeuzevoorlichting aan Allochtone Meisjes en Vrouwen in Utrecht (Educational and Occupational Guidance for Immigrant Girls and Women in Utrecht: Interim Report)* (Wageningen: Lanbouwuniversiteit Voorlichtingskunde).

Hermans, H.J.M. (1992) Telling and retelling one's self-narrative: a contextual approach to life-span development, *Human Development*, 35, pp. 361–75.

Het Amsterdams Bureau voor Onderzoek en Statistiek (The Amsterdam Bureau for Research and Statistics) (1992) *De Amsterdammers in Acht Bevolkingscategorieen (The Amsterdam Population in Eight Population Categories)* (Amsterdam: O&S).

Hooghiemstra, B., Kuipers, K. and Muus, P. (1990) *Gelijke Kansen voor Allochonen op een Baan? (Do immigrants have equal chances of a job?)* (Amsterdam: Universiteit van Amsterdam).

Inner London Education Authority (1983) *Race, Sex and Class 2: Multi-Ethnic Education in Schools* (London: ILEA).

Katz, J.H. (1989) The challenge of diversity, in: C. Woolbright (ed.) *Valuing Diversity on Campus: a Multicultural Approach* (Bloomington, IN: Association of College Unions).

Law, B. (1981) Community interaction: a 'mid-range' focus for theories of career development in young adults, *British Journal of Guidance and Counselling*, 9, pp. 142–58.

Law, B. and Watts, A.G. (1977) *Schools, Careers and Community* (London: Church Information Office).

Local Government Management Board/Institute of Careers Guidance (1993) *Survey of Employment and Training for the Careers Service, 1992* (London: LGMB).

Markus, H. and Wurf, E. (1987) The dynamic self-concept: a social psychological perspective, *Annual Review of Psychology*, 38, pp. 299–337.

Meijers, F. (1991) *Allochtonen en Beroepskeuze: een Vergelijkende Literatuurstudie (Immigrants and Occupational Choice: a Literature Survey)* (Rijswijk: Raad voor Studie-en Beroepskeuze).

Meijers, F. (1992) 'Being young' in the life perceptions of Dutch, Moroccan, Turkish and Surinam youngsters, in: W. Meeus, M. de Goede, W. Kox and K. Hurrelmann (eds) *Adolescence, Careers and Cultures* (Berlin/New York: De Gruyter).

Meijers, F. (1993a) Arbeidsidentiteit: een tangrijpingspunt voor loopbaanbegeleidung in de postindutriële samenleving (Occupational identity: a starting point for careers guidance in a post-industrial society), in: M. de Grauw, L. Parlevliet and R. Spijkerman (eds) *Loopbaanvraagstukken: Tussen Wens en Werkelijkheid (Career Problems: Between Wishes and Reality)* (Alphen aan de Rijn, Samsom H.D. TjeenkWillink).

Meijers, F. (1993b) Tussen angst en woede: beroepskeuzebegeleiding voor allochtonen (Between fear and anger: careers guidance for immigrants), in: Y. van der Sluis (ed.) *Studie- en Beroepskeuzead-visering in Nieuwe Banen: Bij de Start van de Adviesbureaus voor Opleiding en Beroep (New Directions for Educational and Occupational Guidance: On the Start of Regional Guidance Officers for Consultancy on Education and Employment)* (Lisse/Amsterdam: Swets & Zeitlinger).

Meijers, F. (1993c) Who guarantees quality?, in: A. G. Watts, E. Stern and N. Deen (eds) *Careers Guidance Towards the 21st Century: Report of an Anglo-Dutch Consultation within a European Context*, (Cambridge: CRAC/Hobsons).

Meijers, F., van Houten, H.J. and von Meijenfeldt, F. (1993): *Ingepast of Aangepast? Loopbaanstrategieën in Etnisch Perspectief: Een Vergelijkende studie naar Jongeren en hun Ouders (Integration or Assimilation? Career Strategies from an Ethnic Minority Perspective: a Comparative Study of Young People and their Parents)* (Amsterdam: Delphiconsult).

Mellink, E., Voncken, E., Bosma, Y. and Karstanje, P. (1992) *Functioneren en Rendement van het Schooldecanaat (Functioning and Output of Careers Guidance in Education)* (Amsterdam: SCO).

Ministry of Internal Affairs (1992) *Minderhedenbeleid 1993 (Minority Policy 1993)* ('s-Gravenhage: SDU).

Mirza, H.S. (1992) *Young, Female and Black* (London: Routledge).

Projektgruppe Weiterbildung (1990) Jugend in der 80er jahren: berufsstart und familiengründung (Youth in the eighties: the first job and starting a family), in: H. Friebel (ed.) *Berufsstart und Familiengründung – Ende der Jugend? (The First Job and Starting a Family – the End of Youth?)* (Opladen: Westdeutscher).

Roberts, K. (1974) The entry into employment: an approach towards a general theory, in: W. M. Williams (ed.) *Occupational Choice* (London: Allen & Unwin).

Rodger, A. (1952) *The Seven Point Plan*, NIIP Paper No. 1 (London: National Institute of Industrial Psychology).

Roelandt, T. and Veenman, J. (1990) *Allochtonen van School naar Werk (Ethnic Minorities from School to Work)* ('s-Gravenhage: WRR).

Rogers, C.R. (1961) *On Becoming a Person* (Boston: Houghton-Mifflin).

Rosenberg, S.M. and Gara, M.A. (1985) The multiplicity of personal identity, in: P. Shaver (ed.) *Review of Personality and Social Psychology, Vol. 6, Self, Situations and Social Behaviour* (Beverly Hills: Sage).

Schultz, T.W. (1961) Investment in human capital, *American Economic Review*, 51, pp. 1–17.

Simon, H.A. (1983) *Reason in Human Affairs* (Oxford: Blackwell).

Singh, R. (1990) Ethnic minorities' experiences in higher education. *Higher Education Quarterly*, 44, pp. 344–59.

Siraj-Blatchford, I. (1991) A study of black students' perceptions of racism in initial teacher training, *British Educational Research Journal*, 16(4), pp. 35–50.

Super, D.E. (1981) Approaches to occupational choice and careers development, in: A. G. Watts, D. E. Super and J. M. Kidd (eds) *Career Development in Britain* (Cambridge: CRAC).

Swann, Lord (1985) *Education for All: Report of the Committee of Enquiry into the Education of Children from Ethnic Minority Groups* (London: HMSO).

Thomas, D.A. and Alderfer, C.P. (1989) The influence of race on careers dynamics: theory and research on minority career experiences, in: M. B. Arthur, D. T. Hall and B. S. Lawrence (eds) *Handbook of Career Theory* (Cambridge: Cambridge University Press).

Verijdt, H. and Diederen, J. (1987) *Determinanten van Beroepskeuze (Determinants of Occupational Choice)*, OSA Working Paper W39 ('s-Gravenhage: Organisie voor Strategisch Arbeidsmarktonderzoek).

Verweij, A.O. (1991) *Minderheden in Nederland: Toegankelijkheid en Effectiviteit van Arbeidsvoorziening en Volwasseneneducatie (Minorities in the Netherlands: Accessibility and Effectiveness of the Labour Exchange and Adult Education*) (Rotterdam: Instituut voor Sociaal-Economisch Onderzoek).

Vlaming, H. (1991) Project Arbeidsoriëntatie blijkt ongekend succesverhaal (Project Job Orientation seems to be an unprecedented success story), *Werking*, 2, pp. 7–11.

Werdmölder, H. (1990) *Een Generatie op Drift: De Geschiedenis van een Marokkaanse Randgroep (A Generation Adrift: The History of a Moroccan Beer Group)* (Arnhem: Gouda Quint).

Wrench, J. (1992) New vocationalism, old racism and the Careers Service, in: P. Braham, A. Rattansi and R. Skellington (eds) *Racism and Antiracism: Inequalities, Opportunities and Policies* (London: Sage).

Chapter 5

After the Odyssey

New roles for Mentor

Jo Wiggans

Finding a way to define mentoring which fits all its variety of forms is extraordinarily difficult. Mentoring can be simply a process by which one person uses their experience to help another person to learn more quickly or more effectively than they might do without this help. Mentors are often people working in the same organization or at least in the same professional area as their mentees. In all cases, the focus of the mentoring is on the applied learning of the mentee within the working context.

Mentoring has one established central idea. Mentors talk with their mentees, listen to them, develop a purposeful working relationship with them. This relationship is based in a series of 'essential conversations' which explore and work within the boundaries of the aspirations and abilities of the two participants. As a process, mentoring has its own principles and ethics. It requires an act of faith in the first instance, because the mentor must believe that the mentee has the ability to learn and to achieve. Mentors can be visionaries who look to the horizon of the potential of what an individual might be able to learn to do. They are risk-takers – they can never be sure of the outcomes of their work. Above all, mentors believe in the ability of enabling relationships to cut through barriers to learning.

Mentors usually work within the context of a particular job or a particular workplace. Their objective may be to increase and develop the existing ability of the worker or the student on placement or to help a worker to make the transition from one job to another. Mentoring deals in the changes in working lives or in practice learning. It uses experience – of both the mentor and the mentee – to create a dialogue with the changing situation in which the learner (the mentee) is developing and in which the mentor is usually also working. Mentoring helps the mentee to reframe their experience and relocate their individual aspirations and strategies for achieving their goals within a different perception of the constraints and opportunities that are open to them. Explicitly or implicitly, mentoring addresses issues of power as well as knowledge.

THE ROOTS OF MENTORING

The word 'mentor' comes from Homer's Odyssey. When Odysseus set off for the Trojan Wars, he left his son Telemachus in the charge of Mentor, asking that the older man use his wisdom and experience to guide the boy. Later, Telemachus was helped to reach decisions and to respond positively to the situations in which he found himself by the goddess Athena, often appearing in the guise of Mentor.

In the USA, mentoring developed first in management development. In the UK, mentoring schemes have also borrowed from the traditions of apprenticeships and the idea of the novice 'sitting by Nellie' to learn a new trade. As mentoring develops and takes a wider variety of forms, it is losing some of its paternalistic overtones and its emphasis on the direct trans-mission of skills and knowledge. Modern forms of mentoring are based in a dialogue. Athena needed to take a different guise not only because divine powers were necessary to get her to the side of Telemachus on his adven-tures, but also because the child grows to be a man and needs a different kind of guidance, one which continues to challenge him to achieve inde-pendence and maturity, through the ability to solve his own problems in his own way.

In its traditional form, mentoring is designed to help the new recruit to develop their career. Generally, the mentor is more senior within the organization and more experienced. Their 'protegé' is usually younger and relatively inexperienced. Graduate recruits and junior managers, for example, may be offered a mentor to take a personal interest in their individual development. The mentor guides, advises, sponsors and encourages. The 'protegé' has a respected colleague to interpret their observations, to advise on where to go for information and ideas, and to suggest ways of approaching their work. Some of the inevitable mistakes born of inexperience are avoided and the underconfident new recruit is encouraged to be less tentative by the support of their mentor. The evidence seems to indicate that mentors help their 'protegé' to gain confidence, find job satisfaction and focus on achieving their career aspirations (Jackson, 1993; Clark and Zimmer, 1989).

Nursing, social work and youth and community work use mentors, or developmental supervisors, to support student learning in work placements during the period before they gain their initial qualification. In some cases, the mentor is also responsible for substantial elements of the teaching and assessing of the student's performance on the placement. In others, the mentor is simply there to help the student to learn from their experience and to create opportunities for them to gain relevant experience. Teacher education now places substantial weight on the mentoring of student teachers by experienced staff in schools. In professional training and education, where emphasis is placed on learning through hands-on practice in the workplace, the role of the mentor is closer to that of the tutor. In some cases, mentors take responsibility for the delivery of much of the practice curriculum and are the sole assessors of practical competence. At the same time, they encourage individuals to make career choices based on their own preferences, ambitions and abilities and on the evidence of their performance at work.

STRUCTURES FOR MENTORING

Some mentoring schemes are formally structured, with training or briefing for mentors and 'protegés', clear expectations of the relationships, and systematic ways of selecting and matching. Other schemes are more informal so that new recruits may be invited to find their own mentor and the mentors themselves are assumed to have the necessary skills. Difference and diversity is part of its appeal and, arguably, the key to its success. Mentoring has three features common to all schemes: voluntarism, sense of purpose, and context and boundaries.

Voluntarism

A mentoring relationship is a voluntary relationship. Both the mentor and the 'protegé' are active participants in the process. A key element which is advocated in designing mentoring schemes is a 'no fault' opt-out clause, enabling mentor and 'protegé' to acknowledge that the relationship does not and cannot work within the structure of the scheme. Voluntarism is also important because mentors are not professional advisers or counsellors. They are not the only source of information and support but they may be the most approachable because they are close to the mentee in location and awareness. The knowledge and expertise that mentors offer is their own experience of working and of achieving success in their chosen career and the skills they have developed in helping others to achieve, through teaching, training and staff development. Their task is not to explain the range of opportunities and the obstacles that face their mentee, but to help them to negotiate a highly individual way through the field they are entering. Their job is to look after the interests of the one person (or, rarely, more than one) they are mentoring. They need to be ready to recognize the limits of their own knowledge and skills and to refer their mentee to professional guidance or counselling agencies.

In some cases, judgements are made about the suitability of individuals to act as mentors on the basis of past effectiveness, their ability to commit the time and energy needed, their interpersonal skills or perception of their value as a role model. Within organizations, it is considered a mark of recognition to be appointed as a mentor and volunteers may be easier to find. In interorganizational schemes, however, finding enough suitable mentors is often difficult. The work is demanding and mentors must usually be content to find their rewards in the appreciation and achievements of the individuals with whom they work.

Sense of purpose

The essential conversations of mentoring are purposeful and developed and sustained over a period of time through a succession of meetings. Commitment is required from both parties, with a clear focus on the learning of the mentee. Each is prepared to listen to the different point of view of the other, and willing to work carefully through the issues they are discussing. The mentoring sessions develop a pattern, an internal structure, with an ongoing agenda. There will usually be space in the relationship for crisis contact, but generally the sessions are reflective, exploring what has happened and planning and reviewing action. Mentoring guides the mentee through the experiential learning cycle of reflection, action, experience and review (Boud *et al.*, 1985). In order to be effective, both mentor and mentee need to prepare for their meetings and to focus during the meetings. Lack of commitment by either party is one of the main causes of failure of a mentoring relationship.

Context and boundaries

Mentoring is a working relationship, set in the context of a particular organization, profession or job. Although mentors may come to know their mentee very well, and both may learn a lot about each other's personal histories, a mentor is a 'professional friend'. The relationship begins and ends within the context of practice learning. Mentors and their mentees do not have to like each other as people, though it probably helps if they do, but it is essential that they respect each other as workers.

The importance of context also helps to define the difference between mentoring and other forms of guidance and counselling. Mentors work with the actuality of the daily experience of practice. The agenda for their meetings is based less on what an individual may do in the future than on what an individual has been and is doing in the present. It is from discussion of experience of being a practitioner that mentors guide and develop ideas about the directions that may be taken in both the short and the longer term. The participants need to share an understanding of the context in which they are working. Values and perceptions are part of this shared understanding, although there is space for different perceptions, provided these are explored through the mentoring process.

The degree of formality and structure that is required in a mentoring scheme varies according to the context and particularly according to the parties involved in establishing and maintaining the mentoring scheme. In further and higher education, the expectations and boundaries of the scheme are defined by the educational institution and the practice agency as much as by the needs of the learner. In order to ensure parity of experience for students, there must be a formal structure and minimum requirements for the extent of contact, the agenda and recording of meetings. By contrast, mentoring schemes which form part of an induction programme for newly appointed staff in an organization may be deliberately informal, an enhancement to the induction and probationary period.

MENTORING FOR EQUALITY

More recent developments in mentoring include schemes for which the purpose is explicitly to seek to redress inequalities and to deliver support, critical feedback and guidance to people who may be disadvantaged within current career and educational systems or whose expectations and experience are such that traditional forms of learning support and guidance often fail to establish connections and working relationships. There is evidence that these schemes can successfully raise confidence and help individuals to negotiate their own way through the barriers which stand in the way of achieving their goals. The schemes can be categorized as positive action schemes or as schemes for the 'disaffected' or those who are more likely to respond to the informal and voluntary guidance of a mentor.

Positive action mentoring schemes seek to offer support, encouragement and positive role models. These include schemes which aim to facilitate:

- the promotion of women or black or ethnic minority members of staff into senior management positions
- mentoring for black or ethnic minority students on professional qualifying courses by professionals already employed in the professional field
- retention and success in students from minority groups in higher education.

Such schemes are set up in recognition of the institutionalized disadvantages under which minority groups and individuals from under-represented groups are seeking to learn and develop. Schemes for black students, for example, enable such students to obtain support which is reinforcing of personal identity in situations in which there are very few, if any, black members of staff or black professionals in the field and a minority of black students on the course. At North London College, for instance, sixth-form students are paired with members of the black community who have achieved notable success in their chosen field. The mentors are role models, as well as people who offer individual support, advice and guidance. At Leeds Metropolitan University, there is a scheme for black students taking a law degree to be mentored by black lawyers. There are a number of examples of schemes designed to support and enhance the career progression of women (see, for example, Alexander and Murphy, 1992; Reich, 1995).

In each of these and similar schemes, the 'glass ceiling' that has impeded the progression of individuals is defined as part of the structure and culture of the organization or profession. There is no implication that the individuals involved in the schemes are in any way less able, qualified or experienced. There is no adjustment to the requirements for admission to the profession or the criteria for assessment to make it easier for them to succeed. Mentoring offers access to the forms of informal support, encouragement and guidance that are more readily available to others who can see reflections of themselves in the experience and backgrounds of their colleagues or their teachers. It provides a working relationship, in which people who have some important characteristics in common with each other can share their differences and similarities. Its effect, where it works well, is to raise the self esteem of individuals and to encourage them to identify and aim for higher goals. As role model, the mentor is living proof that these goals can be achieved.

In addition, positive action mentoring encourages the expression of creativity and ideas from workers and students who may not expect the spontaneous approval of their colleagues. The mentor may be the first person with whom the idea is explored, or the one who is prepared to offer critical advice about how to adapt or how to present it. Within the workplace, the mentor has an opportunity to give practical support or at least information about where such support might be found. Whatever the context, the mentor has experience on which to draw to suggest strategies for negotiating a way within the system and for overcoming the complex facets and effects of discrimination. Higher education and some professions are the main sponsors of positive action schemes. Many are well-established in the USA (see, for example, Aloia and Smith, 1992; Hart et al., 1992).

The discourse of these schemes rejects the description of the individuals as 'protegés' as paternalistic and hierarchical. Schemes variously call those who are the subject of the mentoring 'mentees' or 'learners'. There is overt acknowledgment of the sharing of experience and the mutual learning that takes place as mentor and mentee work through problems and ideas together. Neither age nor seniority in the workplace are the important factors in identifying mentors.

The second category of schemes includes those designed to help and guide individuals whose ideas about their future career or lifestyle options are limited by lack of achievement at school, by low self esteem and by low expectations. In addition, it is offering increasingly a way of working with people, particularly young adults, who seem to be alienated from the support and guidance of parents, teachers and other authority figures or who have come to mistrust professional interventions in their life choices.

In this context, mentoring offers a way of taking advice, guidance and, importantly, individual support to those people who often do not make full use of professional services and mainstream learning or training provision. Their experience does not fit the patterns of development which generally would be recommended. In fact, the more it does not fit, the more likely individuals are to see professional guidance and support services as inappropriate, in spite of the willingness of guidance and support workers to help and the resources allocated to remedial and compensatory support. The great advantage of mentoring is that it is neither professional nor is it built into the structures of mainstream provision. This mentor is not part of the system which is seen as judging the behaviour of individuals.

The mentor's experience is a vital part of what they offer. There are schemes which use ex-offenders as mentors for young people who have been involved in criminal activity or mentors who have experience of drug-abuse, but it is essential that they focus less on reinforcing this behaviour than on demonstrating the potential for changing direction. Mentors are usually offered a high degree of support themselves, and some form of mentor training is often included in the project. The principles on which this kind of mentoring is founded are similar to those which underlie counselling projects which seek to train and develop survivors of, for example, rape or incest, as counsellors. The shared experience overcomes barriers. However, these schemes share only some of the features of positive action schemes. Where those relationships were collegial, these are founded in respect for the greater experience of the mentor. Probation Services and voluntary projects are the hosts of some of these mentoring schemes.

Training and Enterprise Councils in England and Wales also have encouraged a range of mentoring schemes as part of their objective to build more effective links between schools and colleges and the world of work. Many of these schemes are linked to work experience. In some, the young people are given the option of joining. In others, they are selected and asked to join. In one scheme in Doncaster, for example, year 10 pupils are selected according to criteria which include poor self-management, low self-esteem, weak communication, attributes and skills which are seen as likely to adversely influence their position relative to other school-leavers in work and training (Beattie and Holden, 1994). This scheme actively sets out to address the pupil's value system, to take account of and seek to improve pupil's performance in school and to raise awareness of the realities of the world of work and the expectations employers have of trainees and new recruits.

A PROFESSIONAL PROCESS IN A VOLUNTARY RELATIONSHIP

Many mentoring schemes are time-limited, lasting only a year or less. Most student placements and work-based learning schemes last a few months at most, but a great deal of learning is expected to be achieved in that time. The needs of the mentee are likely to be more effectively and more quickly met by careful matching with a suitable mentor. The right mix of experience and commitment can be difficult to find or there may simply not be enough mentors for some schemes. There are often more women in junior or middle management positions than in senior positions and more black recruits to organizations than black members of staff whose position is already established. We can also make too many assumptions about the potential for experiences in common to guarantee good working relationships. Experience is multi-faceted and individuals not readily categorized. There will, in all mentoring relationships, be some level of dependence on the ability of the mentor to suspend their own values, at least temporarily, in order to see the world through the eyes of their mentee.

If careful contracting, discussing, anticipating difficulties and honesty in expressing doubts and uncertainties are part of the beginnings of a mentoring relationship, the responsibility for ensuring that this happens rests quite clearly with the mentor. There is authority vested in the role of the mentor which carries a responsibility for defining the process and observing the boundaries of the relationship. Failure to negotiate and clarify expectations and purpose is rarely the fault of the mentee. Where it is difficult to find mentors with the kinds of experience that would be most valuable in the programme, some of the pitfalls might be avoided by detailed briefing and by training for mentors. Mentor development and accreditation schemes for mentors are increasing. In all contexts, there is a move towards a more structured approach. As mentoring programmes are formalized, with mentors occasionally receiving payment for their work, some observers are beginning to comment on the increasing 'professionalization' of mentoring (Beattie and Holden, 1994). The voluntary relationship may be threatened by concerns about control and ownership, and where parity in the learning experience offered is an issue, as it must be in any formal educational scheme linked to learning outcomes or assessments. Yet it is the voluntary nature of the relationship which makes it possible to create a bridge between professional guidance and information services, and between formal subject teaching and individuals for whom the professional discourse is alienating or the hands-on practice learning is a priority. Paradoxically, if mentoring becomes a highly trained and quasi-professional role, it may lose some of its effectiveness, its flexibility and its potential for adapting to and unlocking the potential and aspirations of individuals. Whilst it has been important for mentoring to move away from the paternalism of its origins, its distinctive contribution to learning has been in its ability to be idio-syncratic, to use creative and varied methods, and to move from advocacy to information to personal caring within the scope of one relationship and one series of conversations.

Note

Between 1991 and 1994, the author worked on a project at Leeds Metropolitan University, funded by the then Employment Department, to research and develop the practice of mentoring for students undertaking work-based learning modules or practice placements. The project operated across all five faculties of the University. As part of its research, the team collected and considered examples of mentoring practice in a variety of settings in the UK and the USA.

BIBLIOGRAPHY

Alexander G. and Murphy S. (1992) 'A Mentoring Model for Women', in *Diversity in Mentoring*, Conference Proceedings, Chicago, Illinois: Western Michigan University.

Aloia G.F. and Smith J.C. (1992) 'Mentor/Protegé, Relationships with Underrepresented Undergraduate Students at a Large Doctorate-granting University', in *Diversity in Mentoring*, Conference Proceedings, pp. 12–21, Chicago, Illinois: Western Michigan University.

Beattie, A. and Holden R. (1994) 'Young Person Mentoring in Schools – the Doncaster Experience', in *Young Person Mentoring, Education and Training*, volume 36, no 5, pp. 8–15.

Boud D., Keogh R. and Walker D. (1985) 'What is Reflection in Learning?', in Boud D., Keogh R. and Walker D. (eds) *Reflection: Turning Experience into Learning*, London: Kogan Page.

Clark R.W. and Zimmer B.P. (1989) 'Mentoring, Does It Work?' in *Lifelong Learning: An omnibus of practice and research*, Vol. 12, No. 7, pp. 26–8.

Hart J., Ayers J. and Comas J. (1992) 'Building Bridges through Mentoring – Closing the Gap', in *Diversity in Mentoring*, Conference Proceedings, pp. 453–9, Chicago, Illinois: Western Michigan University.

Jackson, C. (1993) 'Mentoring: choices for Individuals and Organizations', in *International Journal of Career Management*, Vol. 5, No.1.

Reich M. (1995) 'The mentor connection', in Kerry, T. and Mayes, A.S. (eds), *Issues in Mentoring*, London: Routledge.

Part II

Modes of delivery

Chapter 6

The tutorial relationship

John Earwaker

An edited version of 'The tutorial relationship', in *Helping and Supporting Students*, Buckingham: The Open University Press (1992).

Teaching staff in their support role have to cope with a range of ambiguities, tensions and conflicting responsibilities. They are, therefore, in quite a different position from that of professional support staff. On the other hand, their position needs to be distinguished from that of a friend. For a member of staff in an institution of higher education to give help and support to a student cannot be equated with one student helping another. Why not?

It is the institutional context which sets limits to the nature of the relationship. A tutor and a student may belong to the same institution, but they belong there on different terms. For both it is their workplace, but whereas for one it is the place of employment, involving a commitment to deliver a service according to a contract, for the other it is the place where the particular services they seek are to be obtained.

It is not just that each occupies a distinct role; the roles are related to each other in such a way that the tutor is presumed to know things that the student does not yet know. This is a necessary consequence of setting up social encounters of this sort where two people come into contact in order that one shall learn from, and with the help of, the other.

This does not, of course, mean that each cannot respect the other; a context of mutual respect is often required for optimum learning. Nor does the student's tacit acknowledgement of the tutor's status with respect to a specific context have to be generalized to cover any more than is covered by the course. It might be possible to think of the teaching/learning relationship as quite detached from everything else, a purely functional affair, so that one consults one's tutor rather in the way that one goes to get one's hair cut. Clearly, this is affected by the subject and level of study; it is very hard to conceive of higher education as narrowly as this. Consequently, there will almost certainly be elements of role strain when tutor and student meet informally outside the classroom and especially when they meet on the specific understanding that the tutor is to offer the student some kind of personal help, whether in the form of advice, guidance or support, since it is the teaching relationship that will be the determinative one. They meet *as* tutor and student in what is essentially a working relationship, not a social one.

INTERVIEWING, COUNSELLING AND TUTORING

Surprisingly little has been written about tutoring and, in particular, the one-to-one tutorial (Bramley, 1977; Lewis, 1984; McMahon, 1985; Lublin, 1987; Jacques, 1989), but there is, of course, a considerable body of literature both on interviewing and on counselling, either of which might be expected to yield useful insights. The fact is, however, that these two bodies of literature take very different approaches. A good interviewer has a clear idea of where the conversation is going, keeps firm control of it, and dictates its direction. A good counsellor, on the other hand, is one who allows the client to determine the content, the direction and even the pace of the conversation. Indeed, according to one very influential theory (Rogers, 1973), counselling skill lies precisely in *not* being directive; the aim is to be, as far as possible, client-centred, never to dominate or to control, but always to enable or to facilitate the functioning of the other. Thus, the best counsellors are those who can draw out of even the most reticent and inarticulate client what it is that the client genuinely feels or wants. Whereas the skilled counsellor is one who keeps an open mind and can follow the lead of the client, the skilled interviewer is one who wastes no time in getting to the point, and who has no doubt about what the point is since it has already been predetermined without reference to the other person.

So is individual tutoring to be understood as a sort of interviewing or as a sort of counselling? If we think of tutoring as a kind of interviewing we shall expect the skilled tutor to have a clear idea of the purpose of the tutorial, and to make this clear to the student. We shall regard as somewhat unprofessional the tutor who approaches tutorials unprepared, who offers students a completely open agenda, whose tutorials range widely over a number of different matters and rarely come to a tidy conclusion. On the other hand, if we think of tutoring as a kind of counselling we shall expect the skilled tutor to be a good listener who allows the student to talk freely without interruption, and who can elicit from the student with a minimum of prompts whatever it is that the student wants to say. We shall regard as somewhat unprofessional the tutor who has a fixed idea about the function of the tutorial, its content or its form, or both, and who tries to help the student by giving clear and firm guidance or a clearly defined set of procedures to follow. By polarizing the issues in this way it is possible to see that the activity of tutoring is, of course, not quite like either interviewing or counselling, even though it may usefully be compared to both, and at different times and in different contexts it may be appropriate for tutors to draw on either interviewing or counselling skills. Tutoring may be conceived as occupying the middle ground between the two, occasionally verging on one or other, but to be identified with neither.

Although little has been written specifically about tutoring, there are other interpersonal encounters, especially professional–lay consultations, which have been quite extensively studied. This work could be relevant to the tutorial in that many of the same issues are present. One interesting study of doctor–patient interaction (Strong, 1979), found that doctors operated in a number of different modes, two of which were termed the 'clinical' and the 'collegial'. Occasionally, the doctor was able to talk to the patient or the patient's relatives on something like an equal footing, using the correct medical terms, and discussing the case in much the same way as with a colleague. This 'collegial' style of interacting was relatively rare. Mostly, the doctors in the study adopted the 'clinical' approach, offering patients crude oversimplifications of their diagnosis and prescribing treatments dogmatically and without any discussion. This may be a useful distinction for tutors to consider. Are there different ways of conducting tutorials? Do some students somehow manage to qualify for a more 'collegial' relationship, in which they are treated as at least potential equals, so that problems are tackled jointly ('What are we going to do about this?') and within a relationship of trust? If so, this might contrast quite starkly with a mode of interacting with students in which the tutor, instead of negotiating the next step with the student, feels it necessary to tell the student what to do.

Among health professionals it is a commonplace to say that we relate to other people differently according to how we define them, as 'well' or 'sick'. This has sometimes been used as a way of distinguishing between psychotherapy and counselling (Arbuckle, 1967): the former starts from the supposition that the client is 'sick' or in some way needs help to recover the status of a normal human being; the latter tries hard to grant 'normal' status from the start, to respect the client's wishes and to involve the client in his or her own treatment as a matter of principle. Whether or not that holds as a distinction between psychotherapy and counselling, it certainly offers a useful way of distinguishing different ways of relating to the people we are trying to help. If we treat them at the outset as people worthy of our respect we shall behave quite differently than if we regard them as people who, however temporarily, or in however limited a context, have no sensible opinions to offer, since their predicament disqualifies them from engaging with us on that footing.

Similarly, among social workers it has been noted that effective provision of help appears to depend on whether or not the client is perceived as 'worthy', i.e. worth helping (Rees, 1978: 107). The client, it is said, has to project and the professional has to recognize what has been called 'a moral character'. The tutor's initial assessment of the student may be crucial. It is not just, or mainly, in terms of ability (brightest in the class) or academic status (a fourth year Honours student) that the student is assessed, but in terms of what might be termed 'moral status'. The tutorial will be conducted very differently according to whether the tutor judges the student to be generally a worthy person, well-intentioned, honest, reliable and hard-working, or whether the tutor suspects that the student is rather lazy, likely to make excuses and that the excuses could be invented.

In these encounters and interviews (patients consulting their doctor, clients being interviewed by a social worker) the patient or client will often be at a severe disadvantage. Similarly, the student going to see his or her tutor is in a weak position. The question of who controls the interaction is, therefore, a crucial one. The interview format suggests that the interviewer is in control: the counselling format suggests, more interestingly, that while the counsellor potentially has considerable influence in the situation this status is being deliberately renounced in favour of giving the client their say and trying to make sure it is heard. It is here that the idea of an agenda may be helpful. For the distinction between interviewing and counselling is not, of course, that one has a clear agenda while the other does not, but that in one case the agenda is determined by the professional helper while in the other it is determined by the client. Who then determines the agenda when tutor and student meet?

THE TUTORIAL: ITS AGENDA AND ITS MANAGEMENT

Will there be an agenda at all? Both teaching and support can appear as no more than just chatting to students; but if a tutorial is being conducted properly there will be nothing casual about it and its purposes might well be made explicit. The tutorial can then be seen as a professional task carried out by the tutor in the course of his or her professional duties and not something done out of kindness or because of a personal interest in the student.

It might, in any case, seem obvious that the agenda of the tutorial, whether dealing with an academic or personal problem, is set by the student and that it should take shape around the student's expressed needs – a question to be answered or a difficulty resolved. Yet this is to return to the remedial model criticized previously. If tutorial contact is seen not as troubleshooting, but as fostering ongoing development, we have to acknowledge that the student may not be in a very good position to assess his or her own development, whether academic or personal, and may need help in finding the most appropriate starting-point.

Tutors may sometimes have to take the initiative in raising matters of concern, possibly setting up a tutorial which the student has not requested. Even when the initiative is entirely the student's, the tutor may wonder whether there is perhaps more to the student's agenda than has been revealed, and may probe a little to find out more. It is, of course, possible that there is more to it than they have said; there may even be more to it than they have so far realized. The student may describe symptoms without being able to determine their underlying cause. They may misdescribe or even misperceive their own problems. You may not appreciate the full extent or the real nature of your problem; you may not even realize that you have a problem at all. The individual is sometimes mistaken and may be helped by having this gently pointed out.

Sometimes, then, the agenda which the student brings gets altered or amended as the tutorial proceeds; the tutor focuses attention onto what lies *behind* what the student has said. If it is an academic problem, something misunderstood, the tutor may be able to convert an inarticulate question into a more pertinent one. If it is a more personal matter, again the tutor may be able to draw the student away from his or her own agenda (e.g. self-pity) and focus attention onto something else which represents a realistic way forward, a practical 'next step'. On the other hand, of course, the tutor may be clumsy, lacking the necessary skills and the agenda might then change in an unhelpful way, such as when the student wishes to talk about something and the tutor (because he or she feels insecure on that subject or because it is a personally painful matter which the tutor cannot handle) diverts attention away from this. This can happen simply by accident if the tutor is not alert to the agenda which the student has brought, and quick to identify it clearly and to bring it into focus.

However, there is another scenario which can be described in terms of 'agenda': that is, when there is a 'hidden' agenda which the student finds it difficult to talk about. Counsellors are familiar with the case of the client who presents one problem when really there is another lurking behind, the first serving simply as a 'calling card'. The skill lies in detecting the hidden agenda, and gently bringing it out into the open so that it can be dealt with. Tutors are not usually trained to do anything like this. Often it does not occur to them that there will be more to uncover besides what the student tells them initially. Doctors are familiar with the patient who consults them about a relatively trivial problem, and then, just as they are about to leave, says 'And while I'm here, doctor ...' and raises a much more serious matter which is for some reason more difficult to talk about. Yet tutors, even if fully convinced that the student should supply the agenda and eager to follow the student's lead, are sometimes quite surprised at the idea that the student might not have told the full story straight out. Exercises in discovering the hidden agenda may, therefore, be some of the best introductions to training for tutors.

What these reflections seem to suggest is that it is not so much that the student sets the agenda, or that the tutor allows the student to set the agenda, but rather that the student, in a sense, *is* the agenda and that it is the tutor's job to ensure that this is so. That way of putting it seems to do more justice to the reality of the tutorial situation, though of course the student is no mere passive subject. The tutor cannot abdicate responsibility for managing the interaction.

However, if we say that the tutor has the main responsibility for managing the interaction, then how is this best done?

When two people engage in dialogue, they are doing much more than exchanging words and information. They are exchanging meanings. Skilled personal interaction involves an awareness that the words spoken and the meaning intended do not always correspond exactly. This is not only true of the inarticulate person who doesn't express him or herself very well, but also of the fluent speaker who uses language flexibly and skilfully. Conversation has to be analysed rather as a game with 'moves'. One may throw down a challenge, hold out an olive-branch or offer congratulations, while the actual words used might be in the form of, say, a question which, written down, would look like a request for information. Person-to-person discussion quickly runs into difficulties if these linguistic subtleties are not recognized.

It is not only that in trying to understand what someone else is saying we have to read between the lines; we also have to read their non-verbal communication which may be more eloquent than their actual words. One of the great advantages of a tutorial is that it provides an opportunity to pay attention to one student at a time; it allows the tutor to concentrate on the needs of a particular individual and to listen to what he or she 'says' in whatever way. If the tutor simply uses it as an opportunity to talk and to teach, this opportunity has been lost or wasted.

When people are in a relatively strong position, we know how they are most likely to behave. They will initiate the interaction and they will determine when it ends; they will set the agenda, ask the questions and decide whether the answers are adequate or not; they will often address the other informally; and they will feel free to interrupt and to change the subject at any point. Non-verbal behaviour, too, will be used to establish and maintain dominance, e.g. not looking at the other so as to give little chance of feedback, ignoring any signs that the other is either agreeing or disagreeing, or is puzzled or confused or embarrassed, occasionally looking at the other too long and too hard, so that they feel their personal space is being invaded (Gahagan, 1984: 62ff.). This could be a description of a typical tutorial. There is no doubt who is in control. The student is likely to defer to the tutor, to wait for the tutor to speak first and signal when the tutorial should come to an end, to let the tutor determine the agenda, to respond rather than to initiate, to follow any changes of direction and to give way whenever interrupted (Gahagan, 1984: 74ff.). Taken together these are unmistakable signs of dominance and submission.

However, a tutorial does not have to be conducted like this, and it should not be conceived as something the tutor 'gives' and the student 'receives', but rather as something which happens *between* two people, an interaction. It involves collaboration and partnership. If there is an analogy with a piece of music, it is not one played by the tutor, and heard and responded to by the student, but rather a duet, played by both together and brought off jointly. Perhaps the most appropriate analogy is that of a dance (Stern,

1977). There are two parties to it; ideally, whatever happens has to be mutually understood, agreed and accepted. Often it is very far from this ideal.

What needs to be underlined here is the fact that, although we may analyse a tutorial as a social encounter, drawing on the insights and language of social psychology to interpret what is going on, nonetheless, the tutorial is a rather special example of such interaction in that it is by definition contrived. As we have seen, the tutor is in the formal sense responsible for managing the interaction. It is, therefore, not quite like a dance or a duet in which the two partners find mutually satisfying ways of performing. It is a dance in which one of the partners 'leads'. Of course, the tutor may be socially clumsy, awkward or shy in this kind of social setting; and the student may be extremely skilled at social interaction. In practice, it is possible that the student may, in effect, conduct the tutorial. Yet that is not what is meant to happen. It is the tutor's responsibility to manage, on behalf of the student, what is essentially an interactive process.

THE USE AND ABUSE OF POWER

People have different tolerances with regard to their personal affairs, and what one person regards as taking a friendly interest, another may regard as an unwarranted invasion of his or her private life. Some students may be highly sensitive on such matters, guarding their privacy quite jealously, so that an innocent enquiry about where they are spending the summer vacation will be felt to be inappropriate and intrusive, and may get a frosty response. Some may have areas of their life which are for some reason 'no go' areas to all but their closest friends, yet in other respects may be quite relaxed and open.

Apart from individual sensitivities and particularly difficult personal circumstances, there are cultural and gender differences which can lead easily to misunderstanding. A female student who told her male tutor that she had to go into hospital for a few days might not expect to be quizzed for details as to exactly what was wrong; yet a male student in the same circumstances would probably interpret such questions as friendly concern. There are wide differences in the amount of psychological space each individual expects for him or herself and habitually allows to others. The extent to which personal matters, concerning family life for instance, are spoken of outside the home can vary greatly. Cultural and religious inhibitions sometimes render whole areas of life 'taboo'. To receive confidences from someone else is to have power over them; by confiding in you, the other person becomes vulnerable to you. While it is only within a safe relationship that such a risk can be contemplated, it is always a risky procedure.

What happens when the tutor tries to share the student's vulnerability by choosing to come off his or her pedestal, admitting to human failings and offering to engage with the student as a fallible human being? A willingness to expose oneself and to let one's own vulnerability show can go some way towards redressing the imbalance of power. Professional counsellors sometimes use disclosure of bits of themselves as a deliberate tool in helping the other. Tutors, by referring only sparingly to their personal lives, not in a self-indulgent way, but with careful control and self-discipline, may enhance their performance of their helping role. A skilful and thoroughly professional performance does not rule out relating to people in a very personal way.

Of course, people who come seeking help with their problems do not want to hear about anyone else's. Yet within a long-term relationship it may be quite natural for the helper to reveal things about him or herself as a way of getting alongside the other. So while as a general rule tutors need to refrain from talking about themselves, it is possible to make discriminating use of one's own personal history to enhance one's effectiveness in helping. A tutor anxious to encourage a student who has just failed an examination, for instance, might reveal the fact that he or she once had to resit an important examination. Such a disclosure might enable the student to relate to the tutor as a person rather than simply as a representative of the institution or of a class of people who do not have problems.

The essential point, though, is that this is still a very 'powerful' thing to do. If the disclosure is done deliberately, not inadvertently, it falls into place as part of the tutor's attempt to act responsibly to 'manage' the encounter for the benefit of the student. Tutors may allow some of their own vulnerability to show, but that does not mean breaking down in tears with someone who is emotionally upset; the aim is to engage with the experience of the other, but without totally identifying with it so as to have no detachment left to offer them.

We can now identify three aspects of interpersonal power as it affects the tutorial relationship.

First, it is not just that in the context of higher education tutors are on a different footing from, and respected by, students, but that they are *entitled* to be. They have the major responsibility for managing the interaction *and rightly so*.

Yet the student is not necessarily disadvantaged by being the weaker party. Within the tutor-student relationship there are built-in assumptions which act in the student's interests. For instance, a tutor cannot legitimately respond to a student's request for help with a shrug, or say 'There's nothing I can do; I have no more influence here than you do.' Within this professional context the power of the tutor is supposed to be available to the student. It is an abuse of this professionally bestowed power if it is exercised irresponsibly or selfishly. It is, indeed, a kind of breach of contract, in the sense that the student as client is, indirectly, buying a service from the tutor. The fact that what students are buying is tutelage, which implies putting themselves under the tutors's guidance, makes no difference. They are entitled to get what they bargained for, no more and no less.

The tutor is in a very different position, able to enter the contract with both eyes wide open. By undertaking to deliver a service for payment, the tutor implicitly acknowledges that it may involve uncongenial tasks, inconvenient duties and tiresome responsibilities. Yet it is understood to be a professional engagement, limited to a specific context; it does not have to impinge upon the tutor's private life. Its content lies to a very large extent in the tutor's own hands, since it is the tutor's own expertise that is to be passed on to the student. It cannot be said to the tutor, as it can to the student, that participation in a particular activity is for his or her own good. That is not why the tutor is there. The enterprise is for the student's good, an altruistic activity in which the tutor has voluntarily undertaken to take part.

One could put this another way by saying that, on the tutor's part, the norms of behaviour are largely set by the notion of professional responsibility, including the responsible use of power and the deliberate sharing of knowledge in a way that respects the other. The tutor's commitment to the course is a professional one; there would have to be extraordinary, overriding reasons to warrant opting out of such an obligation freely entered into. On the student's part, on the other hand, the key concepts are trust and evaluation; enrolment on a course entails an element of surrender to the judgement of others, yet this is constantly checked, retrospectively, by an ongoing process of evaluation. The student's commitment to the course is necessarily provisional, conditional upon satisfactory answers being given to questions like 'Am I getting what I want out of this?' The student is, therefore, not without power, but it is of a different sort from that of the tutor. It is the power of the client to take custom elsewhere, not the institutional legitimacy enjoyed by the tutor.

Second, we should observe that the balance of power in the real world of social relationships may be very different from that predicted by an analysis of the formal role relationships. Those who occupy the most powerful positions do not necessarily have everything under control. On the contrary, they may feel trapped, with very little room for manoeuvre. So while we may say, formally speaking, that the tutor carries responsibility for managing the interaction with the student, we must recognize that, in practice, it may be the student who takes the initiative. Sometimes students will effectively run their own tutorial, may indeed run rings round the tutor. It is even possible that, in the course of what is ostensibly a tutorial conducted by the tutor for the benefit of the student, the student might give the tutor some valuable advice, in much the same way as he or she might occasionally teach the tutor a thing or two.

Of course, students, too, may misuse their power. It is not only tutors who may harass students; students may harass tutors. It needs to be said that students can sometimes be disturbingly manipulative in their dealings with their tutors.

Third, then, is it possible to distinguish different kinds of power? Given that the tutor's power is legitimately, even if not always effectively exercised, where does it get its legitimacy from? What bestows power in this context is not just the recognition from the outset on the part of the student that the tutor is a potential examiner; it is that the tutor is on the inside of the institution in a way that the student is not. The tutor's involvement in the management of the institution and its procedures, however uninterested he or she may actually be in these matters, necessarily skews the relationship and renders it asymmetrical.

Like Stanley Milgram's white-coated experimenters (1974), tutors operate within a social framework in which there is an in-built presumption that they know what they are up to. They may not actually be able to get away with murder, but they undoubtedly derive considerable power from their official position. Tutors sometimes show little awareness of this, and are inclined to play it down, encouraging the use of first names and other signs of informality. However, students are rarely fooled by this into thinking of the relationship as an equal one, for they know that in the last resort the tutor could have a great deal of influence on their future. What they seek is not a pretended renunciation of power, but its responsible exercise on their behalf.

In view of what has been said, how do tutor and student go about coming to terms with each other within an institutional context which, as we have seen, puts them on an unequal footing? For both parties it would be very easy to slip into a relationship which was in some way exploitative, which took unfair advantage of the tutor's position vis-a-vis the student, or in which, more simply, the student relinquished responsibility to the tutor. Tutors need to be clear that, even when there are matters on which they have to insist, such as the meeting of course requirements, there must always be room for the student to make his or her own decision, and to take the consequences for good or ill.

Students in higher education are legally adults and, therefore, the normal assumption must be that they are capable of taking charge of their own lives. Where, exceptionally, their ability to do this has broken down, any interference by others will be by agreement, as temporary as possible, and minimal. It will be designed to get the student back on his or her own feet, functioning independently. This general principle applies to all helping, but it is particularly important where the helper is in a position of authority or influence, or where other factors may intrude upon the situation so that one cannot be sure whether the take-up of offers of help is genuinely voluntary.

It may now be clear why it is necessary to claim not only that the tutorial relationship is an asymmetrical one, in that there is more power on one side than on the other, but that it is *inherently* asymmetrical. The way tutor and student relate in a teaching/learning setting governs the way they relate in other situations within the institutional context. Thus, the inequality of the tutor–student *helping* relationship is intrinsic to the tutor–student *teaching* relationship, and analogous to it. The problem for the tutor is much the same in each case; it is to exercise power responsibly and professionally, to help without helping too much. Those reputed to be the best teachers may actually leave least room for the student to discover anything for themselves; similarly, the tutors who appear most concerned and conscientious may be so quick to anticipate the student's needs that they provide help before the student has had time to ask for it or realized the need for it.

THE PARADOX OF HELPING

In any helping relationship there is always the problem of overdoing it. To help too much is, paradoxically, *un*helpful. That there is a danger of inducing helplessness cannot be denied. Martin Seligman (1975), in his book *Helplessness*, develops an ambitious theory about the ways in which people may learn to be helpless. He offers his theory as an explanation of a range of very different things: slow development in childhood learning, the institutionalization of old people, states of mental depression and the high mortality rate of men whose wives have recently died. All of these may be interpreted as forms of 'learned helplessness'. It would seem a small step to add to this list students who, once given a great deal of support, seem subsequently to be unable to manage without this help and become chronically dependent upon their tutor. Could this be another manifestation of the same phenomenon?

In view of what is sometimes made of the idea of a 'dependency culture' as a reason for dismantling welfare provision, one should be wary of drawing general conclusions from quite limited evidence in other areas. Yet there is no reason to deny that the provision of well-intentioned help can reduce the motivation to help oneself. It is certainly possible that tutors sometimes inadvertently encourage an unhealthy dependency in students who are already somewhat insecure. However, it may not be the sheer *amount* of help which is experienced as disabling but rather the *kind* of help and the *way* it is given.

An over-dependent, clinging relationship creates problems of its own and is difficult to terminate without damage. But who is clinging to whom? Busy tutors, conscious of the needs of their other students as well as all their other responsibilities, may still find themselves devoting an excessive amount of time and attention to one student. This has to be seen not simply as the student's problem (e.g. socially insecure, struggling with the course), nor as the tutor's problem (e.g. pathologically lonely, eager to feel needed), but rather as a problem of the relationship and how it has developed. That said, it must still be reasserted that the tutor has to take responsibility for managing the relationship. The tutor has the difficult and perhaps paradoxical task of assuming most of the responsibility for ensuring that the relationship is not one in which the tutor dominates the student; or, for that matter, one in which the student dominates the tutor.

Occasionally students may pester a tutor for help and support, or perhaps, more subtly, find ways of manipulating the tutor into giving an inordinate amount of time to them. It might appear that for the student to manipulate the tutor was simply the opposite case of the tutor exploiting the student, control having effectively passed out of the tutor's hands and into the hands of the student. Yet a more careful analysis might reveal that the manipulation was another form of dependency; that for the student to try to manipulate the tutor was a sign of weakness not strength. The student is more likely to be wanting to cling than to dominate. The relationship has become so personally important that the student dare not let go, and is constantly manoeuvring the tutor into a helping position for fear that the tutor will not otherwise be available.

Yet there is something of a paradox here too. For when the relationship has become one in which the tutor is virtually on the end of a string, at the student's beck and call, this does not satisfy, for what the student really wants is a voluntary relationship. Constantly asking for help creates a situation in which help is only given in response to demand and can hardly ever be freely offered.

By looking briefly at some of the ways in which helping relationships can become dysfunctional it has been possible to show that helping is a paradoxical activity. So, of course, is teaching. Tutors in higher education normally discourage students from becoming over-dependent for basically the same reason that they resist spoon-feeding in teaching; because in both cases to overdo it is ultimately self-defeating.

This chapter has shown up more than just the unequal status of tutor and student. It has revealed the extent of the tutor's responsibility for managing the helping process and how the tutor's power lies in being on the inside of this process in a way that the student is not. It has also exposed a fundamental principle of helping, that most people most of the time are perfectly capable of helping themselves once their situation can be viewed objectively, and that to provide this objectivity is often the best way, sometimes the only way, they can be helped without being in some way diminished.

Thus, ideally we might think of the tutor who helps a student not so much as a helping agent, but rather as instrumental in facilitating the helping process. It is not that the tutor brings to the encounter a superior wisdom with which to solve the student's problems, but rather that the tutor, by virtue of the role occupied, the human qualities shown and the professional skills deployed, enables the helping process to occur.

There are, indeed, skills which individuals possess or may acquire so as to be more effective helpers. Yet tutoring is not reducible to a set of skills, still less to knowing about interpersonal behaviour. The fact is that tutors are professionally required to be supportive and helpful to students, without necessarily sharing or even fully understanding their point of view. What matters is not whether they know about empathy, only whether they show it.

The trouble is that we can all behave considerately and humanely when we are not too busy, when we are feeling in a good mood, relaxed and unhurried, when the student is someone we know and like, when we are on a 'safe' subject, etc. In such circumstances it is not too difficult to respond to student's needs calmly, thoughtfully and sensitively. However, often it is not like this. Students may ask awkward questions, introduce a very different perspective with which we have very little sympathy or patience; they may surprise us, shock us, or in some way 'put us on the spot' or challenge us, perhaps quite unintentionally; worse still, they may disagree with us, or actually complain to us about something, or perhaps unwittingly touch on what is, for us, a rather sensitive area. On these occasions we may find ourselves responding defensively. In addition to skill, therefore, we need qualities which have traditionally been defined as 'moral': patience, respect for the other, a willingness to put the other's interests above our own, altruism, caring. The tutorial relationship, like any other relationship, works best when these qualities are dependably present.

BIBLIOGRAPHY

Arbuckle, D. S. (1967) 'Kinds of counselling: meaningful or meaningless?', *Journal of Counselling Psychology*, 14, 219–25.

Bramley, W. (1977) *Personal Tutoring in Higher Education*. Guildford: Society for Research into Higher Education.

Gahagan, J. (1984) *Social Interaction and its Management*. London: Methuen.

Jacques, D. (1989) *Personal Tutoring*. Oxford Centre for Staff Development: Oxford Polytechnic.

Lewis, R. (1984) *How to Tutor and Support Learners*. London: Council for Educational Technology.

Lublin, J. (1987) *Conducting Tutorials*. Higher Education Research and Development Society of Australasia, University of New South Wales, Australia.

McMahon, T. (1985) *Developing Tutorial Skills*. London, Further Education Unit.

Milgram, S. (1974) *Obedience to Authority: an Experimental View*. London: Tavistock.

Rees, S. (1978) *Social Work Face to Face*. London: Edward Arnold.

Robinson, D. (1971) *The Process of Becoming Ill*. London: Routledge and Kegan Paul.

Rogers, C. R. (1973) *Client-centred Therapy: Its Current Practice, Implications and Theory*. London: Constable.

Seligman, M. E. P. (1975) *Helplessness: On Depression, Development and Death*. San Francisco: W.H. Freeman.

Stern, D. (1977) *The First Relationship: Infant and Mother*. London: Fontana/Open Books.

Strong, P. M. (1979) *The Ceremonial Order of the Clinic: Parents, Doctors and Medical Bureaucracies*. London: Routledge and Kegan Paul.

Chapter 7

Counselling in groups

Bernard Ratigan

An edited version of: 'Counselling in groups', in *The Handbook of Counselling*, Chapter 6, London: Routledge (1997).

INTRODUCTION

Aristotle wrote that human beings are, by nature, social animals. Yet the lay person's view of counselling is that it is in essence an individual activity, or more properly, dyadic: client and counsellor. Although psychotherapy and counselling emerged as individualist disciplines, in the second half of the twentieth century there has been an enormous growth in the use of group methodologies in a variety of settings. The range is wide and includes:

- formal, long-term groups designed to help bring about major changes in members' functioning
- brief but intensive groups
- skill training and staff support groups
- groups with a focus on helping members solve, resolve, or accept problems, make adjustments, or cope with trauma.

Group counselling covers a wide gamut.

This chapter surveys the major theoretical and clinical perspectives underpinning various forms of group counselling. It includes some descriptive material to illustrate the nature of the counselling process as it can occur in group settings. Issues in group counselling are considered, including the goals of the group, inclusion and exclusion factors, the role of the group counsellor, the 'work' of group members, the development of different types of group over time, how change actually occurs in groups, the limitations of the various types of groups, and effective leadership profiles. There follows a review of the different purposes for which counselling and counselling skills are used in groups and an attempt to identify the different types of group setting where counselling has a part to play. The chapter concludes with a consideration of likely future developments. These include questions to do with training, the increasing use and appropriateness of group counselling, and the convergence of methodologies.

PRINCIPLES

All the major theoretical approaches to individual counselling and psychotherapy are represented and practised in group counselling. This chapter takes as the primary differences between counselling and psychotherapy the following: length of time over which the group meets, the depth at which the members' material is treated, the use of transference, and the purposes for which the group is convened. A pragmatic distinction is preferred in which counselling emphasizes work with non-patient groups, is of shorter duration, with little explicit use of the transference and where there is a greater degree of task orientation. Throughout the chapter, though, these distinctions will be continually blurred and the literature of psychotherapy and counselling equally utilized.

The history of group counselling is not extensive and has developed rapidly in the second half of the twentieth century (Roberts, 1995). During the Second World War attempts were made to develop group treatments for soldiers which led to important work at the National Training Laboratory at Bethel, Maine in the USA and the Tavistock Clinic and the Tavistock Institute in London (Trist and Murray, 1990; 1993; Lyth, 1988 a and b). The application of psychoanalytic insights to group processes provided one of the major perspectives in group counselling (Foulkes and Anthony, 1957). The work of Rogers was also of significance in the development of group counselling. From his work with individual clients important ideas evolved about the nature of human development and necessary conditions for growth and change which have profoundly affected group counselling (Thorne, 1988). Humanistic psychology has a strong base in group methodologies, as for example with Gestalt and psychodrama. The development of stress counselling groups is reported in Palmer and Dryden (1995).

Group counselling offers a fundamentally different experience to the client from that of individual one-to-one counselling. In his magisterial work, Yalom (1995) identified eleven factors which distinguish the curative factors operating in group counselling and provide a background to all its forms:

- The instillation of hope is central to all forms of psychological therapy, and to religion and medicine.
- Universality: one of the most significant learnings by members of groups is that they are not alone in either their experience or concerns.
- Imparting of information: although in the beginning group members often expect that, as in school, they will be taught facts, they come to realize that this is of relatively small importance.
- Altruism: group membership often releases in participants previously hidden or forgotten capacities for helping others.
- The corrective recapitulation of the primary family group: groups can help members to work through and in some ways heal hurts sustained in earlier life.

- Development of socializing techniques: participation in a group provides the opportunity for learning, and practising, different ways of relating to others in a live setting.
- Imitative behaviour: by watching others' behaviour and listening to them, group members can discover their own distinctive personal styles.
- Interpersonal learning: through interaction with others, members are often able to grow and change. Groups provide an opportunity for both emotional and cognitive understanding.
- Group cohesiveness is the result of all the forces acting on the memories to remain in a group and is not a curative factor *per se* but a necessary precondition for effective change.
- Catharsis and ventilation of feelings are not themselves sufficient for change, but may play a significant part in the process and can therefore also be curative factors.
- Existential factors such as the need to take responsibility for oneself, the fact of individual isolation, contingency, the inevitability of mortality, and the capriciousness of existence are all themes which are often more easily tackled in group settings rather than in individual therapy.

In one of the most significant pieces of large-scale research in this field Yalom established what members of groups themselves saw as the most helpful factors. In order of importance they were:

1 discovering and accepting previously unknown or unacceptable parts of myself
2 being able to say what was bothering me instead of holding it all in
3 other members honestly telling me what they think of me
4 learning how to express my feelings
5 the group's teaching me about the type of impression I make on others
6 expressing negative and/or positive feelings towards another member
7 learning that I must take ultimate responsibility for the way I live my life no matter how much guidance and support I get from others
8 learning how I come across to others
9 seeing that others could reveal embarrassing information and take other risks and benefit from it helped me to do the same
10 feeling more trustful of groups and other people.

Applications

There are a wide variety of types of groups in existence ranging from those in clinical settings offering long, slow treatment to educational and management training settings with short lives and focused agendas. Historically, the group-analytic movement established a model of groupwork in which a group of strangers would come together on a weekly or twice-weekly basis, often over a period of years, with the leader (usually called the 'conductor') acting as analyst to the group (Roberts and Pines, 1991). The conductor would usually only comment on the group process in so far as it revealed the transference material emerging in the free associations of the group members (or patients) about themselves, the other members, and, especially, the leader. It will be seen that such groups are derived from the psychoanalytic ideas of Freud and the theory underpinning them owes much to the work of Bion (1961).

Then there are groups derived from the work of Rogers, who eschewed what he saw as the deterministic ideas of Freud and instead emphasized the importance of the personal encounter between client and therapist in both individual and group settings. From using these ideas in small-scale encounter groups in the 1960s, Rogers and his associates have extended the concept of group counselling through to much larger gatherings of people from widely diverse ethnic and language backgrounds. Similarly, the group-analytic perspective has developed methods for exploring the big issues that divide and exercise people. Some of the most exciting developments in groupwork ideas and practice in the 1990s have demonstrated the power of groups to facilitate communication between people otherwise separated by conventional barriers of nationality, class, ideology, sexual orientation, gender, race and language.

Psychology and education combined to produce a range of group methods which employ theories based upon cognitive-behavioural and social-learning approaches. One of the increasingly widely practised forms of groupwork is assertiveness training. Although there are a number of models in existence the unifying idea behind them is that individuals working together in a group with a leader are systematically trained to develop skills which will help them in their relationships with others. There is considerable emphasis on participants identifying situations in their own lives in which they are not assertive – that is, in which they are passive or aggressive. By enacting these scenes with tuition from the leader and the active support and encouragement of other group members standing in as significant others in the participant's life, skills are acquired (Dickson, 1982).

Assertiveness training is of particular interest because it includes within it a number of other methodologies, for example instruction and psycho-drama. When groupwork ideas were first being contemplated in the years before and during the Second World War, group leaders would sometimes give lectures on aspects of mental health. This practice has now dwindled with the realization that the kinds of changes being worked for in group approaches need something more powerful than information and instruction. Psychodrama has a long and distinguished history. It is an especially potent form of group counselling because of its immediacy, the role of the director (sic), and its capacity for getting at traumatic material in group members' lives, current and past (Blatner, 1973). It is especially applicable in forensic settings. Because it is such a powerful, and potentially explosive, medium it requires specialist training and supervision.

Among some of the most significant changes that have taken place in western society this century have been those in the relationships between men and women. The women's movement is essentially founded upon ideas that have been arrived at in groups. Single-sex groupings are not, of course, new. Indeed, through much of human history boys and girls have been educated and trained in single-sex groups and much human activity is carried out separately. What is especially interesting in terms of group counselling is that both women's and men's groups are now regularly convened to develop and raise consciousness and to give their members the context and possibility of exploring issues that are hard or impossible in mixed-gender settings. In viability, one of the perennial issues in single-sex counselling groups is the emotional and sexual emotions between members. This century has begun to see the recognition of the complexity and range of human sexuality and sexual orientation. Well-run groups provide safety for people to explore the often painful parts of themselves which may have lain unrecognized or hidden for years and sometimes decades. Such exploration can have the most profound implications not only for the group member but also for his or her partner, parents, children and friends.

Group therapy really began to take shape during the Second World War as part of the treatment given to those suffering neurotic disorders. It is in other total and neo-total institutions that group counselling has grown, if not flourished. In the prison system, for example, there has been some recognition of the power of groups as a therapeutic agent of change. Two particular modalities are worthy of special note. Psychoanalytically derived groupwork methods are used to treat some of the most disturbed and disturbing prisoners (Cox, 1978). Methods derived from psychodrama are also practised in work with prisoners. Again, the focus on drama seems to give such methods a special significance and power. Although there are very few psychiatric therapeutic penal facilities in Britain, there is a need to expand groupwork treatments to make them available on a much wider basis.

Groups, then, are having an increasingly important impact on the treatment of the emotionally disturbed and ill. Even in organically orientated psychiatric units there is recognition of the importance of establishing a therapeutic milieu, even if this proves difficult in practice (Whitely and Gordon, 1979). Therapeutic communities all have group therapy at their centre and out-patient groups are routinely organized in NHS specialist psychotherapy departments as well as increasingly by community mental health teams (Hinshelwood, 1987; Kennard, 1983). Another important development is the range of self-help groups in the community. Examples abound: groups for alcohol and other substance abusers, for those with eating disorders, for the bereaved, for those traumatized by violence or sexual attack or abuse, for the recovering mentally ill, for those affected by HIV, for those coming out as gay or lesbian, for those who consider themselves to be sexual compulsives, for the divorced and many others. Although some of these groups would eschew notions of leadership on ideological grounds, they are, of course, subject to many of the same dynamics and processes as more formally convened groups with trained, professional leaders. Indeed, it is clear that as in any other form of therapy the important distinction is not between the professional and the amateur but between the more effective and less effective leader.

Lastly, groups are used extensively in training for the therapeutic and other helping professionals such as social work, education, and management. It is increasingly recognized that the formation of people for such professions requires more than cognitive learning and specialist skills. The power of the group can be utilized to show beginners the need for personal knowledge which, paradoxically, is often best acquired in interaction with others. The painful process of change and the acquisition of personal insight and sensitivity is often enhanced and made more powerful by the exposure to the group experience.

ISSUES

Goals of the group

Counselling groups are convened for many reasons although it is important that they are convened for a purpose. What the group is for will condition how it is conducted, led or facilitated. Group counsellors have themselves to understand the group's purpose so that they can make this explicit to the participants. Of course, stated and actual goals can diverge considerably and once groups begin they develop a life, culture and personality of their own which is as likely to fluctuate as is any human being.

The role of the leaders

Group counsellors have important but often subsidiary roles when compared with their individual colleagues. The work starts with the conception of the group, when it is called into being and for what purpose the group is convened. Group counsellors have many important housekeeping and boundary-holding functions. They need in particular to ensure that the potential client population is aware of the availability of the group. There are key questions about selection:

- is the group appropriate for all those who would wish to join?
- what are the criteria for selection?

- what is the optimum size of the group, the maximum and the minimum?
- over what period of time will the group meet and meet and how frequently?
- how long will sessions be?
- once started is it open so that new members may join as some leave, or is it closed?
- where will the group meet?
- are there rules or guidelines about the participants meeting outside sessions and what is to happen if this does happen?
- what are the rules about confidentiality?
- what are the rules about smoking, eating or drinking in sessions?
- what is the policy to be on absence and its notification?
- what supervision arrangements do group counsellors need to support their work?

This list is not exhaustive and the reader is referred to Whitaker (1987) for an extended discussion of these and related issues.

The work of the counsellor includes many external functions which, though of apparently small significance, do much to ensure an efficiently and carefully run group with a good therapeutic culture. Examples of these include getting and keeping the same room each week; ensuring that there are enough chairs and that the chairs are there for every session in the same configuration. Small matters but of great importance.

Once the group has begun, the work of the counsellor will vary depending on his or her primary theoretical orientation, the purposes for which the group is convened, and the particular point it has reached in its developmental natural history. In all groups, though, counsellors will pay particular attention to both what is said and not said, to helping the group stay in the here-and-now and to boundary matters like time, breaks and endings. Two important concepts of relevance are holding and leverage. Holding refers to that special quality of relationship that a leader has with the group which parallels that of the good (enough) parent able to communicate to the infant and child that they are viewed unconditionally. Through reliability and a non-retaliatory stance the leader can help to sustain a productive therapeutic atmosphere. By applying the principles of leverage the effective leader can identify just how much force to apply where and for how long to maximize change. It is a skill acquired with experience under supervision and from making inevitable mistakes.

Groups are complicated and suffused with complex interactions. Two leaders are almost always better than one. They provide support for each other, they are able to adopt differing roles in the group at different times, one perhaps more active than the other, and they are able to offer to the group and each other differing perspectives on what is going on. For mixed-gender groups it is particularly helpful if the leaders are of different genders:

many issues relating to male–female relationships, to parents, and sexuality can thus be given greater prominence.

The final issue facing group leaders is that of supervision. The powerful forces at work in any therapeutic relationship are multiplied many times over in a group. It goes without saying that group leaders must themselves have embraced the training tripos of theoretical instruction, a personal experience of group membership and of doing supervised work. Supervision is necessary from the moment the idea of the group is conceived and called into being. One of the advantages of having two leaders is that peer supervision is much easier to arrange. Some kind of supervision is, however, essential for the well-being of the group and the leaders.

The work of group members

The 'work' of participants in groups will vary with the purpose of the group. One of the unifying concepts throughout most group modalities is that of remaining in the here-and-now. This means trying to say what members are experiencing in the present moment. This is especially difficult for most neophyte group participants and requires considerable effort, as many human interactions avoid this. A good group culture can be invaluable in transmitting the importance of staying in the here-and-now. Members soon sense when the group is not 'working' and say so.

The basic ground rule for group members is uninhibited conversation. This is the group equivalent of free association in individual work. It is an encouragement for continued communication in the face of antagonism. Conflict, both within and between members, is one of the distinctive features of most forms of group counselling. The asymmetry of the power relationship between counsellor and client in one-to-one work is transformed in group counselling, so that in groups clients can often more quickly experience and express angry or fearful feelings towards leaders. A member who attacks a leader may be a spokesperson for others and the public character of the occasion tends to ensure that retaliation will not take place. Further, in individual work, the only source of information is the counsellor; in a group, the other members also serve as sources of feedback, as models, as guides and as encouragers.

The expression of anger can be a particularly useful medium of learning, growth and healing, especially with those people who have been traumatized, have never learned how to express their anger adequately, or have become skilled at converting it into depression or some psychosomatic condition. Members' anger with one another and with the leaders, is often an important turning point for both the individuals concerned and for the group's development as a therapeutic agent for change. Although painful, being angry with one another is often a way of saying 'I am taking you seriously', and even 'you are important to me'. For those group participants who experience themselves as more or less unimportant, to be able to get close to saying these words can be profoundly significant.

Group members tend to discover that in many ways they are more similar to each other than they expected. Behind the masks of everyday life, of surface coping, even the most seemingly well-adjusted group members will usually have undercurrents to explore. Sullivan's (1953) one-genus postulate, 'everyone is much more simply human than otherwise', although conceived in the context of individual psychotherapy, seems even more apt in the context of groups.

The distorted views that group members have of themselves, other members and leaders provide one of the richest sources of material for productive work in a group. The distortions are a result of the life experiences of the participants. Frank (1974) has identified two, mirror and transference reactions, that are especially common, important and useful. Mirror reactions are those where group members tend to detect and disapprove of traits in someone else that they deny in themselves. In the group they can be helped to see them as their own. Transference reactions occur when members inappropriately transfer on to or put into other participants or the leaders those feelings which are, or more usually were, appropriate to others in their lives. Through the process of the 'reflective loop' members can be helped to see and work through their distortions and difficulties over and over again. Members of groups come to demonstrate what Frank has called their 'assumptive world'. Instead of merely talking about their life and concerns they *become* them and so demonstrate them in the group. In the group they create the relationships and the difficulties which they experience in the outside world. The group can then become a workshop or laboratory where steps can be taken to change with the powerful support of the other group members and the leaders.

How groups develop over time

Counselling groups, like other forms of life, have a natural history: a beginning, a middle and an end. Early sessions are often characterized by hesitancy, fear, dependency, difficulties in staying in the here-and-now, and high expectations. It is a time for building group norms that emphasize the importance of openness and sharing but not too much too soon. Sometimes it is more useful if participants are able to hold back on what seems very pressing until a sufficient degree of trust has been built up. Likewise, confrontations, although important and often therapeutic in effect, are often the characteristic of the more established, safer atmosphere of the mature group. In these matters there is usually a tension between the need to disclose and the fear of disclosure: done too soon and a fragile therapeutic alliance can be destroyed; left too late, and an anti-therapeutic culture may preclude any real sharing and be very difficult to shift.

In more mature groups, participants are gradually able to free themselves of inhibitions and resistances to talking openly, more able to stay in the present and more able to give and receive feedback and to exercise autonomy both within and outside the group. There is also an increasing ability to risk doing the things, being the person they wish, and sharing the words and feelings which are hard to express but which are necessary for change and growth.

All groups have to face issues to do with ending. Even in long, open groups in which members stay as long as they need, there are endings. Most counselling groups are of fixed length and a well-run, mature group will be helped to face the questions of ending well in advance of it actually happening. It is a time for reflection on the gains made, the insights, the sense of belonging, the good and the bad times shared. It is also a time for sadness, loss, anger and frustration. The well-run group will be helped to face these issues and to work through them. As in individual work, breaks and endings will generate many, often lost or repressed, memories of other losses experienced by group members in the past. Members will be surprised at the powerful feelings encountered and, with help, be able to speak of them and work through the pain of the losses.

How change occurs

There are a variety of factors at work in groups which facilitate, and inhibit, change. Ideally, participants come to see themselves more fully and are able to try out new ways of being and relating to others and thinking about themselves and their worlds. In the safety of the group they are offered space and time which can provide the context in which these changes can occur. It is a complex (and not fully understood) nexus of factors which both allows the participants to experience the safety necessary for change to occur and for the anxiety or tension which is the spur to move towards change (Yalom et al., 1975; Bloch and Crouch, 1985). Developments, learning, insight, and growth occur in an episodic rather than a linear manner. Merely being in the group is clearly not sufficient for change to occur; involvement in other processes, such as risking saying what one is feeling, sharing secrets, giving and receiving feedback, catharsis, confrontation, modelling, and the corrective emotional experience can all be important. An important process in group counselling is the reflective loop of doing, looking back on what was done, and then understanding. As groups mature, members often take over this function from leaders.

Limitations of counselling groups

Group counselling provides a therapeutic and learning environment in which many human problems can be worked on to good effect. People for whom a one-to-one relationship is essential will not benefit from groups. Those who will probably not do well in groups are those suffering from psychotic illness and severe depression, those who can only see their difficulties in physical terms, the paranoid who are overly suspicious, the narcissistic who need all the attention for themselves, and the schizoid who are too cut off from other people. Once people have been helped to move from these categories, group work can often provide an important and potent ingredient in their return to well-being. In essence, groups are more for interpersonal rather than intrapersonal development (Rattigan and Aveline, 1988).

It is also often difficult to persuade potential participants that a group really is the treatment of choice and not a second best to individual therapy. The culture of individualism in our society is often strongly embodied in those with difficulties, especially interpersonal difficulties.

The power and flexibility of group counselling is that it can be used to help participants over a whole range of concerns. There are very few people who could not benefit from the forum for open genuine communication which group counselling can provide.

FUTURE DEVELOPMENTS

Human beings are born into group life and need other people for physical and emotional nourishment, sustenance, and hope. Although the history of counselling has emphasized work with individuals, it is becoming clear that group work will become more significant. There are many reasons for this. It appears that not only are groups somewhat more economic, they can sometimes provide a more effective form of help than individual work. The empirical work to establish this, fraught with many methodological difficulties because of the complexities of what goes on in groups, is yet to be fully undertaken (Bednar, 1970).

What is clear from observation is that in a group a person is able not only to describe difficulties but, when they are of an interpersonal nature or have an interpersonal dimension, they can also demonstrate them. Groups are good at mobilizing a range of sources of help, not least other group members.

As our society seemingly becomes more fragmented and individuals experience the trauma of alienation, there is an increasing need for the use of psychological techniques to help construct what so-called simple or primitive societies did naturally through social structures and rituals (Roose-Evans, 1994). We need to help ourselves create mechanisms which provide safe space and dedicated time to ensure our physical, emotional and spiritual well-being and growth. In a society which is rapidly changing, where individuals and families are often separated, where there are conflicting values, goals and identities on offer, counselling in groups can assist in bringing people to, and keeping them at, a psychologically healthy state. One of the most simple yet profound satisfactions reported by group members is that of 'just being together'.

CONCLUSION

This chapter has reviewed group counselling in Britain as it appears to one practitioner currently working in the NHS and who has been heavily influenced by person-centred, existential, and psychoanalytic ideas. Others with differing orientations would, doubtless, have given different accounts. What is clear is that group counselling has come a very long way in the last fifty years and that it has an exciting and productive future ahead. It is likely to become not only much more important within counselling, but also within society as a resource for personal development in, for example, education, community development, religion, and in the workplace, as well as in clinical settings. People live in groups: should they not then be treated in groups?

BIBLIOGRAPHY

Alladin, W. (1988) 'Cognitive-behavioural group therapy' in M. Aveline and D. Dryden (eds) *Group Therapy in Britain*, London: Routledge, pp. 115–39.

Aveline, M. (1986) 'The use of written reports in a brief group psychotherapy training', *International Journal of Group Psychotherapy* 36: 477–82.

Aveline, M. and Dryden, W. (eds) (1988) *Group Therapy in Britain*, London: Routledge.

Bednar, R.L. (1970) 'Group psychotherapy research variables', *International Journal of Group Psychotherapy* 20: 146–52.

Bion, W.R. (1961) *Experiences in Groups and Other Papers*, London: Tavistock.

Blatner, H.A. (1973) *Acting-In: Practical Applications of Psychodramatic Method*, New York: Springer.

Bloch, S. and Crouch, E. (1985) *Therapeutic Factors in Group Psychotherapy*, Oxford: Oxford University Press.

Cox, M. (1978) *Structuring the Therapeutic Process*, Oxford: Pergamon Press.

Dickson, A. (1982) *A Woman in Your Own Right*, London: Quartet.

Foulkes, S.H. and Anthony, E.J. (1957) *Group Psychotherapy: The Psychoanalytical Approach*, London: Penguin Books.

——(1989) *Group Psychotherapy: The Psychoanalytical Method*, London: Penguin Books.

Frank, J. (1974) *Persuasion and Healing*, revised edn, New York: Schoken Books.

Hinshelwood, R.D. (1987) *What Happens in Groups: Psychoanalysis, The Individual and the Community*, London: Free Association Books.

Hyde, K. (1988) 'Analytic group psychotherapies' in M. Aveline and W. Dryden (eds) *Group Therapy in Britain*, London: Routledge.

Kennard, D. (1983) *An Introduction to Therapeutic Communities*, London: Routledge.

Lyth, I.M. (1988a) *Containing Anxiety in Institutions: Selected Essays*, vol. 1, London: Free Association Books.

——(1988b) *The Dynamics of the Social: Selected Essays*, vol. 2, London: Free Association Books.

Palmer, S. and Dryden, W. (1995) *Counselling for Stress Problems*, London: Sage.

Rattigan, B. and Aveline, M. (1988) 'Interpersonal group therapy' in M. Aveline and W. Dryden (eds) *Group Therapy in Britain*, London: Routledge.

Roberts, J.P. (1995) 'Reading about group psychotherapy', *British Journal of Psychiatry* 166: 124–9.

Roberts, J.P. and Pines, M. (eds) (1991) *The Practice of Group Analysis*, London: Routledge.

Roose-Evans, J. (1994) *Passages of the Soul: Ritual Today*, Shaftesbury, Dorset: Element.

Sullivan, H.S. (1953) *The Interpersonal Theory of Psychiatry*, New York: Norton.

Thorne, B. (1988) 'The person-centred approach to large groups' in M. Aveline and W. Dryden (eds) *Group Therapy in Britain*, London: Routledge.

Trist, E. and Murray M. (eds) (1990) *The Social Engagement of Social Science, volume 1: The Socio-psychological Perspective*, London: Free Association Books.

——(1993) *The Social Engagement of Social Science: A Tavistock Anthology, volume 2: The Socio-Technical Perspective*, Philadelphia: University of Pennsylvania Press.

Whitaker, D.S. (1987) *Using Groups to Help People*, London: Routledge.

Whitely, J.S. and Gordon, J. (1979) *Group Approaches in Psychiatry*, London: Routledge.

Yalom, I.D. (1995) *The Theory and Practice of Group Psychotherapy*, 4th edn, New York: Basic Books.

Yalom, I.D., Brown, S. and Bloch, S. (1975) 'The written summary as a group psychotherapy technique', *Archives of General Psychiatry* 32: 605–13.

Chapter 8

Telephone counselling

Judith George

INTRODUCTION: THE CONTEXT OF TELEPHONE COUNSELLING

Counselling and advisory support for students is an integral feature of well-designed educational provision. It is the strand of support by the institution and its staff which helps students cope with the practical, emotional and personal barriers to their progress in learning, and which complements academic support in enabling students to make the most of their opportunities and abilities. This support begins with pre-entry advice about admissions, about choice of course, about pre-course reading or placement work, about finance and housing and a host of practicalities. It continues with the help given to students from a variety of sources as they adjust to a new life and a new culture: by academic staff, personal tutors, counsellors, and so on. As the students progress through their courses, these sources of help continue to give guidance and advice on choice of courses, on how to become a more effective learner, and on practical or personal difficulties. The right support at the right time can make all the difference to the progress and development of an individual learner – and even to how well they make the transition from study to an appropriate job, or to further education or training.

The challenge to a telephone counselling service is to make it as effective in all the aspects of interaction as the rich medium of face-to-face contact. This includes the main specialist face-to-face advisory services – course choice, careers and vocational guidance, financial advice, accommodation, and personal problems. Less obviously, advisory support, in a real sense, is provided almost unnoticeably and subliminally from a range of other sources. These might include the information which circulates informally round an institution, the osmosis of conversations in a corridor or half glimpsed notices on a board – about deadlines and important dates, about what you are responsible for and what not, about who will help you with what. A student's aspirations or expectations are imperceptibly moulded by the values and attitudes imparted by tutors, and by peer support and pressure. And a traditional setting in itself may well remove the cause of many needs for counselling or at least some form of student support. The very physical presence of a building, of lectures happening, and of staff and peers milling round instil confidence, and give a sense of 'belonging' and identity.

In discussing telephone counselling, we should bear in mind that the very nature of the system which necessitates counselling to be by phone is also likely to lack some of the intrinsic underpinning of a conventional college setting, which pre-empts formal counselling; it is thus likely to create a more diffuse and complex range of possible counselling needs in students. The better the preparatory advice, the introductory meetings, and the information flow about practicalities, the less this need will be there. But again and again feedback on what students value from telephone contact tells us that, even when the agenda is an academic one, it is the affective gains which are of most importance to them. George (1984; see also Cowan, 1997a) documents the importance of the sense that they are not alone and isolated, that they belong to a group, and that they have peers (and tutors) who share their values and enthusiasms. Any counselling or advisory telephone contact, therefore, is likely to have this additional and underlying agenda.

The great expansion of distance education in the past decade has led, in practice, to as diverse a provision of telephone or distance counselling support for students as there is of face-to-face counselling in conventional institutions. These can range from the support which consists of a telephone admissions advisory service which then withdraws, leaving only course tutors whose sole remit is to mark and return assignments and who are virtually uncontactable if a student is in any difficulty. At the other end of the spectrum is the counselling support given by The Open University and an increasing number of institutions delivering courses on a distance format, where an educational counselling remit is often part of a tutor's role, supplemented by specialist advisers, where necessary, and by educational helplines, and by careers and vocational guidance services, who work more and more by telephone.

At the moment, the use of video-conferencing and computer-mediated conferencing for counselling is limited, and the full potential of these media has not yet been fully researched. Reaction to video-conferencing, for example, has sometimes been a sigh of relief that all the challenges set by voice only contact will be resolved, once visual contact is established. Initial findings, however, seem to indicate there are another set of challenges in this medium – in handling the group dynamics, for instance (Cowan, 1997b). Further work needs to be done before we can map the strengths of these media with confidence.

WHY COUNSEL BY TELEPHONE?

The usual answer is simply because students are unable to obtain the advice they need face-to-face. They may be studying at a geographic distance; they may be housebound by circumstance or disability; they may be working shifts or very long hours. For almost all purposes, the face-to-face contact would offer a richer medium for interaction. But, given the very circumstances which make them distance students in the first place, it is likely that the telephone represents their only option for obtaining the help, advice and support they need.

The challenge to an advisory and counselling service, given the needs of such students, is to open this line of access to them effectively, and to make the best use of this medium. The word 'challenge' is used advisedly. Experience in The Open University in Scotland is that students often regard the phone as an expensive form of contact, to be used only in emergencies and only briefly even then. Even among Open University tutors, it is not uncommon to hear a tutor declare that it is not possible to teach their subject by phone! And even if people are used to using the phone more comfortably in their daily work, they often do not appreciate that, as holding a conversation with a colleague is significantly different from counselling a student, so being able to hold a work discussion by phone is different from giving advice and counselling by phone. Even trained counsellors need to reflect on the demands of a very different medium, and think purposefully about how to adapt their skills and counselling style to this context.

Similarly, it is unusual for students to have the skills development in telephone contact which staff receive. Moreover, in any contact, it is likely that they are in a situation where, of its very nature, they lack confidence, are in difficulties, or have the kind of problem which needs sympathetic prompting to get them to explore it, even in a face-to-face situation. The telephone counsellor must be aware of the additional counselling demand; to help the student help themselves when they are perhaps opening up a conversation about a personal failing or difficulty, in the total lack of all the visual cues which might induce a feeling of confidence or security, with a stranger who is only a voice.

The advantages, on the other hand, can be considerable, if the medium is well used. It is a comparatively cheap, familiar, and 'low tec' medium, to which most people have access at home; it also provides instant and interactive contact. Macdonald and Mason (1996) report that, for all the convenience of computer-mediated conferencing, students still feel a need for the warmth of a human voice which a phone provides. George (1984 and 1993; see also Cowan, 1997a) suggests that, well used, a phone interaction can be more focused and purposeful than face-to-face contact. It is also increasingly possible to use fax or e-mail communication to follow up the phone conversation with additional information or written confirmation.

WHAT ARE THE SIGNIFICANT FEATURES OF TELEPHONE CONTACT IN RELATION TO COUNSELLING?

The essential feature of telephonic communication is that it is non-visual. The impact of the absence of visual contact on the nature of any interaction can be considered under three general headings. The first impact is upon the ease of establishing an effective rapport and relationship between counsellor and student; the second, upon the pacing and structuring of the interaction itself; the third, upon the access to reference materials or further data for discussion between the two.

The establishment of an effective rapport and relationship

Visual cues and body language are critical factors in establishing an effective relationship between counsellor and student, as they are between tutor and student. The smile and gestures of welcome, the detail of seating arrangements, and the body language of empathic attention reassures the student, and creates an atmosphere of security and of serious consideration of that particular student's needs.

Much of the focus in counselling training and reflection on practice is on listening and on the verbal skills of reflecting, echoing, etc. However, if a counselling training exercise – say, a role play of counsellor and student, with an observer of the interaction – is reproduced *without* visual contact, it will immediately become apparent how much of what we are 'hearing' is in fact data from constant minute observation of body language and visual signals, which supplement and interpret the actual words and voice tone, often without our realising. Similarly, the response we are making as counsellors is as much through these kinds of non-stop visual cues as through the form of question or statement we use, or the structure we give to the interaction.

The pacing and structuring of the interaction

Similarly, the constant visual interaction between counsellor and student provides the feedback which paces and structures the advisory session. Body language or the lift of an eyebrow, as much as an open question, invites the student to expand on a statement; student and counsellor can communicate without a word that they move on to the next topic.

Visual signals form a significant strand of communication, distinct from the purely verbal one, whereby counsellor and student can set or dismantle an agenda, determine the pace at which a topic is tackled, decide when and whether discussion on that is finished, and negotiate content and shape of the interview.

Access to reference material or further data

In a face-to-face advisory interview, the counsellor is usually working in her own office or interview room, with access to a database or shelves of relevant reference materials. At any moment, she can reach out for a brochure, a screen print-out, or some other source of relevant information. On occasion, of course, there will be information which is not immediately retrievable in this fashion, and which will have to be accessed at a later stage.

By contrast, the situation on a telephone advisory interview is *always* like the latter situation. Unless student and counsellor have spoken beforehand to agree their agenda and to obtain any reference material they need, the counsellor will have to evolve a different strategy for backing up suggestions by reference to the relevant documents.

HOW CAN THIS VOICE-ONLY MEDIUM BE USED MOST EFFECTIVELY FOR COUNSELLING?

Experience in The Open University in Scotland suggests that, though neither telephone counselling nor telephone tuition have the richness of face-to-face interactions, experienced staff can be most effective (George, 1984 and 1993; Cowan, 1997a). Indeed, the flexibility and ease of access which the phone allows can compensate for some of the losses of visual contact, and offer a service which students value.

This experience also suggests that the process of becoming a good telephone tutor or counsellor is one of adaptation of some conventional skills and strategies to a non-visual context. The starting point for such a process of development and adaptation lies in looking at these strategies, and considering how we can find a purely verbal version for any contribution made by visual contact.

Again, it is helpful to consider this question under the three headings set out above.

The establishment of an effective rapport and relationship

Experience suggests that the optimum starting point for telephone counselling or tutoring is a face-to-face meeting between student and counsellor or tutor (George, 1984 and 1993). Students report that they find it far easier to speak to someone to whom they can put a face and have met already, however briefly. Even if this meeting has been merely a general introductory meeting for new distance students at a remote centre, this contact is sufficient to make a student feel more relaxed about phoning for help at some later stage. A course brochure which includes photographs of staff provides something of a substitute for direct contact.

Such contact, however, is not always possible. It is then important to think of the elements of a first contact which build the rapport with a student and set the right tone for a counselling interview, and then ensure that these are translated as far as possible into the voice-only contact. Such elements might be the counsellor establishing him- or herself as an accessible, welcoming and friendly person, with a genuine and non-judgemental interest in the student and her situation.

The voice is a powerful tool. Rutter and Robinson (1981) found that speaker and listener are transmitting a wider range of signals than they are usually conscious of. Voice tone conveys a wealth of feeling with accuracy – warmth and interest, enthusiasm, concern, query, puzzlement. Experience suggests that a good guideline for telephone counselling or teaching, at least in the early stages of a contact, is to treat the interaction more like a dramatic performance, accentuating important characteristics or features as one would in a face-to-face teaching situation; projecting the voice, speaking clearly and somewhat slower than in a face-to-face conversation. Actually smiling relaxes the facial muscles, and the voice sounds warmer and more friendly.

Words of welcome and introduction are backed by visual reinforcement in a conventional format of interview. To achieve the same effect with voice alone, it is advisable to be somewhat fuller in what you say than you normally would, and to have thought carefully beforehand whether there is any important aspect of yourself as counsellor which is conveyed visually, and needs to be put into words. An extreme example might be that you are sight impaired; you need to consider letting the student realise this, however directly or indirectly, to avoid future embarrassment or difficulty.

Use of names is also important in setting the tone of contact. The use of first names sets an informal tone, though it may be inappropriate in some contexts. As a telephone session proceeds, there are also points at which the exchange would be eased by a smile or a friendly gesture in a face-to-face setting, and where the intention of such visual communication needs to be translated into a laugh, a joke or whatever is appropriate. Silence, too, can be a source of tension and distraction in phone contact. Students are likely to interpret a silence or pause on the counsellor's part as stemming from their having said something foolish or inept (Cowan, 1997a). However, if they could see the counsellor's expression, they would know that s/he was just being thoughtful. Similarly, the counsellor needs to be ready to ask the student to interpret his/her silence; and to create time for silence explicitly if s/he feels that the student needs a moment to gather thoughts or reflect on what has just been said.

The telephone is an invasive form of communication. Students may well be hesitant about what they see as 'interrupting' the tutor or counsellor at home, for example; and this hesitation may well be confirmed when they, in fact, do ring at an awkward time, and the tutor's own hesitation sends them the message that they are invading privacy and are unwelcome. Setting clear times during which the counsellor will be available helps in this difficulty, although it is important that the counsellor should also observe the dedicated time. If there is a genuine reason for the call being inconvenient, the counsellor should explain what it is, arrange to call back at a definite time, and keep to that arrangement.

The pacing and structuring of the interaction

Central to the skills of a counsellor are the strategies of facilitating a student to explore a situation or difficulty, to determine what the various options or choices might be, and to come to a decision. Beginnings, middles and ends of such interviews are all important to the success of such an interaction; skills such as reflecting and summarising are important.

In a face-to-face interview, the process of counselling is steered to a considerable extent by the feedback each gives the other by visual cues. Facial expressions of puzzlement or enquiry, the body language of anxiety or confident resolution inform the counsellor of what is happening for the student and prompt an appropriate response. Similarly, the counsellor's expressions and gestures can indicate attentiveness and a wish for the student to continue speaking, or suggest that it is time to move on to the next item.

In both telephone teaching and counselling, George (1984; see also Cowan, 1997a) found that experienced staff thought it most important to find substitutes for this visual feedback which structures and paces an interaction. This again means putting far more into words than happens in a face-to-face interaction. Good practice here often consists of creating an explicitly agreed and clearly defined agenda, checking at each stage how the student is feeling about the progress of the call and what their perception is of what has happened in relation to that particular agenda item, summarising carefully what has been agreed or what is to happen next. All these would be aspects of a good counselling or advisory interview in conventional circumstances. On the phone, it is all the more necessary for the counsellor to create the framework of discussion verbally and to keep checking that both are agreed and comfortable about where they have got.

Access to reference material or further data

Part of an advisory interview is often seeking further information in some reference work or handbook. If an agenda has been agreed on and the timescale permits, it may be possible to post out any material the student may need to refer to – or to give them time to go and collect copies for themselves. Use of a fax machine can be a useful supplementary tool here.

If this is not possible, the counsellor will have to think of an appropriate way of conveying the necessary information to the student; for example, giving a solid few minutes of factual input, followed by a ten minute break for the student to assimilate what they have heard and to reflect upon it.

PRACTICAL CONSIDERATIONS

Consideration of basic practicalities can improve the quality of the telephone support the student receives. Especially if students are home-based, they often do not think, in relation to telephone learning or seeking advice, about certain practical aspects; the position of the phone – is it in a badly lit, drafty hallway, and could extension wiring at least allow them to sit in the understairs cupboard? Have they something to rest papers on, and write on? Would a call 30 minutes later allow the family to have finished watching the soap on the TV, and win them more peace and quiet? Have they explained to the family what the call is about and why it is important that they have this uninterrupted time? Similarly, the tutor or counsellor needs to think about their surroundings, and to get the best arrangement possible.

Finance is another important aspect to consider. Is the institution or the academic department prepared for the sudden and dramatic increase in the telephone bill? Arrangements need to be made to reimburse tutors if they are expected to use their home phones. Students too need to know the financial implications of phone contact and whether they or the institution are expected to bear the cost of the calls. These are issues which are surprisingly often forgotten, and cause annoyance and frustration.

HOW EFFECTIVE IS YOUR TELEPHONE COUNSELLING?

The drive towards quality assurance and audit over recent years has focused attention on the responsibility of the professional to evaluate their own performance; to become the critically reflective practitioner, as defined by Schön (1993). The need increasingly is for counsellors or tutors to have available to them a range of formative and illuminative techniques of evaluation, which they can use easily and unobtrusively to match their work against the criteria they or others have set them; or to obtain answers to certain particular questions about their style or their effectiveness. In the counselling field, the work of Kagan (1975, for example) has offered a methodology whereby counsellors can explore the experience of their counsellees, and reflect on the illuminating mismatches in perception of what was happening between counsellor and counselled. Recent action research projects have begun to widen the range of what is available to the tutor or counsellor as practicable techniques (George and Cowan, 1997).

It is doubly important to seek sound feedback for telephone counselling or student support. In addition, the lack of visual feedback during a telephone interaction means a lack of the data which face-to-face contact provides in abundance. The concentration of this medium, moreover, often makes a counsellor too busy to monitor voice tone or the pattern of exchange as the call proceeds.

As George and Cowan (1997) describe, questionnaires are certainly a good starting point, especially for broader or more practical questions; timing, relevance, achievement of objectives and so on. A tape of an interview or support session (taken only with the student's permission, of course) can provide data for either the counsellor or for a colleague to gather information which will inform the counsellor's self judgement on strengths or weaknesses. A three way link can actually allow a colleague to 'sit in' as they might on a face-to-face session, with similar purpose. Drawing a concept map at the end of a session – probably immediately after the call and then reporting in a resumed contact – helps the student consolidate what has been achieved and identify any loose ends; it also 'maps out' for the counsellor what has happened for the student, perhaps with more of a tendency to report cognitive than affective or interpersonal happenings. An interview with a student by a colleague immediately after a call can produce useful data, especially when the colleague emphasises the positive and creative purposes of such reporting. And finally, a telephone version of Kagan's Interpersonal Process Recall, though somewhat labour intensive in relation to phone contact, can produce, as it does for face-to-face teaching or counselling, rich and powerful insights into the student's experience.

STAFF DEVELOPMENT

A recent telephone action research project in the Open University in Scotland had, as its intended purpose, the establishment of guidelines for good practice from the investigation of the work of tutors acknowledged as excellent telephone tutors, across a range of facilities and disciplines (Cowan, 1997a). The actual outcome was that every tutor, on the basis of the data which the project fed back to them about what was happening on their calls, significantly altered their style and the organisation of their agendas. Whether the term is 'continuing professional development' or 'staff development', there is the need for individuals to constantly review data on their performance against the criteria they set themselves, to have the chance to experience or hear of good ideas from others, and to feed the consequent changes into their working practices.

One pattern for such continuing development could start with a basic skills workshop. This might best be a face-to-face one – for all the advantages of numbers and mutual support – which enables participants to explore the medium, first through a 'warm-up' exercise of partners building matching Lego shapes without visual contact, and then through observed telephone interactions, from which participants draw guidelines for themselves. Advanced workshops could run on a similar framework of reflection on observed practice. Both can be supplemented by the support of a mentor, through sitting in on calls and/or interviewing students. The data gathered will enable them to judge for themselves their strengths and weaknesses.

In addition, as George (1996) reports, staff should be supported and encouraged to develop the action research techniques which will enable them to become the custodians of their own standards, and to take responsibility for the quality of their professional practice. Such autonomy is as important to the distance tutor or counsellor as it is to the distance learner.

POSTSCRIPT

Video-conferencing or interactive computer visuals are fast becoming a more available and familiar reality. But the low-tec phone, for its cost, familiarity and availability, is a medium for teaching and for counselling students in a distance system which remains simple and effective, and which could only be replaced for more than a monied minority by a public system of technology access which in the UK seems beyond resource in the current situation.

BIBLIOGRAPHY

Cowan, J. (1997a), *Open University in Scotland Telephone Tuition Project*, Edinburgh: The Open University in Scotland.

Cowan, J. (1997b), *Open University in Scotland Videoconference Project*, Edinburgh: The Open University in Scotland.

George, J.W. (1984), *On the Line: Counselling and Teaching by Telephone*, Milton Keynes: Open University course P519.

George, J.W. (1993), 'Effective teaching and learning by telephone', in *Distance Learning in ELT*, eds. Richards, K., and Roe, P., Review of ELT vol. 3.2, Modern English Publications with the British Council.

George, J.W. (1996), 'Action research for quality development in rural education in Scotland', in *Journal of Research in Rural Education*, vol. 12, no. 2, pp. 76–82.

George J.W., and Cowan, J. (1997), *Tutoring by Phone: a Staff Guide*, The Robert Gordon University.

Kagan, N. (1975), 'Influencing human interaction: eleven years with IPR', *The Canadian Counsellor*, vol. 9, no. 2, pp. 74–97.

Macdonald, J., and Mason, R. (1996), *Information Handling Skills and Resource-based Learning*, Milton Keynes: Open University OTD.

Rutter, D.R. and Robinson, B. (1981), 'An experimental analysis of teaching by telephone: theoretical and practical implications for Social Psychology', in *Progress in Applied Social Psychology*, (eds) Stephenson, G.M., and Davis, J.H., vol. 1, 345–75.

Schön, D. (1993), *The Reflective Practitioner: How Professionals Think in Action*, New York: Basic Books.

Chapter 9

Guidance and counselling in The Open University

Alan Tait

INTRODUCTION

This chapter aims to give an overview of guidance and counselling in The Open University UK (OU), and to provide some understanding of how it has developed over time. It will also offer some frameworks of analysis and identify the primary terms and concerns which have been employed within the OU itself. An account of the media used will be given, acknowledging one of the most important frameworks of analysis, i.e. that the OU has developed guidance and counselling for adult learners in an open and distance learning system. Finally, the chapter notes the move from the OU's practice of counselling towards more widely understood models of educational guidance and customer care.

THE OPEN UNIVERSITY

The OU was established in 1969 with an initial mission to offer undergraduate degrees on a part-time basis to adult students who would not need entry qualifications, and a longer term mission to develop 'updating, refresher courses, and occupational conversion courses' (Planning Committee, 1969: 4). From its first year of teaching in 1971, when it had just under 20,000 students, it had grown to some 140,000 students by 1997 (The Open University, 1997). The OU did much to establish what was termed distance education, later open and distance learning (ODL), and as the first open university had a uniquely important role in bringing about the modernisation of the correspondence education tradition through the employment of a range of media and methods. These comprised well-produced and structured learning materials; TV and radio programmes; video and audio-cassette, and more recently CD-ROM; local opportunities for face-to-face meetings with tutors, counsellors and fellow students; telephone teaching; and residential schools. Individualised student support through local tuition and counselling was introduced from the beginning, as was the development of correspondence teaching as a serious teaching and learning interaction. More recently, computer-supported communication has been introduced for some courses, with more than 20,000 students participating in 1997. While in 1971 almost all students were restricted to the UK, the OU's geographical reach now includes the European Union and other Central and Eastern European countries, with schemes of study also in countries as far apart as Ethiopia, India, Singapore, South Africa, and the USA. Further, the Master's Programme in Open and Distance Education has recruited a student body which is global in make up, and principally electronically supported. This is the pen portrait of historical development within which guidance and counselling has been conceived, developed and transformed in the OU. Many of the OU's defining characteristics have since become common to other Higher and Further Education institutions in the UK, including the recruitment of adult students to Higher Education on a much more flexible basis in terms of entry requirements, the development of independent learning strategies and the employment of a range of technologies to support learning. The OU remains unique however in its first come–first served, open entry policy at undergraduate level.

GUIDANCE AND COUNSELLING IN THE OU: AN OVERVIEW

The OU Planning Committee was prescient in 1969 when it said:

> Because of the range of choices inherent in the degree pattern, the 'openness' of the University, and the possibility that many students may wish to enrol who are not at a stage when they could profitably pursue degree studies, we consider the development of the counselling service to be of particular importance. It will . . . be the means by which the University can reduce to a minimum the number of students who embark upon courses only to find they cannot continue with them.
>
> (The Open University, 1969: 14)

Two points immediately arise out of this paragraph. First, the recognition of the implications of open access and of a counselling service that aims to support learners coming from non-traditional backgrounds in terms of qualifications for university entrance; and second, the related concern of drop-out and the role of counselling in containing it. From this beginning has grown the dominant counselling model of the Undergraduate Programme, along with a range of complementary services, including pre-study enquiry and advisory services, summer school counselling, vocational guidance, and support to students with disability. The core role of the counsellor was proposed by the first Director of Regional Tutorial Services to the OU Planning Committee as:

> rather akin to the academic supervisor in the traditional sense. He (sic) is an educator and he must have an understanding of the total educational process that the student is engaged in. Conceived of in this fashion, the counsellor is as much a part of the tutorial process as the tutor proper.
>
> (Robert Beevers, cited in Grugeon, 1987:197)

OU counselling was seen as the essential support to all students in order to create an individualised programme of study. As one of the first Senior Counsellors wrote:

> Counselling is therefore essentially a concern with a true balance of objectives, with a meaningful integration of communicable knowledge with the felt needs of the learners.
>
> (Davison, 1975:23)

Counselling is seen here as both integral to the teaching and learning process, and dependent on the developmental dimension of the whole person over time 'whose learning takes place in the context of past experiences, present circumstance and future hopes and aspirations' (Fage and Heron, cited in Bailey *et al.*, 1996: 32). These counselling objectives could only be fulfilled though a relationship based on the period of studentship in the university, not through a relationship which is course-based with a succession of different tutors from one year to another or a drop-in or telephone service from an unknown adviser.

Planning proceeded on the basis that graduates interested in supporting adult learners could be identified and employed as counsellors, and that distance, in the sense of separation from the institution, could be overcome in this way. No such assumption could be made about finding tutors on such a widespread basis; they needed subject-specific academic competence for each course. It has been suggested that the combination of the Oxbridge tutorial model, with its emphasis on small group or individual interaction, together with elements of the British adult education tradition, provided the larger framework of ideas and values in the design of the OU's counselling system (Tait, 1996: 61). By the time the first year of teaching had begun in 1971, the OU had appointed counsellors across the whole of the UK, an achievement in the provision of learner support for adult undergraduate students which can in retrospect too easily be taken for granted.

THE PRACTICE OF GUIDANCE AND COUNSELLING IN THE OU

We can summarise the original vision of counselling within the OU as having had in practice the following inter-related and mutually supportive concerns:

- the support of student academic progress, success and the containment of drop-out
- institutional induction and study skills
- the student course choice and programme planning processes
- advocacy for the student within a complex bureaucracy
- the development of the individual student on a personal and local basis over a series of courses and over time.

In terms of its organisation, counselling was perceived along two main lines. First, as integral to the teaching role for first year undergraduate students, though where differentiated it was taken to refer to induction, study skills, administrative problem-solving (e.g. fees issues, summer school attendance requirements, study scheduling issues), and course choice and degree planning. Second, as an activity which was non-course-based for students for the remainder of their undergraduate careers over as long as eight or so years. The combination of information distribution based on computer systems together with the direction to tutors and counsellors to be interventionist represented a central aspect of the commitment to the support of student progress. It was intended to substitute for the day-to-day monitoring of student progress which, at its best, can take place informally on a campus.

Counselling within the OU, whatever the medium, has been seen primarily within the framework of study, and counsellors have been strongly directed not to work outside their skill areas as experienced teachers. They have been directed to suggest referral routes to students with particular personal difficulties e.g. in the area of marital or domestic relations, redundancy, mental health problems, alcohol or other abuse etc. (The Open University, 1988: 43).

Vocational guidance

It was recognised from the beginning that vocational guidance was necessary for OU students, many of whom were mid-career or in pre-career (the latter especially women who had carried major parenting responsibilities). The OU's own research revealed that some 60 per cent of its students had an interest in changing career direction (Woodley et al., 1997). The OU committed itself to a strategy which would recognise the fact that its students were 'at a distance'. This included the generation of a small amount of materials itself and buying in a greater number of materials (for example occupational and career specific booklets from the Association of Graduate Careers Advisory Services), and making these available by post to students on request and at residential school. Computer-supported careers advisory programmes, such as CASCAID and later JIIG-CAL, could be assessed in the same ways. In addition, for a small subset of OU students external face-to-face careers counselling from local careers offices or other university careers services was purchased.

The slim commitment on the part of the OU to the vocational guidance needs of its students makes a contrast with other sectors of Higher and Further Education, where in many instances adult students are now in a sizeable minority or even a majority in a single institution. Adult students in such universities and colleges are able in principle to access careers centres with the full range of services.

Support to students with disability

The OU has a record of significant achievement in the provision of opportunity to students with disability. There were in 1997 some 5,500 students with what are now termed special needs. Each Regional Centre has dedicated professional support to this area of work, supported by a central office at the OU headquarters. At Residential School, services are provided including student helpers and equipment, together with a focus on the needs of such students whose special needs have been assessed beforehand. While the accessibility of conventional campuses to students with physical disability has improved significantly in recent years, home-based study may still represent for some the only viable option.

MEDIA AND DISTANCE

As an institution working in the ODL context, counselling in the OU has not been predicated solely on the one-to-one face-to-face meeting that is thought of generally as the counselling encounter. The media used by the OU in counselling are principally:

- counselling materials
- telephone
- face-to-face, individually or in a group
- computer-supported communication.

Counselling materials are variously used throughout the OU's regional structure and are sent out on a routine basis, e.g. triggered by the period when students choose the following year's course, or by the student's withdrawal from the course or vulnerability to exam anxiety, or by some other event or issue. Other materials are developed by course teams and offer study advice about how to engage with a particular assignment or prepare for an examination. The materials are intended to be used on a self-study basis, and thus can be seen as support to guidance and counselling rather than representing the interaction itself (Simpson, 1988). Interaction by telephone or correspondence may follow as a result of student response, or less often as a result of counsellor intervention.

The telephone is the medium through which the majority of guidance and counselling activities take place on an individual basis and because of this it has received considerable attention. Directions to OU counsellors suggest the main advantages of the medium lie in its speed and convenience, while disadvantages include the lack of visual clues and the lack of context (neither party knowing what is going on at the other end) (The Open University, 1988: 49). Group counselling on the telephone has been little developed.

Face-to-face meetings with individuals make up the smallest part of the OU's counselling offer, taking place by and large as an exception when a student has particular issues or problems to discuss (the exception to this is counselling at residential school when this is the predominant medium). Counsellors are trained to use basic listening skills, and within the broader guidance dimension of this activity to distinguish between information-giving, advice and counselling.

Most recently, along with the growth in tutoring and student–student interaction through electronic mail and computer-conferencing, the electronically supported media have also begun to be used for complementary counselling services (Jennison, 1997). Information on courses is being offered electronically and advisory services made available from regional centres for students who want to ask questions in the process of choosing their paths of study. While at the time of writing demand is not high, it is clear from wider social trends, as well as fast-developing OU policy in this area, that electronic communication, essentially interrogation of electronical databases and asynchronous correspondence, will represent a substantial medium for counselling in the future. Domestic usage of electronically supported communication is not however as widespread as the telephone, and there is clearly a difficult balance between technology adoption and equal opportunities policy.

FRAMEWORKS OF UNDERSTANDING

Moore's (1984) examination of what had been written about counselling in the OU from within the institution provides a useful starting point to examine frameworks of understanding. The frameworks can be organised and further elaborated as in Figure 9.1. The overarching categories in Figure 9.1 combined in terms of understanding and values to produce the counselling services that obtained for the first twenty-five years of the OU. The Open and Distance Learning context has contributed an understanding that students could not have a service predicated on the need to be on a campus, although some of what has been termed counselling has taken place on a face-to-face basis in study centres or residential schools. While counselling in the OU has attempted to overcome the distances caused by the legacy of social histories as well as the physical barriers imposed by geography, this has combined with the assumption that counselling can be distinguished from that developed in other educational institutions because of the adult status of students (Beevers, cited in Mills, 1981). The location of the counselling role within the teaching and learning process, as noted, brought with it explicit advice to those involved not to see themselves as personal counsellors in the sense widely understood elsewhere.

The restrictions relating to personal counselling were based primarily on the assertion that adult students studying from home had their own sources of support, viz. family, friends, colleagues and access to local services, which made their situation different from that of conventional eighteen year olds on a campus, often living away from home. There was also the doubt that such services could be delivered through an ODL system, as well as, paradoxically, the concern that resources could not cope with potential demand. However, the emergence of very demanding students disabused the OU, or at least those immediately concerned, of the view that adult students did not from time to time have severe personal problems affecting their capacity to manage study, and that they were often not able to find adequate support in their immediate environment, which might indeed represent the very locus of the problem. These problems might arise in the main course of study or in the 'hothouse atmosphere' of summer school, and derived from domestic relationships, unemployment, financial difficulties, physical disability, serious long-term illness, and any combination of these and others (Kirk, 1977; Bailey and Moore, 1989). The assumption that students were

Overarching categories

ODL context   adult students   learning

Subordinate categories

distance ◄— student progress ◄— continuity of concern ◄— drop-out ◄— independent learner

Figure 9.1 Frameworks of understanding for counselling in The Open University (adapted from Moore, 1984)

mature enough not to need a personal counselling service, or that they could easily avail themselves of it elsewhere, has never been successfully challenged, even though andragogy, or the schematic difference posited in learning between children, young people and adults, has since been widely discredited (Hanson, 1996). Such an assumption stands in sharp contrast to the counselling services available to the many adult students in other universities. This leads to the question as to whether the term 'counselling' was the most useful that could have been adopted. The development of other services, such as those to enquirers, as well as specialist services to students with disability and in what was termed vocational guidance, makes it plausible that guidance would have been better understood as the overarching term. Counselling in the conventional sense has represented in fact the smallest element within a range of guidance activities.

The concentration on counselling in learning acted to focus counselling on the educational process, especially on the development of skills and knowledge for newcomers to higher education without the conventional 'A' levels or Highers, and on the support of course choice and degree planning in what was a radically new kind of 'menu-based' undergraduate programme. While the term counselling has sometimes presented difficulties both for students and the OU institutionally, the OU's pioneering concentration on counselling and learning at the same time has raised the profile of support to learning and to individual development as a complement to course teaching in ways that have been influential elsewhere.

The overarching structure in Figure 9.1 governed the subordinate framework of ideas, and involved in more detail the attention paid to distance or remoteness in the straightforward geographical sense, and the concomitant use of varied media, practices and forms of organisation. The broad commitment to student progress which grew out of the location of counselling within the learning process was combined with 'continuity of concern' (Cook, 1977), which contained within it a commitment to personal development over time within the framework of a programme of study. Student progress also contained within it the narrower but necessary commitment to containing or reducing drop-out, which from the beginning of the OU has been recognised as a threat to individual well-being in an open access programme as well as to institutional credibility. The broad notion of the 'independent learner' was much discussed during the 1980s and early 1990s, and represented the idealised robust student which the OU's teaching and learning system should aim to create. Counselling activities within the OU had to attempt therefore to engender autonomy through support to individuals (a not unfamiliar conundrum in mainstream counselling also).

While the framework of OU ideas about counselling has been influential in more than twenty other distance teaching universities around the world, it is clear that within higher and further education in the UK the OU has had to seek its own path. For example, what in other institutions is termed 'tutoring' is closer to what the OU has termed counselling. As Earwaker puts it:

> In British higher education 'tutor' has for a long time seemed the natural way to refer to the member of teaching staff who takes a personal interest in a student . . . there are several different kinds of responsibility . . . Course tutor (responsible for running a complete course), Year Tutor (responsible for one year of a course), Personal Tutor (responsible for keeping a watchful eye on the student's work and progress on an individual basis).
>
> (Earwaker, 1992: 45–46)

The centrality of pastoral care to counselling in higher and further education identified by both Earwaker (1992) and Bell (1996) is foreign to the OU. While pastoral care and the interest in maturational and developmental processes was conceived in the context of eighteen- or nineteen-year-old school leavers, Earwaker (1992: 13) argues that 'it is not just for eighteen year olds that the experience of being a student is intertwined with, and perhaps even indistinguishable from, the experience of being a developing person. All students, whatever their chronological age and degree of maturity, can experience higher education as a process of personal development.' The experience of access courses to higher education through the 1980s and 1990s, with student cohorts very similar in many ways in terms of age distribution and educational experience to those of first year OU undergraduates, would support Earwaker's observation. Bell (1996: 42) reports that the dominant view of student counsellors in higher and further education was that 'counsellors never give advice'. Her account of the psychodynamic or person-centred orientations governing counselling for students also reveals how far what the OU terms counselling is from what is denoted by that term elsewhere. In terms of Earwaker's analysis, the OU stands on the side of amateurs in the counselling field in education as opposed to the professionalisation which has dominated North American and subsequently British developments (Earwaker, 1992: 101).

CONCLUSION: FROM EDUCATIONAL COUNSELLING TO GUIDANCE AND CUSTOMER CARE

Despite the observation that more theory was needed (Moore, 1984: 89), counselling in the OU has remained pragmatic with little research undertaken to demonstrate its effectiveness. The published accounts of counselling are predominantly descriptive and characterised by what Moore (1984: 89) termed 'polemic about its inherent goodness'. While there have been small-scale studies of student reaction to various forms of intervention (Simpson and Stevens, 1988) and extended internal policy studies (Fage, 1992), the difficulty of identifying the contribution of counselling to student progress has been recognised from research and managerial perspectives (Thorpe, 1988: 118).

The far-reaching review of OU counselling policy which was concluded in 1996 therefore did not have substantial research-based evidence available concerning its effectiveness, and arose from a complex range of internal and external factors. From the external perspective, developments in the organisation of educational advisory services had come to complement the OU vision of counselling, particularly the work of the National Association for Educational Guidance for Adults (NAEGA), and the Unit for the Development of Adult and Continuing Education (UDACE). Other significant external influences have included the work of the Higher Education Quality Council, mapping guidance and student support through pre-entry, entry and induction, and the on-programme phases (Higher Education Quality Council, 1995). As they become more influential in higher education, key skills in the fields of literacy, numeracy, communication and information technology may be supported through guidance activities as well as course materials (National Committee of Inquiry into Higher Education, 1997). These developments have necessitated a general engagement of the OU with the outside world, and a diminution of its somewhat inward nature which characterised the institution until the 1980s.

A range of internal changes contributed more specifically to the need for a review. First, the wider range of programmes developed during the 1980s did not introduce a counselling system on the undergraduate model but rather developed piecemeal. For a number of programmes of study, a counselling role where at all explicit was the extension of the tutor role on a course by course basis without the continuity of concern from one identified student counsellor over the full period of study (Brindley and Fage, 1992). This model subsequently has become predominant within overall OU provision. Other factors included the view that locally based, part-time staff could not be expected to be conversant with the increased complexities of the OU's courses and regulations; that continuity of concern had become a relationship too often honoured as a principle rather than delivered in a meaningful way in practice; and that the increase in student numbers together with the downward pressure on funding meant that support with lower unit costs had to be sought (Fage, 1992).

The development of a series of guidance services with focused expertise in Regional Centres, staffed by small teams of advisors and student support assistants, combined with a reduction in the expectations in particular of the non-tutorial related kind (i.e. what had been hitherto termed post-foundation counselling delivered on a local basis in the undergraduate programme) were seen as the key to moving forward (Tait, 1996). The concern with drop-out and with assisting students in managing the rules and regulations of the organisation have been maintained and received new emphases within the framework of customer service and retention (Gaskell and Simpson, 1995) guided by the principles of service industries (Sewart, 1993). The objectives in the establishment of the new counselling and student support services include greater speed in terms of response to students from full-time dedicated staff, the provision of more accurate and regularly updated information, and clearer lines of accountability within more developed managerial structures.

We can see that the organisation of services in other areas of both higher education and educational guidance, and indeed the increased emphasis on customer service in all organisations which has taken place in the recent period, has changed what had been uniquely developed within the OU as educational counselling. The overall picture reveals that while the opportunities for sustained personal relationships on a local basis have declined, the availability of up-to-date information and guidance from advisors from regional centres has increased. We may note also the increased professionalism of a reduced number of guidance workers replacing the widespread availability of amateur educational counsellors, that is counsellors for whom experience of adult teaching was the prime professional prerequisite. Student guidance is also being developed through World Wide Web-based provision, which is expected to support both enquirers and students in the future as the new technologies are adopted (Phillips, *et al.*, 1998). Thus, asynchronous electronically mediated services, supported by a telephone enquiry service may in their turn be able to diminish the geographical and social distances which OU counselling was intended to remedy at its inception.

NOTE

I would like to thank the colleagues who have given so much help with earlier drafts, and in particular David Grugeon.

BIBLIOGRAPHY

Bailey, D. and Moore, J. (1989) 'Closing the Distance: Counselling at The Open University Residential Schools'. *British Journal of Guidance and Counselling*, 17, 3: 317–30.

Bailey, D., Brown, J. and Kelly, P. (1996) 'Academic Advice, Personal Counselling, and On-programme Guidance in The Open University', in *Higher Education Quality Council, Personal Tutoring and Academic Advice in Focus*, London: HEQC.

Bell, E. (1996) *Counselling in Further and Higher Education*, Buckingham: The Open University Press.

Brindley, J. and Fage, J. (1992) 'Counselling in Open, Adult Higher and Continuing Education: Two Institutions face the Future', *Open Learning*, 7, 3: 12–19.

Cook, R. (1977) 'Counselling Continuity and the Committed Tutor-counsellor', *Teaching at a Distance* 9: 54–9.

Davison, J. (1975) 'Educational Counselling in Academic Studies', *Teaching at a Distance*, 3: 16–25.

Earwaker, J. (1992) *Helping and Supporting Students*, Buckingham: Society for Research into Higher Education, The Open University Press.

Fage, J. (1992) *A Strategy for Counselling – Expansion, Quality and Change in the 1990s*, Milton Keynes: The Open University Regional Academic Services, mimeo.

Gaskell, A. and Simpson, O. (1995) *Customer Defection in the OU: 'Bailing Out' Revisited*, East Anglian Regional Projects, Research and Other Developments, mimeo, Cambridge: The Open University, East Anglia.

Grugeon, D. (1987) 'Educational Counselling and Open Learning', in Thorpe, M. and Grugeon, D. (eds) *Open Learning for Adults*, Harlow: Longman.

Hanson, A. (1996) 'The Search for a Separate Theory of Adult Learning: Does Anyone really Need Andragogy?', in Edwards, R., Hanson, A., and Raggatt, R. (eds), *Boundaries of Adult Learning*, London: Routledge.

Higher Education Quality Control (1995) *A Quality Assurance Framework for Guidance and Learner Support in Higher Education: the Guidelines*, London: HEQC.

Jennison, K. (1997) *Mutual Support on the Virtual Campus*, in Conference Papers of the 1997 International Council for Distance Education World Conference, Pennsylvania State University.

Kirk, P. (1977) 'The Tip of the Iceberg: Some Effects of Open University Study on Married Students', *Teaching at a Distance*, 10: 19–27.

Mills, A.R. (1981) *The Development of Counselling in The Open University of Great Britain*, mimeo, Cambridge: The Open University, East Anglia.

Moore, M. (1984) 'Counselling in Teaching at a Distance', *Teaching at a Distance* 25: 87–91.

National Committee of Enquiry into Higher Education (1997), *Higher Education in the Learning Society*, The Dearing Report, Summary Report, NCIHE/97/850, London: HMSO.

The Open University (1969), *Report of the Planning Committee*, London: HMSO.

The Open University (1988) *Open Teaching*, Milton Keynes: The Open University.

The Open University (1997) *Open University Planning Office*, Personal Communication, Milton Keynes: The Open University.

Phillips, M., Scott, P. and Fage, J. (1998) 'Towards a Strategy for the Use of New Technology in Student Guidance and Support', *Open Learning*, 13: 2.

Planning Committee (1969) *The Open University, Report of the Planning Committee to the Secretary of State for Education and Science*, London: HMSO.

Sewart, D. (1993) 'Student Support Services in Distance Education', *Open Learning* 8, 3: 3–12.

Simpson, O. (1988) 'Counselling by Correspondence in Distance Education', *Open Learning*, 3, 3: 43–5.

Simpson, O. and Stevens, V. (1988) 'Promoting Student Progress', *Open Learning*, 3, 2: 56.

Tait, A. (1996) 'Conversation and Community: Student Support in Open and

Distance Learning', in Mills, R. and Tait, A. (eds) *Supporting the Learner in Open and Distance Learning*, London: Pitman.

Thorpe, M. (1988) *Evaluating Open and Distance Learning*, Harlow: Longman.

Woodley, A., Simpson, C. and Jelfs, A. (1997) 'Early Results from the 1997 Costs Survey', *Institute of Educational Technology Internal Report*, Milton Keynes: The Open University.

Chapter 10

British systems of careers software: past and present

Malcolm Hunt

An edited version of: 'The present and future use of IT to support guidance', in *The Future Use of Information Technology in Guidance*, NCET/CRAC/NICEC Seminar Report (1994).

Over the last ten years there has been a growing awareness of the role of Information Technology in guidance work. In this chapter I intend to consider current developments in computer-assisted guidance; to suggest areas where existing provision might be enhanced; and to examine the role of new and emerging technologies in supporting guidance provision in the future. This chapter will also consider the potential of the technology and look, as it were, over the horizon, based on our present knowledge of developments and emerging trends.

THE CURRENT POSITION

It is possible to identify a number of important recent developments in various sectors of the guidance community, with respect to the use of Information Technology in guidance. These include the White Paper *Education and Training for the 21st Century* (HMSO, 1991), which provided the resources for schools and colleges to purchase computers and related software to enhance their careers library provision; the development of the *PROSPECT* system for use in higher education and the consideration of a version for the sixteen to nineteen age group; also, the establishment by a number of TECs of guidance shops in town-centre locations offering access to career software packages, principally for use by adults.

A review of computer-assisted careers guidance systems in Britain identified over seventy systems and software programs for use in careers education and guidance (Offer 1991, 1992). They range from basic information retrieval systems through to more complex learning systems, and are summarised in Figure 10.1. By far the largest group (44 per cent) are information-retrieval and processing systems, followed by work simulations, self-presentation aids and software to support administration and recordkeeping.

It must be said that the currently available systems are not without their problems. There is much that can still be done to enhance current provision, given that some packages were developed a number of years ago. There

Types of career software	Definition	Examples of British systems and careers software
Information retrieval	The task of the computer is to find the 'page' on which information is located in response to certain criteria selected by the client from a menu of search factors. Packages include databases of educational courses or occupations.	ECCTIS ·microDOORS · CAREER BUILDER · CHOOSING HE COURSES · CHOICES · CID · COMPUTAJOB · COMPUTER SIGNPOSTS · COUNTDOWN · EUROPE IN THE ROUND· DISCOVER (ISCOM) · JOBFILE EXPLORER · **GRADUATE CAREER BUILDER** · HEADWAY · SUBJECT WISE · NVQ DATABASE · THE NATIONAL GRANTS DATABASE
Information processing and matching systems	The computer identifies occupational or educational opportunities which satisfy a number of criteria chosen by the client. Matching is often achieved via the use of an interest questionnaire or established test. In the case of the older matching systems, there is little opportunity for the user to change their reponses as they are elicited via paper-based questionnaires/assessment tests, sent to a computer centre and the results delivered by batch processing.	CASCAID HE · JIG-CAL · CAREER BUILDER · CASCAID/JOBWISE · CENTINEL-MX · CENTIGRADE · DISCOURSE (ISCOM) · FUTURES · GRADSCOPE · HEADWAY · JOBALERT · JOBSKILL · LIFELINE · CPS · ADULT DIRECTIONS · GUIDELINES · KUDOS
Decision aids	This type of software seeks to help the user examine and structure the various preferences which form part of a decision or to compare various choice options. The packages differ from information systems, as they concentrate on the process rather than the content of decision-making, and on reviewing rather than generating occupational titles. They are content-free and aim to help the user to analyse the factors involved in decision-making.	MAUD · SELSTRA · RESOLVE · DECIDER · CAREERGRID · EXPLORER · GRID MAP
Work simulations and games	These allow the user to experience some of the management decisions involved in running a business or manufacturing industry. This type of software often involves a competitive element with an emphasis on experimental or active learning. Many are business games suited to group activites and not all are specifically designed for careers education. Some have cross-curricular applications.	PRODUCTION LINE · **COMPUTAVISIT** · HOTEL · **MICRO-FIRM** · SECRETARY'S DAY · SUPERMARKET · THE GAME'S THE THING · **TOURISM AND LEISURE** · COCA · ENCOUNTERS · MICROLIFE · SURVIVE · WARD MANAGEMENT SIMULATION · ENTERPRISE BUSINESS PLAN
Self-presentation aids	These are designed to help the user with jobseeking skills such as interviews, action-planning, making applications and writing curriculum vitae.	CV+ · CVII · COMPUTER CV · MOVING ON · FORMS · REVIEWING SKILLS/ACTION PLANNING · CAREER BUILDER · ROA PROCESSOR · PORTFOLIO · PERFECT CV
Psychometric tests and checklists	Many of the packages in this group are computerised versions of paper and pencil tests, measuring such characteristics as personality, ability skills, interest or aptitude. Theaccompanying manuals give statistical data covering the reliability and validity of the measure.	VOCATIONAL PREFERENCE · HANDWRITING ANALYST · LEWIS COUNSELLING INVENTORY · LIFELINE · SCREEN TEST · GENERAL OCCUPATIONAL INTEREST INVENTORY

Figure 10.1 Computer-assisted career guidance systems and software classification

Types of career software	Definition	Examples of British systems and careers software
Learning systems	These are concerned not just to retrieve and process information, but to do so in ways which help the user learn relevant skills and concepts such as decision-making, self-assessment and the ways in which the world of work is organised. In order to do this, such systems are interactive, and the more comprehensive learning systems include a range of modules incorporating many of the systems mentioned above, such as decision aids and information-processing facilities.	PROSPECT
Others (including dedicated databases)	Any other software including dedicated word processors, software designed to assist in administration, including tasks relating to work experience, interview schedules and record keeping.	CAREERS ADMIN II · CAREERS AND WORK EXPERIENCE MANAGEMENT SYSTEM (CAWEMS) · CLASSIFY IT · CLCI LABEL MAKER · ENTERPRISE/ BUSINESS PLAN · LOCAL INDUSTRY PACKAGE · **TOURISM AND LEISURE** · WORK EXPERIENCE ADMIN · INTERVU
	Note Where systems perform more than one clear role, such as information retrieval and information processing, they will appear under more than one heading (eg CAREER BUILDER).	
	Software in bold type has recently been withdrawn by publishers, but may still be available in schools and colleges. It should be noted that packages are being withdrawn or updated all the time and new software developed. The reader is advised to check details with suppliers	

Figure 10.1 Computer-assisted career guidance systems (*Cont.*)

is scope to improve the user interfaces and to develop new types of software. Doubts have also been cast on the value of some programs (Crowley, 1992; Law, 1990; Offer 1992). Nevertheless, leaving these issues to one side, it is perhaps worth reflecting on the rich range of systems of software currently available to the guidance community, despite the fact that careers education and guidance work has always had to fight hard for recognition both nationally and within individual organisations or institutions.

THE 'MINI'/'MAXI' DEBATE

Watts (1992) suggests that there are three main views about the future use of computer-aided systems in guidance. One view is that developments should be limited to information-retrieval and information-processing, although this fails to acknowledge the useful role of the computer in supporting the wider guidance process. A second view is that there should be a range of 'mini' systems, each covering specific functions of the guidance process: what Offer (1991) refers to as 'build your own hi-fi', where practitioners select a mix of systems which meet their distinctive needs and local priorities. This encourages diversity and choice but has the disadvantage of providing only limited interaction between systems and creating potential discrepancies with respect to conceptual and terminological issues. The third approach is that of the 'maxi' systems, typified in Britain by the *PROSPECT* system. It seeks to cover as many of the aims and functions of the guidance process as possible, with appropriate interlinking between the various sections. While this approach has much to recommend it, it too has its problems. In particular, the high cost of establishing and maintaining such systems has led Ward, Stevens and Twining (1992) to comment that a possible way to develop a system such as *PROSPECT* might be on a European scale, rather than individually in each member state.

It can be seen that there has been a trend to developing software for specific target groups, such as adults in the case of *Adult Direction* and *Guidelines*, and for the less able, *CID*. In some respects this reflects developments in guidance policy, highlighting the need for adult guidance and a growing awareness that current software does not always suit individual needs or situations. Despite these developments, other sectors still do not appear to be particularly well served. For example there is a need for systems to support clients within industry, clients in mid-career and clients with special learning difficulties, where new developments such as touch-screen and pointing devices may prove beneficial.

IMPROVING EXISTING CAREERS AND GUIDANCE SOFTWARE

What many information systems and databases still lack is the provision of guidance 'front-ends' to make them more transparent and easier to use – for example, additional facilities to support the database, such as self-assessment programs or modules which allow the user to use the software more effectively. Similarly, although information systems and databases have been improved to provide users with enhanced data to support decision-making and improve opportunity awareness, there remains a need for more effective decision aids or systems to help clients process this information. Decision aids do exist, although a recent NCET survey into the use of software in careers work in schools suggests that such programs are not widely used. Reflecting on this situation, Offer notes that while some people may prefer to discuss options and choices with a counsellor, the process does seem 'ideally suited to computer modelling if only to produce a tool in teaching methods of decision making' (Offer, 1992).

TRAINING

The increasing use of computers in guidance over recent years has raised a number of issues concerning training. The need to improve the general training available to guidance practitioners and careers specialists has been identified by Cleaton (1987) and HMI (1988). Given this situation it is not surprising to find that training in the use of IT in guidance work is very limited. While careers officers may receive basic training in the use of such systems as *CASCAID* and *JIIG-CAL*, and certain system developers provide courses in the use of their particular software, access for practitioners to courses which consider the broader issues concerning the use of IT in guidance is restricted. This must be a major concern if the existing hardware and software is to be used effectively (Rayman, 1989; Johnson and Sampson, 1985).

When considering the issue of training, it is worth considering how IT might have a role to play in supporting the training, not only of careers and guidance specialists but also of non-specialists such as librarians and subject teachers in schools, who are increasingly being involved in guidance work. It is only in the last few years, with the development of the TVEI and Careers Education and Guidance Interactive Video Disc projects, that the full potential of IT, and in particular, multimedia systems has begun to be exploited. The TVEI disc seeks to provide teacher trainers with a resource of TVEI case studies, comments and information for use in staff development activities. The CEG disc offers training for non-specialist teachers and those in initial teacher training in careers and guidance work. Research has demonstrated the effectiveness of interactive video for interpersonal skill training, in-service teacher training and in education generally (Beautment, 1991; Wright and Tearle, 1991; NCET, 1989). It would appear to have a valuable role to play alongside existing training provision, such as the Open College pack, *Co-ordinating Careers Work*, and taught courses.

IMPROVED DATA STORAGE AND THE USE OF CD-ROM

The information needs of guidance have been much enhanced with improvements in computer hard disk storage capability. The capacity of the computer to store and retrieve information has developed considerably, as witness the large number of information systems currently available and the specific reference made to certain educational and occupational databases in key careers education and guidance documents (DES, DoE, 1987; HMI, 1988). The potential of the CD-ROM as a medium for database delivery is well illustrated by the recent development of the *ECCTIS* database, while enhanced memory capacity combined with developments in programming techniques can be seen in the graphics features and extremely flexible access to data possible in *Europe in the Round*.

MULTIMEDIA

CD technology also offers the potential to deliver multimedia: that is to say, the provision of still and moving pictures, sound, text and graphics. The potential of multimedia to support guidance work has already been mentioned in the context of training through the use of interactive video. Other multimedia platforms which are being used to develop guidance packages include *Compact Disk Interactive* (CDI). Whereas CD-ROM operates through a computer, CDI uses a player not unlike a standard video recorder in appearance, connected to an ordinary television set. As the disk plays, the user can control the action by clicking a remote control to go into certain sections or to find the answer to questions. Hirschbuhl, writing about developments in America (Hirschbuhl, 1992), describes a multimedia sampler which gives information about college courses and academic disciplines. In Britain, CDI Training and New Media have developed *Welcome to Work*, a generic induction course for school leavers in their first job, and for mature workers returning to the job market.

While the use of multimedia could enhance a number of existing careers software packages, it would seem especially appropriate in the development of work simulation programs.

SOFTWARE DEVELOPMENTS

A further characteristic of multimedia development has been the increasing use of sophisticated software such as *Windows* and *Hypercard* combined with the mass storage offered by optical technology, to provide a powerful learning tool. Such authoring software provides the user with flexible access to a large amount of data and enables 'a wide range of learners to choose their own pathways through complex materials' (Megarry, 1991). Use of programs of this kind may go some way to enhancing interactivity and improving the somewhat rigid search routines and inflexible approaches which have been identified as a potential drawback with certain 'matching' and assessment systems (Wooler, 1985; Wooler and Wisudha, 1985).

One aspect of the use of computers which has not yet been exploited to any degree is the potential offers to promote group interaction and dialogue.

To some extent work simulation software can be used with small groups of students, and networking careers software may promote work in threes or pairs. The development of electronic mail, voice annotation, computer conferencing and groupware which has been used successfully to promote co-operative learning and to help groups of people communicate effectively. Industry also has the potential to support guidance work. It has a role to play in tutorial work within an institution and could allow tutors/practitioners and clients who cannot meet face to face to keep in touch with each other.

ACCESS

Many of the arguments in support of computer-based systems in guidance are concerned with improving access, and in turn increasing the quality and extent of guidance provision (Watts, Humphries and Pierce-Price, 1988). A number of new technological developments would appear to have the potential to advance this process still further. Increasing miniaturisation has resulted in the development of portable computers, notebooks and palmtops, offering not only greater mobility of hardware, but an increased access to IT for clients and practitioners. There would also appear to be a number of possibilities for the use of portables in supporting guidance work in rural areas or outreach situations.

Within schools the implications for the use of portables go far beyond the educational values of portability. An NCET study made the following observations:

> The advent of portables has made us think about what education would be like with far greater numbers of computers than we have at present. How do classrooms operate with portable computers available at all times when they are far less physically obtrusive than desktop computers? How can pupils and teachers benefit from ownership of their own personal electronic workspace? How should schools respond to the private ownership of computers by pupils or parents?
>
> (NCET, 1992)

This latter point raises the issue of the use of Information Technology in the home. One major option for technology companies is to develop the consumer market. Reference has already been made to the potential of multimedia systems, and CDI in particular is being developed and marketed as a technology to sit in the living room alongside the television and hi-fi. Link with this the development of satellite broadcasting and cable television which many schools and colleges are beginning to exploit, and the potential for bringing aspects of guidance into the home would appear to be considerable (Groombridge, 1993; NCET, 1992).

In some ways this is not a new phenomenon. It raises very similar issues to those posed by the use of the French video text system Minitel (Aubert and Guichard, 1989) and to a lesser degree, the Prestel systems in Britain. In particular it may be argued that they allow the development of self-help and active approaches in the area of access to educational and occupational information. They also illustrate how self-guidance techniques can help to combine formal guidance with informal guidance in the home and community.

INFORMATION TECHNOLOGY AND CURRENT GUIDANCE ISSUES

Having spent time considering what technology might offer, it is also worth reflecting on what is lacking in current developments and considering some of the issues which confront the guidance community, that IT might support in the future. On the matter of assessment, there would appear to be some scope for useful software development. Do we for instance have all the assessment software we would like? There is clear evidence that IT may have a useful role to play in supporting this aspect of guidance work. Other developments include the use of dedicated word processors such as the *Action Planning* and *Record of Achievement* processors, for assisting a client in the process of writing an action plan. A number of developmental projects have also produced logging and tracking systems to monitor client progress through courses. While existing guidance software such as job-generating software, educational and occupational databases may be helpful in identifying qualifications or training which a client might wish to undertake, there are few pieces of software which seek to support the APL assessment process.

The potential of the computer for tracking might be used to monitor user interactions, giving not only statistical data, such as rates of use, but also valuable research data, such as the various paths that users make through a given system. Such an idea is not new, although few systems designers or researchers appear to have exploited this facility (Katz and Shatkin, 1983; Sampson, 1983).

Other areas for consideration are the role of IT in record-keeping, and administration. Many institutions have installed large management information systems such as *SIMS* and *CMIS* which hold information about clients which guidance staff would wish to access in support of their work. The loading of large quantities of client data onto computer systems could be assisted by the use of scanners or optical mark readers. Indeed, they are already used in the batch-processing of client forms in systems such as *JIIG-CAL*, but their use in other aspects of guidance would not appear to have been fully investigated.

Finally, turning to the Single European Market, guidance services are having to adapt to the changes in national labour markets, including the impact of demographic and technological developments. There is likely to be an increasing demand for reliable sources of comprehensive and up-to-date information on education, training and employment opportunities, as the process of 'Europeanisation' changes the hitherto rather nationally-orientated focus of guidance services. Indeed, we have already seen the establishment of a number of 'European Careers Centres' in certain European Community countries, including the British centre in Bradford.

The case for the increased use of computers, databases and self-help information systems has been supported in a number of documents on European guidance matters (Banks *et al.*, 1989; Plant, 1989, 1991; Watts, 1989). Newton (1989) argues that computer-assisted careers guidance systems can provide easy access to all forms of information across frontiers, using the enhanced data storage offered by CD-ROM and supported by on-line information services and satellite links; they can also assist in the harmonisation of databases, and facilitate educational and occupational mobility across Europe.

CONCLUSION

In examining the present and future role of Information Technology in guidance, I am very conscious that we do not live in a perfect world. Merely identifying the potential of a given technology does not make it a reality, as it is subject to social and political influences. On the technical side, a major war is raging as to which will be the main multimedia platforms of the future. The pace of innovation is relentless. Any new developments will have implications for resourcing, guidance policy, organisational practice and implementation, which the guidance community, government policy-makers, decision-makers, careers publishers and software developers will all have to confront. What is clear is that, through the adoption of micro-computers, IT has now come of age in the guidance world, and that in the future it has the potential to support and enhance our work still further.

BIBLIOGRAPHY

Aubert, J. and Guichard, J. 'MINITEL and Careers Guidance', in Watts, A.G. (ed.) *Computers in Careers Guidance*, CRAC/Hobsons, 1989.

Banks, J.A.G., Raban, A.J. and Watts, A.G. *The Single European Market and its implications for Educational and Vocational Guidance Services*, CRAC/Hobsons, 1989.

Beautment, P. 'Review of Interactive Video Systems and their possible application to Training in the 90s' *Interactive Learning International*, 7, 45–54: 1991.

Cleaton, D. 'Survey of Career Work,' *NACGT, Newpoint*, 1987.

Crowley, A.D. 'Computer-Aided Careers Guidance: an Investigation Involving an Artificial System,' *British Journal of Guidance and Counselling*, 20, 3: 1992.

Department of Education and Science and Department of Employment. *Working Together for a Better Future*, COI, 1987.

Groombridge, B. 'Auntie's secret strengths,' *Education*, 15 January, 1993.

Her Majesty's Inspectorate. 'Careers Education and Guidance from 5 to 16,' *Curriculum Matters 10*, London HMSO, 1988.

HMSO. Department of Education and Science and Department of Employment: *Education and Training for the 21st Century*, Vols 1 and 2, May, 1991.

Hirschbuhl, J.J. 'Multimedia: Why Invest?', *Interactive Learning International*, 8, 321–3: 1992.

Johnson C.S. and Sampson, J.P. 'Training Counsellors to use Computers,' *Journal of Career Development*, December, 1985.

Katz, M.R. and Shatkin, L. 'Characteristics of Computer-Assisted Guidance,' *The Counseling Psychologist*, 11(4), 1983.

Law, B. 'Daft Computer-Assisted Guidance Needs Remedial Help!', *NICEC Bulletin*, 37: 1990.

Megarry, J. 'Europe in the Round: Principles and Practice of Screen Design,' *Educational Training and Technology International*, 28 (4) November: 1991.

NCET. *Interactive Video and Learning in Schools – a Report to the Department of Education and Science*, NCET, January 1989.

NCET. *Extending Your College into the Future – Using Satellite and Cable Technology in Further Education*, NCET, 1992.

NCET. *Choosing and Using Portable Computers*, NCET, 1992.

Newton, W. 'Towards 2000 via 1992: Implications of likely technical and other developments,' in Watts, A.G. (ed.) *Computers in Careers Guidance*, CRAC/Hobsons, 1989.

Offer, M. 'An Introduction to the Use of Computers in Guidance,' Information and Advice Unit, Employment Department, 1991.

Offer, M. (ed.) *Careers Software Review*, NCET, 1991.

Offer, M. *Careers Software Review: 1992* Update, NCET, 1992.

Offer, M. 'Developments in the field of vocational guidance software from Cambridge to Nürnberg 1989–1992.' Paper presented at the Third European Conference on Computers in Careers Guidance, 1992.

Plant, P. 'Technology is the Answer: What was the Question?', in Watts, A.G. (ed.) *Computers in Careers Guidance*, CRAC/Hobsons, 1989.

Plant, P. 'Networking on a grand scale: Vocational Guidance in the EEC,' *NICEC Training and Development Bulletin*, 38: 1991.

Rayman, J.P. 'Factors that limit the effectiveness of CACGS services.' Paper presented at an International Teleconference on Technology and Career Development, Florida State University, Tallahassee, FL, 1989.

Sampson, J.P. 'Computer-Assisted Testing and Assessment: Current status and implications for the future', *Measurement and Evaluation in Guidance*, 15: 1983.

Ward, C., Stevens, B. and Twining, J. 'Top of the Agenda – a report on the Nürnberg Conference on Computers in Careers Guidance,' *EDUCA* 128, December 1992.

Watts, A.G. (ed.) *Computers in Careers Guidance*, CRAC/Hobsons, 1989.

Watts, A.G. 'The Politics and Economics of Computer-Aided Careers Guidance Systems.' Paper presented at the Third European Conference on Computers in Careers Guidance, 1992.

Watts, A.G., Humphries, C. and Pierce-Price, P. 'PROSPECT (16–19): A Feasibility Study,' NICEC, 1988.

Wooler, S. 'Let the Decision Maker Decide! A Case Against Assuming Common Occupational Value Structures,' *Journal of Occupational Psychology*, 58 (3): 1985.

Wooler, S. and Wisudha, A. 'An Educational Approach to Designing Computer-based Career Guidance Systems,' *British Journal of Educational Technology*, 16 (2): 1985.

Wright, B. and Tearle, P. 'The Development of Classroom Management Skills using Video Disc Technology,' *Interactive Learning International*, 7, 55–66: 1991.

Chapter 11

Information technology in careers education and guidance

An historical perspective, 1970–1997

Marcus Offer

Understanding the history of the use of the computer in guidance helps to highlight the important issues involved as well as demonstrating the increasing challenge posed for professional practice and identity.

In the mid 1970s (Watts, 1986) there were only seven main computer-aided guidance systems in existence in the UK. All but one of these were 'batch-mode' – they used paper questionnaires to gather data that was then turned into punched tape or cards for input to a mainframe computer. They usually involved a process of matching users' preferences or attributes to occupations and produced output interpreted to clients by a careers adviser.

Some careers advisers already felt threatened by the use of the mainframe computer. A machine that could generate large numbers of apparently appropriate occupational and course suggestions, individually tailored to a client's statements about themselves, might replace an adviser who saw that as their main function in the guidance interview. The coming of the microcomputer to the guidance field in the early 1980s spread the fear and excitement more widely. Whereas the batch process was firmly under careers service control, now it was possible that educational providers and even individual users might be able to afford to outflank the careers adviser's cherished monopoly of information in the occupational field. The BBC microcomputer was popular with schools, and amateurs and publishers of all kinds tried their hands at careers guidance-related software, not just to rival the large mainframe systems but to do other things these 'matching' systems had not. In 1982, there were perhaps three or four programs for microcomputer that were relevant to guidance. By 1987 there were 108 items on the list, categorised into eleven sub-groups, including 'games or simulations' and 'decision aids' (content-free programs that helped to elicit and structure the ideas of someone making a decision between two or more jobs or courses). However, the 'matching' programs and information databases still dominated the list (Offer, 1987). A key difference was the interactivity of the microcomputer programs over the older mainframe systems, seen by some as parallel to a more recent emphasis on the value of the process of experience – the computer feeding back to the client the effects and implications of his/her decisions and opening up discussion on the process of decision-making itself.

At the same time there were bigger players at work. The development of the PROSPECT-HE computer system [now widely used in most British universities] was commissioned by the UK government in 1986. This provides a comprehensive suite of interlinked programs to deliver all the four 'learning outcomes' of guidance (self-awareness, opportunity awareness, decision learning and transition learning (Law and Watts, 1977). PROSPECT was more like the systems already used in the USA for some years than anything that was available elsewhere in Europe. Such systems became known as 'maxi-systems'. They attempted to offer in one purpose-built package, as many of the relevant inputs to the guidance process as possible and enabled the user to some extent to carry with them data and personal profiles from one program to another within the system. 'Mini-systems' on the other hand, generally only offered one or two of the learning outcomes of guidance and did not always link these together.

A second important development was the first European conference on 'The role of Computers in Guidance and Counselling' held in Brussels in 1985. It was the first of a series of conferences to take place every four years. The second conference in 1989, in Cambridge, was attended by 128 participants from eighteen countries (Watts, 1989). The relevance of IT to guidance was sufficiently recognised by now to warrant expenditure and policy-making at an international level.

In 1990 the National Council for Educational Technology (NCET) in the UK published the 'Careers Software Review' (Offer, 1990). By now there was some retrenchment of numbers of programs in the UK, partly due to the rise of the IBM PC which eventually rendered the old BBC microcomputer and the careers software written for it obsolete. Programs were more 'professional' and commercial. Sixty programs were reviewed for the NCET, but the dominance of matching and information retrieval systems was persistent, while decision-aids and games had apparently declined in importance and use. The review used a classification system of eight categories – Games and Simulations, 'Matching' Programs, Information Retrieval, Decision Aids, Dedicated Word-processors (e.g. for CV or application letter writing), Cross-Curricular Applications, Psychometric Tests, and Programs to Teach Job Seeking Skills. This provided a simple indication of the ways computers could contribute to the guidance process.

A survey of European Union and EEA countries seven years later (Offer, 1997a) identified over 300 items of software available for use in careers education and guidance in Europe. The survey used essentially the eight categories of the earlier NCET review substituting 'Self assessment programs' (those that produce, for example, an interest profile from a questionnaire) for 'cross-curricular applications'. There were wide discrepancies between European countries in terms of what and how many computer-assisted guidance systems (CAGS) were available to guidance services, guidance workers and teachers. Over half of those listed were UK products. France and Germany, the next more prolific in terms of CAGS availability, showed thirty to forty such systems in the list. This form of support for careers education and guidance had expanded greatly, and by comparison with the 1980s, the CAGS were relatively expensive and sophisticated, commercial or professional packages, on a par with other educational and commercial software using similar graphic interfaces and often requiring state-of-the-art computer hardware.

ECONOMIC, CULTURAL AND POLITICAL CONTEXTS

This growth points to issues of importance. First, the different ways in which guidance services were delivered in different countries at that time. In Germany it was largely a monopoly of the state, while in France, most CAGS systems listed appeared to target school or college-based students, and implied support by the trained psychologists in the mainly education-based services, with a strong emphasis on testing. This was supplemented, for other French guidance seekers outside the education arena, by the use of the public information network Minitel (Aubert and Guichard, 1989) which delivered some of the things that in other countries were offered by stand-alone CAGS. In Germany, as well as the effect of a central buyer and developer of software able to plan for the entire country, there was a strong tendency towards a pan-European, transnational development of guidance. This had led to the development of the EURO-PC project – a networked system linking European careers resource centres across Germany electronically, with access to relevant software for each partner country, thus supplementing the purely German offering of CAGS with the largest single collection of international CAGS on-line in Europe. Add to this the fact that Germany's offering in terms of other CAGS systems included such giant database systems as CoBer (careers information and guidance) and KURS-Direkt, and the highly sophisticated psychometric test delivery system, DELTA, and the UK's lead in sheer numbers of CAGS fades into insignificance. German CAGS were comparable in size, comprehensiveness and significance in use, to the USA's 'maxi-systems'. However, unlike the US systems, they tended to be designed primarily as systems for careers advisers' use rather than for direct access by clients. SIS (vacancies for job seekers) and KURS-Direkt (on-line course information), both also accessible via the Internet, are notable exceptions to this rule.

The fragmentation of the UK careers software market mirrored the fragmentation of careers and guidance services there, and, to some extent, the 'free market' policies that produced and supported it. However, UK careers and guidance services had been decentralised for a long time. Each local education authority, and now each careers company, could make their own decision about what CAGS to buy and how to use them, and each school, college or university could do likewise. There was thus a market of relatively small buyers to support the number of suppliers and their competing systems.

There were, in the UK at least, and perhaps also in Europe as a whole, relatively fewer systems that offered a complete package of guidance interventions to compete with CoBer or typical American CAGS such as SIGI or DISCOVER. The expense of acquiring such a system seems to need more ability or willingness to invest on a larger or longer-term scale than was likely in the UK in the 1990s.

DIFFERENT NATIONAL EMPHASES: LEARNING OUTCOMES OF GUIDANCE

Equally interesting was the comparison between countries in terms of what guidance outcomes or interventions could be supported by their available CAGS. Suppose we allocate to CAGS programs a code based on the learning outcomes of guidance – 1. Self Awareness, 2. Matching, 3. Opportunity Awareness, 4. Decision Learning and 5. Transition Learning (support for job search and the implementation of decision) (Law and Watts, 1977). Many systems will offer more than one of these. However, Opportunity Awareness was, in all countries, the most favoured guidance outcome to be addressed via IT – nearly half (45 per cent) of the 304 items in this 1997 list of European CAGS, contributed to this category. Self Awareness came next. A quarter of all CAGS available in Europe support this in some way, many of which involved psychometric tests. Programs that match the self to opportunities, thus bridging the gap between the two outcomes, represented about 12 per cent of all CAGS.

This begins to suggest attitudes to the potential of CAGS. IT, it may be hypothesised, was seen in the first instance as a means of managing information. Certainly where newer, or poorer, countries make their first ventures into CAGS purchase or development, it is the information role that takes the highest priority. Relative wealth or stage of development, however, is not the only criterion – in Germany, too, information management and retrieval dominated the very large systems in use: nearly two-thirds of all German CAGS (excluding the EURO-PC project) had this purpose, five times more than those that contributed to self-awareness. In Italy the ratio was even clearer in favour of opportunity awareness: about 14:1. In the UK by contrast there was a much greater balance – the ratio is more like 2:1 – and in France it became 1:1. French CAGS frequently presented computer-assisted testing and often explicitly proposed support by a careers counsellor. Self awareness was to be mediated by interaction with the professional guidance counsellor. Direct public access to information, on the other hand, would more commonly be via public systems such as Minitel – not accounted for in the list – and this is one reason for the balance shown.

To this cluster of guidance outcomes must be added that of 'transition learning'. The aspects of transition the currently available CAGS were capable of supporting included support for job search, finding finance for learning and training, and computer-based training programs in the art of writing CVs and résumés and handling the job interview. About 15 per cent of CAGS in the principal European user countries made an input under this heading. But again, there were wide differences between countries. Whereas 25 per cent of UK CAGS made such an input, none of those listed for France did so.

The missing outcome is decision learning. Systems to support this were not only very rare but also hardly used. There were some interesting examples, notably in France, but overall they represented about 3 per cent or less of the total CAGS.

These figures are not reliable, and must be treated as very rough indicators of what is available and, particularly, in use. It is important to note that no account has been taken of numbers of users per system, or of level and frequency of use. However, anecdotal evidence suggests that these statistics reflected attitudes and structures beyond the nature of the programs themselves. There is room for more research here.

CONSTRUCTS OF GUIDANCE: HUMAN VERSUS MACHINE, EXPERT DELIVERY VERSUS SELF-HELP

When we turn towards the United States with its approximately ten-year lead in the use of CAGS in guidance, there is a further contrast. Most European systems are 'mini-systems' designed to deliver at most one or two guidance outcomes. American systems on the other hand, tend to attempt comprehensive, integrated coverage. Is it that attitudes to technology in the United States are generally more positive than in Europe? The construct 'human versus mechanical' is likely to surface very rapidly in discussion of CAGS in any European gathering of careers counsellors. The construct carries clear positive and negative poles. There is not the same reaction to books, videos or even audio tapes, which are clearly seen as less threatening to the professional's own position – these are 'merely' information resources. Where CAGS deal with information management and retrieval, they also are no threat. The fact that European 'mini-systems' are also smaller, less ambitious and typically address only one or two guidance outcomes, further supports the same hypothesis. Yet the US systems appear to coexist happily alongside human counsellors while offering a very much more extensive guidance intervention than most of their European counterparts.

The construct alters if we look at it from a different angle. The French tendency to emphasise the role of the counsellor in support of CAGS systems for self-assessment, fits the natural ethics of psychometric test feedback to which all properly trained users of psychometric tests subscribe. In the States, the relationship between psychometric testing and CAGS also appears strong. The pattern of CAGS use proposed by such US experts as Sampson (1996, 1997a) appears to draw on this. He emphasises the need for reliability and validity in CAGS as in psychometric systems, and in his Center for the Development of Technology in Counselling and Career Development, the protocol is for clients of the Center to engage in a brief diagnostic conversation with a guidance counsellor before any use of CAGS. This is followed up during or after the session by the counsellor who acts as a supervisor and resource person for any client working with CAGS. The readiness of the client to use a particular CAGS may even be assessed by a psychometric diagnosis (Sampson et al., 1994) where the counsellor judges that the client has needs that might make it dysfunctional to attempt immediate use of some CAGS. Sampson and his colleagues have developed a whole literature around these issues (see Peterson et al., 1996). This seems to imply an essentially psychometric model of the guidance process, into which CAGS fit seamlessly as one remedy for conditions diagnosed by prior screening. Even the running of the recently developed 'one-stop centers' in many American states is to some extent informed by this (Sampson, 1997b), despite the fact that they are intended to offer 'customer choice' including self-help services.

By contrast, the development of CAGS use in Europe, especially in the UK, and less so in France, has been more 'pragmatic'. Direct access to information has been the driving force behind a number of initiatives – the TAP (Training Access Points) database in the UK for example, or the BIZ-computer (BerufsInformationsSystem – 'Careers Information System' – Bundesanstalt für Arbeit, Nuremberg) in Germany. These have fitted into a 'walk-in' model of guidance provision where the risk that clients might not be 'ready' for such access was seen as negligible compared with the need to reach a wider audience. A careers adviser might or might not be on hand – in the case of TAP more often not (NTICS, 1995) but the user usually had direct access to the CAGS system unless they specifically requested help. The same applies to information via Minitel and other public networks in France and Scandinavia. The construct this time is 'information versus guidance' where information is an elementary but harmless pre-guidance activity and, in any case, external to 'real' guidance. This can be contrasted with UDACE's view (1986) where informing is one of the seven activities of guidance, and integral to it. Not surprisingly, therefore, the development of CAGS based on such constructions ('human versus mechanical' and 'guidance versus information' or 'pragmatic versus theoretical') took a different form than the development of CAGS in the

USA or (the key exception perhaps) the development of the few 'maxi-systems' such as PROSPECT-HE in Europe. The use of the computer is either 'just about information' and therefore outside the one-to-one guidance process, or simply another way of delivering psychometric testing and subsumed under the same rules and the same 'expert delivery' model of guidance.

This model of professional practice in the use of the computer in guidance may also account for the very cautious way in which the American Association for Counseling and Development (AACD) (quoted in Watts, 1996) requires its members to ensure that 'the client is intellectually, emotionally and physically capable of using the computer application . . . that the . . . application is appropriate for the needs of the client . . .'.

PSYCHOMETRIC TEST OR LEARNING SYSTEM, ESSENTIALISM OR CONSTRUCTIVISM?

This is the kind of approach normally taken to psychometric testing. Most such tests will have reliability and validity data to back their claims to predictive value. Many of the computer programs that offer self-assessment questionnaires, in form not unlike a psychological test, do not. On the one hand such programs generally share the underlying 'trait-and-factor' theory behind psychological testing: individuals are seen as having stable features equating to the requirements of occupations, also stable. Unless such stability is assumed, prediction becomes very difficult indeed, and prediction on this view is what guidance is supposed to be about. However, there is no point in helping someone to decide they are a square peg and advising them therefore to look at square holes, if they, or the holes, are going to become round tomorrow.

On the other hand, computer programs often offer the facility to make repeated passes through the program, with the input of different data each time. One learns thereby the effect of presenting oneself differently to the world, the result of having or not having certain skills or qualifications, of taking one route or another – and the job or course suggestion will vary accordingly. This is a very different process from psychological testing. There is no necessary assumption of an essential self. The user constructs alternative futures. This may not often be the way computer-assisted guidance works in practice, but it is the real potential of one category of CAGS when creatively used and taps into a real advantage of the computer as a resource for guidance. The conflict between such a constructivist position and a more traditional psychometric one, has led to some unacknowledged confusion over what computer-assisted guidance is, and how to use it among users and advisers alike.

TECHNOLOGY-PULL OR GUIDANCE-PUSH?
THE DEVELOPMENT OF MULTIMEDIA AND
'MAXI-SYSTEMS'

In part, this may be because we are aiming at a moving target, and one not necessarily moved by us. Technology (in the form of technologists with resources for development) does not stand still and wait for users to come up with ideas about how it might be used. New developments in other fields more friendly to technology have implications for guidance services too. The history of the development of CAGS in Europe, particularly the UK, is a repeated cycle of new developments – the rise of the microcomputer, the advent of CD-ROM, the development of multi- and hypermedia, and finally the dynamic expansion of the Internet – interspersed with attempts by guidance services and counsellors to catch up with what has already happened elsewhere and is now impacting on their area. In Germany or France the ability of central government agencies to plan such developments nationwide, has meant a more coherent pattern of use and development than in the UK. However, the core constructs seem to have been similar and models borrowed from psychometric testing and information science, seem to have been more powerful than purely guidance-related theories of career choice, counselling and development.

The Internet has thrown a large stone into this pool. Before tackling the issues it raises, it is worth retracing our steps to see how the pragmatic development of CAGS in Europe led us to arrive at this point.

The rise of multimedia is a good example. The first multimedia occupational databases in Europe appeared around 1992 – in the UK, France, Germany and Switzerland. Given the huge emphasis on information management in early use of CAGS, it is not surprising that when it became possible to use visual and aural elements as well as text as part of a computer system, the first uses of such innovation were to add illustration to the description of occupations or courses or institutions in the databases of the day. Still photographs of people doing the work or of life at the universities or colleges where they trained added interest and a new dimension to the information. Thanks to parallel developments in the use of multimedia in computer-based training, the 'illustrated database' was soon joined by the 'talking head', the delivery of guidance-related learning (how to handle a job interview, with the trainer on screen telling you how to do it). Now the possibility of taking part in a simulated interview exists, with input by keyboard or microphone. Interaction had arrived. This meant, also, that instead of simply reading about a job you could 'talk to' a practitioner on screen about it, and they could 'talk' back in a videoed or animated 'conversation'. The illusion of participation can be part of even more extensive games and simulations. Developments at the time of writing (1997) in the USA mean that it will be possible in the future to undertake simulated 'work experience' in selected occupations via multimedia systems (Krumboltz, 1997). Finally 'virtual reality' allows the guidance seeker to enter artificially created 'landscapes' and directly 'explore' career choices much more actively than before, e.g. the Swiss CD-ROM, 'Job City' (Offer, 1997a).

Somewhere in this process the rather artificial distinction between 'information' and 'guidance' has broken down. What happens is much more complex and interactive than simple informing. This occurred not because of the development of guidance theory and practice, but because technological developments were turned into innovative products which outflanked mainstream ideas (in career counselling circles) of what 'human' versus 'mechanical' guidance was about.

A similar process can be observed from another angle. In Europe, as we said above, the CAGS available have been, on the whole, more limited in scope, and less integrated, than those developed in the USA. A debate arose about the relative merits of 'maxi-' versus 'mini-' systems (Watts, 1992). The trend has been towards adding programs to existing programs so as to create 'mini-systems' with a range of guidance inputs (an approach dubbed the 'LEGO' model by Offer (1997b). A database of occupations may add a self-assessment module, or a CV-writing package. At the same time, in the UK there is a tendency to make links between systems (even between those of different suppliers) so that, for example, completing the self-assessment in one CAGS you can move seamlessly with your profile to search the occupational database of another, possibly on the same CD-ROM. Such connections are especially important where opportunity databases (jobs, courses, vacancies) are linked together with labour market information so the user can find a course, check the labour market prospects for graduates, and find related occupations. Moreover, where CAGS each cover small parts of the whole guidance process, menu systems are important to front-end the suite of programs, the 'mini-systems' built out of them. They provide for the user a coherent framework within which to seek answers to questions efficiently and signposts to the further questions raised by those answers. There is a marked convergence in this between Europe and the USA where integrated systems have been dominant from the start. However, few in Europe consciously planned these developments *ab initio*.

In part because of this *ad hoc*, reactive approach, the technological development of this period has not been accompanied by a correspondingly sophisticated or unifying development of guidance theory and practice.

THE COMING OF THE INTERNET: WORLD-WIDE CONNECTIVITY OR INFORMATION OVERLOAD?

The Internet takes this development one stage further. It has been around for a number of years but it has taken careers guidance services a little while to realise the bus is leaving and, at the time of writing, something of a scramble is taking place to get on it. In the process, the continuing need for a theory of the relation between information technology and guidance seems likely to get trampled underfoot.

It is now theoretically possible for all information technology resources of the guidance services of all countries to be accessed directly by their clients from their own homes. Several major CAGS are already accessible via the Internet. In a sense all that prevents this is the ability of any household to afford the hardware that gives such access, and the willingness of the suppliers to make resources available in this way. The cost of access to the individual is no small problem and the quality of the telecommunications infrastructure in some countries would be a further brake on developments. However, the potential is enormous.

The World Wide Web is, of course, not the only use of the Internet relevant to guidance. E-mail and newsgroups both have implications. Job search and application via the Net represent a major new development. The construction of an electronic CV as well as the use of electronic means to search for vacancies, vet applicants, and shortlist people for interviews, are increasingly important new skills.

E-mail as a means of international communication has obvious benefits for careers advisers talking to colleagues in another country, but the possibilities of delivering guidance locally by this means are less appreciated. The HERMES sub-project within the transnational ESTIA project (a European gateway linking national careers resource centres in the UK, Sweden, Finland and France – see Aalto and Kankaanranta, 1996 or Offer, 1997a) is exploring this avenue. Counselling, person to person via E-mail (or IRC – Internet Relay Chat) is similar in some ways to telephone counselling. Sampson comments (Sampson, 1997b and Sampson et al., 1997) that some clients may be more willing to undertake one-to-one counselling in person after becoming more secure in the relationship via E-mail or video-conferencing, from the familiarity of their own home. In this way the 'human' versus 'mechanical' problem is resolved – technology simply makes human contact more available! Group guidance is also possible, both by video-conferencing, and, a new form, also requiring new skills, by group e-mail or newsgroup (Offer and Watts, 1997).

NEW TECHNOLOGY, OLD ISSUES: CONCLUDING QUESTIONS

Exciting as these developments appear, the same issues arise as with stand-alone CAGS, and indeed, with the use of other guidance resources as well. What is important about the use of information technology in guidance is the way in which it continually raises questions about what we do in guidance and why we do it that way. These questions are not primarily about technology but about guidance. They are professional issues with economic, social and political overtones. The IT-illiterate are not, therefore, excused from answering them.

For example, what is the truly human skill of guidance counselling (as opposed to the technological capabilities of the computer)? What can a human being do that a machine cannot?

Given that guidance and information technology are both in part about 'informing', what place does information have in guidance and how is it constructed from mere data? The tendency to see 'information' as a simple answer to a basic problem and essentially external to 'real' guidance, must also be examined. How anything becomes personally relevant 'information' given unlimited world-wide access to 'data' is precisely part of the difficulty.

To what extent can or should the 'needs' of an individual guidance-seeker be 'diagnosed' by experts and what does this do to the power-relationship between guidance professional and client? Are the dangers of 'direct access' to information unmediated by a guidance or information professional real or imaginary?

What role does the guidance professional have in relation to the use of the Internet for guidance purposes by his or her clients? What is the role of professional guidance services when so much of what they offer can effectively be obtained via information technology direct to guidance seekers, now even in their own homes? Guidance services may reach out even more effectively than before, beyond the confines of the guidance centre, and hopefully to some new groups of clients – using video-conferencing for example (Closs and Miller, 1997). However, the technology, and perhaps even the data, are now beyond their control.

Is guidance practice merely reactive to technological developments or can it play a proactive role in shaping and promoting them? Access to the technology still raises political, social and economic issues, and the coherence and quality of the guidance delivered by these means is also more difficult to assure. A description of the guidance process is needed which links together the vast resources now placed at our disposal by information and communication technology and includes human beings and their real human skills as one of those resources (Offer, 1997 a and b). It should suggest to both the client and the professional which resource is most appropriate for which needs and at what point in the process. The guidance community might then have a tool to shape the technology of the 'information society' rather than simply react to its development.

BIBLIOGRAPHY

Aalto, P. and Kankaanranta, K. (1996) *'Towards Information Society – Information Technology Applications in Guidance and Counselling'*, Helsinki: Centre for International Mobility – CIMO.

Aubret, J. and Guichard, J. (1989) 'Minitel and Careers Guidance' in Watts A.G. (ed.) *Computers in Careers Guidance*, Cambridge: CRAC/Hobsons.

Closs, S.J. and Miller, I.M. (1997) *Careers Guidance at a Distance, An evaluation of desktop video conferencing technology*, Department for Education and Employment.

Krumboltz, J.D. (1997) 'Virtual Job Experience', Paper presented at the National Career Development Association Convention, Daytona Beach, Florida, January 1997.

Law, W.G. and Watts, A.G. (1977) *'Schools, Careers and Community,'* London: CIO.

NTICS (National Training Information Central Support) (1995) *Training Information Services Individual Commitment: A Summary Report of Research into TEC and LEC Training Information Services and TEC Individual Commitment Strategy'*, Sheffield, Employment Department.

Offer, M.S. (1987) *Careers Education and Guidance on Microcomputer*, Winchester: Hampshire Guidance and Careers Service, mimeo.

Offer, M.S. (ed.) (1990) *Careers Software Review*, Coventry, NECT – National Council for Educational Technology.

Offer, M.S. (1992) 'Developments in the field of vocational guidance software from Cambridge to Nuremberg (1989–1992)', Paper presented at the third European Conference on Computers in Guidance, Conference Documentation: *New tendencies, challenges and technologies in transnational careers guidance,* Nuremberg: Bundesanstalt für Arbeit.

Offer, M.S. (1993) *Software in Guidance: A European Review*, Report to the Commission of the European Communities (Agreement No 92-20-FOP-0066-00).

Offer, M.S. (1997a) *Supporting Careers Guidance in the Information Society. A Review of the Use of Computer-Assisted Guidance and the Internet in Europe*, Dublin: Irish National Centre for Guidance in Education.

Offer, M.S. (1997b) 'Developments in the use of Information Technology in Careers Education and Guidance from Nuremberg to Dublin, 1992–1996', Paper presented at the conference, *Guidance in the Information Society*, Conference Proceedings, December 1996, Fourth European Conference on Information and Communications Technology in Guidance, Irish National Centre for Guidance in Education, Dublin.

Offer, M.S. and Watts, A.G. (1997) *The Internet in Careers Work*, NICEC Briefing, Cambridge: National Institute for Careers Education and Counselling/Careers Research Advisory Centre (CRAC).

Peterson, G.W., Sampson, J.P., Reardon, R.C. and Lenz, J.G. (1996) 'A Cognitive Information Processing Approach to Career Problem Solving and Decision Making', in *Career Choice and Development*, Brown, D., Brooks, L. and Associates, 3rd Edition, New York: Jossey-Bass.

Sampson, J.P. (1996) *Effective Computer-Assisted Career Guidance: Occasional Paper Number 2*, Tallahassee: Center for the Study of Technology in Counseling and Career Development, Florida State University.

Sampson, J.P. (1997a) *Helping clients get the most from computer-assisted guidance systems*, Paper presented at the Australian Association of Career Counselors, 7th National/International Conference, Brisbane, Australia, April 1997.

Sampson, J.P. (1997b) *Maximising Staff Resources in Meeting the Needs of Job Seekers in One-Stop Centers*, Technical report Number 22, Tallahassee: Center for the Study of Technology in Counseling and Career Development, Florida State University, January 1997.

Sampson, J.P., Peterson, G.W., Lenz, J.G., Reardon, R.C. and Saunders, D.E. (1994) *Career Thoughts Inventory: Improving Your Career Thoughts. A Workbook for the Career Thoughts Inventory*, Psychological Assessment Resources Inc.

Sampson, J.P. Jr, Kolodinsky, R.W. and Greeno, B.P. (1997) 'Counselling on the Information Superhighway: Future Possibilities and Potential Problems', *Journal of Counselling and Development*.

UDACE (Unit for the Development of Adult Continuing Education) (1986) *The Challenge of Change. Developing Educational Guidance for Adults*, Leicester: NIACE.

Watts, A.G. (1978) 'The role of the computer in careers guidance', *International Journal for the Advancement of Counselling* 9: 145–58.

Watts, A.G. (1986) 'Using Computers in Careers Guidance in Schools', *Journal of Occupational Psychology*, 51(1).

Watts, A.G. (ed.) (1989) Computers in Careers Guidance, Cambridge: CRAC/Hobsons.

Watts, A.G. (1992) 'The politics and economics of computer-aided guidance systems' in *New tendencies, challenges and technologies in transnational careers guidance*, Conference Documentation, Third European Conference on computers in careers guidance, Nuremberg: Bundesanstalt für Arbeit.

Watts, A.G. (1996) 'Computers in Guidance' in Watts, A.G., Law, W., Killeen, J., Kidd, J.M. and Hawthorn, R. *Rethinking Careers Education and Guidance*, London: Routledge.

Part III

Accessibility, client-centredness and impartiality

Chapter 12

Guidance, access and networking

Amy Blair and Lyn Tett

INTRODUCTION

Adults are returning to education in the UK in ever-increasing numbers. More adults are participating now in formal and informal learning opportunities in all sectors – schools, further education colleges, community education providers, and higher education institutions – than at any time in the past. Higher education institutions, particularly, have seen a change in new entrants to full-time and part-time degree courses, which face the challenge of welcoming and serving a greatly changed constituency of students. By 1996, the momentum towards increased participation appeared to be slowing (*Times Higher Education Supplement* no. 1211, January 19, 1996), so if the promise of widened access is to be realised, ways must be found to encourage and sustain adult students in their studies – including improved systems of guidance.

ADULTS IN HIGHER EDUCATION

Although all formal educational settings are seeing changes in their client group, it is arguably in higher education that the notion of widening access has generated the most interest, and where the greatest cultural changes have had to be addressed. The so-called 'access debate' centres upon the perceived shift of HE from an elite system in which social norms are preserved to a mass system in and by which social norms may be transformed.

Thus, the traditional view of undergraduates as teenage school leavers is being challenged. The participation of individuals from previously under-represented groups – including adults, the disabled, and some minority ethnic communities – has led to attempts to identify common factors which might enable or prohibit return. Such identification has been impeded by the disparate nature of such students, whose common characteristics are elusive. Indeed, such students are often united only by the characteristics they *fail* to share. This paradox is discussed by Metcalfe (1993), who defines non-traditional students as all those with non-standard social characteristics and entry qualification. Although widening access means increasing the representation of these groups, the pressure towards this increase is often diminished by low numbers, for 'unless such students represent a sizable participating group, they tend to become invisible in the larger mass of undergraduates and there is little pressure on academics to change their teaching styles or on institutions to reorganize their provision' (Bown, 1988: 26). Yet it is often the existing nature of such provision that can discourage such students from participating in or completing courses. Adults, by definition, fall out with HE's traditional constituency by virtue of age. In addition, adults may come from minority ethnic communities or lower socioeconomic groups, thus, in effect, layering disadvantage upon disadvantage. Many arguments about widening access apply doubly to adults.

GUIDANCE AND SUPPORT

One important way in which institutions can help students – particularly adults – is through the provision of guidance and support services (HEQC, 1994; SOEID, 1996). The importance of such services has been recognized in the charters for higher education and in the national systems for quality assessment and audit. Additionally, current trends in the delivery of the curriculum in higher education, such as flexible provision and modular courses, mean that course pathways are no longer pre-determined. Clear lines of communication and guidance are necessary if students are to benefit fully from the advantages promised by these innovations. Yet such guidance is highly variable in quality and under increasing pressure as a larger and more diverse student body places a strain on existing resources. Research into guidance and support in Higher Education (Blencowe *et al.*, 1996) has highlighted some of the challenges that guidance services currently face, including pressures on resources and the demands of a more diverse student body. The opportunity has been provided to rethink the provision of services and the principles upon which they are based. Key among these principles are the enhancement of the quality and accessibility of guidance provision through collaboration and networking.

COLLABORATION AND NETWORKING

Collaboration and networking amongst education institutions such as further education colleges and schools is growing. Franchizing is becoming commonplace and organizations are working together to provide coordinated services such as community education. The Higher Education Funding Councils of the United Kingdom, too, have placed high on their agendas collaborative strategies for the delivery of a wide range of services, including guidance and support for students. It is anticipated that, by working together, institutions of all kinds can provide more effective and higher quality provision for all who might benefit from it.

Why is collaboration desirable? The considerable literature on management and capital identify the benefits of collaboration that may be found in any context (see Huxham, 1996). Three principal benefits, known as 'collaborative advantage', emerge from ideal collaborative systems. The first aspect of collaborative advantage is added value. Through joint funding, coordinated planning and combined effort organizations are often able to achieve 'more' with 'less'. Secondly, collaborative systems operate to increase efficiency and quality through the economies of scale and scope that are afforded by pooling resources and effort. The third aspect relates to the complexity of problems with which policy makers are increasingly concerned. It is nonsensical to argue that important goals such as achieving wider access can be tackled by any one organization acting alone.

The collaborative ideal, however, faces many challenges. In higher education, particularly, repeated rounds of funding cuts have forced many institutions, and faculties within them, to compete for students. Indeed, higher education in the United Kingdom – based traditionally upon the selection of an elite constituency – can be seen to have competition as one of its most basic principles. In the past, there has been little collaboration between institutions bidding for limited numbers of students and dwindling resources. Proponents of collaboration argue, however, that as access widens the climate for competition diminishes, since recruitment will become more important than selection.

THE RESEARCH STUDY

It was in this context, where new ways of providing guidance were increasingly recognized as desirable and scrutinized for effectiveness, that the Scottish Higher Education Funding Council sponsored the following piece of research. The study had two central foci. The first was the guidance and support currently available to adults on first-degree courses in seven higher education institutions in one Scottish city. This was explored through interviews with thirty-eight higher education staff, including student services staff, academic tutors and admissions tutors. The second focus was the way in which this support might be enhanced in the future, both within individual institutions and on a collaborative basis. For this purpose, we worked with respondents to examine the ways in which they might collaborate with colleagues in other HEIs to provide these services in one geographical area in Scotland.

PRE-COURSE GUIDANCE

We know that adults' reasons for choosing to participate are complex and varied and numerous studies have attempted to identify these reasons (Morstain and Smart, 1974; Cross, 1986; Kelly, 1989). Adults' return to education is, generally, the product of an interplay of forces in an elaborate social, cultural and educational context (see Blair *et al.*, 1995). Key among these forces is the knowledge of educational opportunities, for if potential participants do not know that the opportunity to return exists, then other barriers become irrelevant. It is at this stage that institutions can helpfully offer guidance and advice. Indeed, the National Institute for Adult and Continuing Education posit that one of the aims of educational guidance is to help *create* demand by ensuring that all adults are encouraged to engage in learning (NIACE, 1986). Yet guidance for returning adults is often not offered by higher education institutions (Blencowe *et al.*, 1996; Howieson, 1992). This is of particular significance for many adults who choose their provider before they choose their course (Blair *et al.*, 1993). By choosing providers first, adult students limit their course options to those offered by one or two particular institutions. In addition, innovations such as modularization and the accreditation of prior (experiential) learning add a new imperative to pre-course guidance, if they are 'not to reproduce the exclusiveness of conventional higher education' (Imeson and Edwards, 1990: 61). APEL itself is meaningless without the assessment of the experience it seeks to recognize both in enabling the learner to recognize and formulate the basis on which their experience is to be assessed, and alerting the learner to the options available as a result of that assessment.

If adults tend to choose their provider before their course, and if course choice itself is dependent upon the evaluation of prior learning and experience, then institutions' guidance systems for helping adults choose the appropriate programme become very important. Providers differ greatly in the support they offer at this stage, however, and it is all too easy for adults to choose the 'wrong' courses at the start of their studies (CNAA, 1989; Munn *et al.*, 1992; Howieson, 1992; Blair *et al.*, 1993). This can affect success later on. Qualifications may prove inappropriate for a chosen career; subject content may be pitched at the wrong level; or there may be a mismatch between students' and providers' aims for a particular course. Thus, pre-course guidance is an investment providers can make early on to maximize students' later success.

PROVIDERS' VIEWS OF PRE-ENTRY GUIDANCE

In our study, we were interested to discover what pre-entry guidance institutions offered to inquirers seeking to return to higher education. We also sought to explore respondents' views of the effectiveness of this guidance.

The first point of contact for all enquiries (apart from those to The Open University, which has a regulated system for dealing with all enquiries) was the switchboard, from where prospective students were routed to 'appropriate' individuals. General enquiries were most often put through to the registry or the individual responsible for sending out prospectuses. If the inquirers believed they knew the course they wished to study, they might be directed to the admissions tutor or another member of that department. Respondents reported that while this system was rather ad hoc, it seemed to work effectively and enquirers appeared satisfied with their reception.

In fact, no institution apart from The Open University took a systematic approach towards enquiries, ensuring potential applicants received, at the minimum, the information they sought. Institutions had no mechanism for individuals who, as one respondent put it, 'don't know the questions to ask' and, moreover, did not have systems to handle inquirers outside term time, when academic staff might be difficult to contact. No records were kept of enquiries or the route they had taken through the institution.

Institutions relied heavily upon prospectuses for information-giving – although non-traditional applicants often find these documents intimidating and unhelpful (Blair *et al.*, 1993). A very few institutions had a prospectus for mature students: most relied on a paragraph or section in the main publication. Open days were also cited as a source of information, although some respondents suggested adults might be overwhelmed by the atmosphere of these occasions, which were geared to and 'swarming' with teenagers.

Of course, information-giving is only one, small facet of pre-entry guidance. If inquirers were looking for advice or support rather than information, it was down to individuals who happened to be at the end of the telephone to provide it to the best of their ability. Although most respondents stressed they would do what they could to help such inquirers, they admitted their knowledge of opportunities outside their own department was limited. Some pointed out that competition for students meant an institution could not be expected to provide impartial advice.

What guidance was offered to students who were applying for courses? Again, there was the same reliance on prospectuses and telephones at the pre-entry stage. Some departments interviewed all non-traditional prospective applicants, but most did not. A number of respondents pointed out that adults, particularly, at this stage often needed financial advice – but that staff conducting these interviews were unqualified to give it. Opinion was dichotomized between those who viewed guidance for adults as infantilizing and those who saw the potential for guidance's enabling and supporting role. Many talked of their 'natural empathy' with adult applicants and felt this was an appropriate position from which to offer advice – whether prospective students shared this view is open to question.

FUTURE POSSIBILITIES

Since adults tend to choose their provider before their course of study, the guidance and support offered by HEIs for adults at the initial stages of return is vitally important but in most institutions there was no system for offering such advice. Of course, many enquirers fail to reach the person best able to help, either because of poor luck or because they do not know the 'right' questions to ask. It would not be difficult, we believe, for institutions to ensure all enquiries from adult students were routed through to the appropriate individual. An internal audit of enquiry procedures would quickly identify any 'gaps'– particularly during holidays when many academic staff are away from the institution (HEIs might benefit from an examination of the enquiry procedures at many colleges of further education, where enquiries are dealt with by named individuals at all times). Named individuals with specialist knowledge of adults' needs – such as advice about qualifications or finance – should be known to anyone likely to answer the phone to an enquirer. These individuals may well be outwith the institution, either in another HEI; the community; or government agency. HEIs could collaborate to produce such a list of names, some of which will inevitably be relevant only to a particular institution. A certain amount of awareness-raising among staff would be necessary for such a system to work efficiently – yet such staff development could be used to generate the system itself.

ON-COURSE AND EXIT GUIDANCE

What guidance and support do institutions offer adult students whilst on their courses and when leaving them – and do adults have different requirements from younger undergraduates? We know that a variety of personal and institutional factors affect learners' success on course, including the quality of providers' guidance services (see Norris, 1985). This guidance must necessarily deal with a wide range of issues: teaching and learning; finance; personal welfare; and possible routes into work or other educational providers. It may take a number of forms: academic tutors or advisors; student support services; and explicit courses or modules designed to support students in their learning. Past commentary has stressed that this support must be appropriate, accessible and visible, and proactive as well as reactive (Imeson and Edwards, 1990; Lowden and Powney, 1993; Blencowe et al., 1996). Howieson (1992) found particularly that there was a low awareness among adult undergraduates about the role and availability of student services' support – and the tendency to believe that these services were geared solely towards younger students. There is also evidence (Blair et al., 1993; Blencowe et al., 1996) that some adults can feel the use of institutional support services is demeaning or a sign of failure; such students would far rather attempt to deal with their problems on their own.

It has been suggested in some quarters that completion rates for entrants with non-traditional qualifications (most of whom are adult students) are somewhat lower than those for more standard entrants (see Gallagher and Wallis, 1993, for a survey of the literature). Although Munn *et al.* (1992) argue that reasons for student withdrawal are complex and that no 'quick-fix' is possible, clearly institutional support can help mitigate the effects of these factors – and encourage students to continue their course – if the institution's ethos encourages its use. Conversely, exit guidance for those who are leaving 'early' becomes important as they decide what use might be made of their educational experience in the labour market or other forms of education.

PROVIDERS' VIEWS OF ON-COURSE GUIDANCE

What systems did higher education institutions have in place to support adult students during and upon leaving their courses? All institutions followed roughly the same model of on-going support for students, although the precise nature of these systems varied: in some institutions, even different faculties or departments worked in slightly different ways. No institution made special provision for adults: respondents argued that adults did not wish to be treated differently than younger undergraduates and that, at any rate, 'good' practice for any single group was 'good' practice for all. Generally, students were assigned 'first contact' academic or year tutors, responsible for general welfare. In addition, there existed at least three groups of profes-sional guidance staff: student welfare advisors; student counsellors; and careers advisors. Interestingly, academic and guidance staff seemed to have slightly different views of this model.

Figure 12.1 Academic staff view of the guidance system

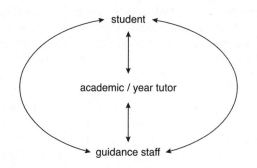

Figure 12.2 Guidance staff view of the guidance system

Academic staff tended to describe a reactive linear model, with clear lines of referral in response to particular problems as in Figures 12.1 and 12.2.

In both models the relationship between academic and guidance staff in terms of information-sharing and feedback differed greatly in individual cases because of the confidential nature of the issues. But what role did these figures play in adult learners' seeking to access guidance in their institutions?

ACADEMIC TUTORS

All institutions operated a first-contact system of academic or year tutors, although the precise nature of these systems varied in terms of responsibility and the ways in which students were assigned to their tutor. Commonly, however, named members of academic staff held responsibility for the academic and pastoral care of a given number of students (full or part-time), and met with each of them once or twice a term to monitor progress. In addition, students were expected to approach this person with any academic or personal difficulties for advice or referral to another service.

Respondents in academic departments all spoke highly of this system. Such tutors were seen as the first line of contact for students with academic difficulties, either through regular of extraordinary meetings. A number of respondents stressed the benefits of a system where students felt free to come for advice if they felt they needed it, describing their provision as 'informal' or 'open-door'. Whilst in some smaller departments an academic tutor might be responsible for less than ten students, in larger faculties tutors might be responsible for fifty or more, though this was not necessarily believed to impact on effectiveness. Some tutors believed that a special empathy could exist between tutors and their adult students, by virtue of shared 'adulthood'.

Academic staff reported that the tutorial system worked effectively, although little formal monitoring was carried out. Most used completion rates and stated reasons for withdrawal as a measure of guidance success, although these figures were not always available at the appropriate times. Generally, though, the absence of complaints was viewed as evidence of success.

This view of success was not always shared by student counsellors and welfare officers. Counsellors often felt that adults, in particular, were unwilling to visit their tutors with a problem and would be more likely to bypass the system, preferring instead to see a counsellor straight away. A fear of being branded as a 'problem' or 'difficult' student often meant that adults preferred to go outside their department for advice. It was unclear in interview how far academic staff were aware of their students' perception of such a departmental culture.

STUDENT WELFARE OFFICERS AND COUNSELLORS

Student support services within institutions fell into two categories: student welfare and student counselling. Student welfare services helped with such practical matters as financial advice; housing; and health; whereas counsellors were more responsible for students' emotional and psychological well-being. Sometimes, the two services shared staff: in small institutions, the same team performed both functions. Student welfare officers and counsellors were most likely to identify adults as having 'special' needs arising from their many external commitments and concerns. Such guidance professionals often believed that academic tutors could do more to support their students, and some institutions were offering training to raise such individuals' awareness of guidance issues.

Interestingly, all student counsellors and welfare officers reported that they saw proportionately more adults than younger undergraduates in the course of their work. A number of possible reasons were given for this, including the aforementioned 'labelling' by departments and adults' feeling that tutors were not in the best position to provide advice. In addition, adults were seen as more reflective and more likely to view counselling as a possible source of support – although for some, there was a stigma associated with counselling that made them less likely to seek support (see Blencowe et al., 1996).

Counsellors also agreed that outcomes for adults could be different than those for younger students: whilst younger undergraduates often sought one-off help for individual 'crises', adults often requested longer periods of counselling for difficulties that had built up over time, or were part of a larger pattern. Counsellors identified particular problems faced by adults, including isolation; difficulties with group work (when required to work and be assessed with younger students); and 'persecution' (in the words of one respondent) by younger students – where adults were seen as being 'too conscientious' with course work and group projects. Other research (Crozier and Garbet-Jones, 1996) confirms this experience of ageism by younger students. In our study, counsellors believed adults came to student services, rather than academic staff, with such problems.

We asked counsellors and welfare officers whether provision for students was monitored in any way. Unlike the record-keeping by many academic tutors, student counselling services' monitoring systems were consistent across institutions and involved extensive records – although the uses of these data varied greatly from provider to provider. This leads us to think that some form of collaborative monitoring of students' guidance needs might be useful for helping institutions audit provision and determine priorities.

CAREERS ADVISORS

Exit guidance was seen to be the remit of academic, or year, tutors and careers advisors. Careers services varied in size from institution to institution, but all offered seminars on job-hunting and CV-writing as well as one-to-one counselling. The stage during which careers officers became involved with students varied: some saw their role beginning with pre-course guidance (though limited resources often put pressure on this function) – and some saw their role as never ending. Others resisted this notion, believing their responsibilities were centred firmly around students' third and fourth years. In many ways, the challenges facing careers officers and the definitions of their roles were extremely complex: certainly, there was a good deal of disagreement amongst respondents as to the roles careers advisors should play in guidance and support for students. Respondents were likely to associate particular job-seeking difficulties with adults and tended to feel their responsibility towards adults was different – if not greater – than that towards younger undergraduates.

FUTURE POSSIBILITIES

Currently, institutions can point to the ways in which they meet most guidance needs, even if in practice students have difficulties accessing the support they require. The exception to this rule is counselling for students leaving their courses early. Very few institutions are able to 'catch' such students in time, unless the students themselves make their plans known in advance (which they often do not do). Students at risk of non-completion must be identified in time for full discussion about possible options to take place.

The resources needed for such guidance can be offset against the penalties caused by student wastage, since at least some of these students will stay on their course given the right sort of advice and encouragement. Institutions might find it beneficial to investigate systematically discontinuing students' reasons for leaving, as institutional factors such as lack of guidance in making appropriate modular choices may well play a part in their early exit. Since other students may well be affected adversely by the same factors, such research would profit from a collaborative approach. Formal exit counselling for all students should be built in from the beginning of courses as well as clearer exit points with recognised levels of credit and greater ease of transferability to other institutions.

We have pointed to the role of academic tutors in the guidance process and their widely varying remits and responsibilities. Naturally, in most cases they perceive their primary function as an academic one of teaching and research. For this reason, it is important to ensure academic and year tutors are not responsible for the pastoral care of too many students: 'chatting' time is important if tutors are to understand the pressures created by current conditions. At a minimum, general guidance time should be built into regular contacts with year or academic tutors: the progress of students' personal development plans, where these exist, would be a useful focus for such discussions. Open door policies must be genuine and evaluated for effectiveness. Departments should properly monitor student satisfaction with guidance procedures and share the lessons learned with colleagues elsewhere in the institution.

Academic advisors must be properly trained and have close links with the counselling services. To this end, the establishment of 'one-stop' centres with a high profile might be a useful way of doing this, especially since the distinction between academic support and other forms of guidance is often unclear.

Few institutions make full use of one of their most valuable resources – other students. Staff–student liaison groups and student representatives are readily available sources of feedback on the quality of guidance systems. Peer mentoring and peer support could provide much-needed guidance for adults entering higher education for the first time. As always, improved communication between departments and the different arms of the guidance service is necessary if progress is to be made.

We have pointed out that the sorts of networks already provided by counsellors' and careers advisors' professional organizations help to expand knowledge of 'what is possible' outside individual institutions. Everyone involved in guidance and support would benefit from similar forums. A guidance network for HEIs might be a useful setting for a wide variety of activities: sharing information on good practice; providing mutual support for institutions and practitioners; identifying training needs; and even providing staff development opportunities. The network could also form the springboard from which future collaborative projects could be launched. That would enable greater resources of time as well as money to be available for guidance activities.

TOWARDS A GUIDANCE POLICY

We have described respondents' perception of a crisis-led, reactive guidance and support system for adult students which one of our respondents referred to as the 'deficit' model of guidance. Despite individuals' intentions, we perceived an underlying lack of corporate philosophy upholding guidance as a pro-active, student-centred process. If guidance is to be more than mere crisis management attitudes at all levels need to change. One respondent described guidance in higher education as follows:

> Traditionally in higher education, guidance has been seen almost as an emergency service. It is the ambulance at the bottom of the cliff for those who fall down it. It may be helpful to think of guidance as the fence at the top of the cliff (putting emphasis on prevention of problems) while continuing to provide the ambulance for those who need it.

What is needed for a fence at the top is a wide variety of provision, including help for potential students formulating questions; clear advice and support from appropriate individuals at the early stages of adults' return; introductory interviews; peer mentoring; clear and accessible course handbooks; good communication amongst all those involved in student guidance; and effective, embedded exit guidance. Such provision would be the responsibility of a range of staff including tutors, guidance staff, course organisers, student representative groups, and university administration. It would be overseen, supported, and monitored by a committed member of senior management. The first step towards such a future must involve the whole institution working towards a shared understanding of guidance and individuals' roles and responsibilities in supporting students. We believe the collaborative formation of a strategic guidance policy is one way in which such a first step might be taken. Its goal would be to ensure consistency in the guidance offered to all students. In the following discussion, we outline the ways in which such a policy might be formulated and some ideas about what it might include.

FORMULATING POLICY

Policy can be a powerful tool: it can both shape and reflect principle and provide a starting-point for strategic planning. Yet policy fails in this function if individuals are unaware of its significance in their practice. If staff are ignorant of policy's origins, its informing influence is quickly lost. The importance of this ownership, particularly for guidance, where all staff must be expected to play a part, has important implications for the way in which guidance policy must be formulated. We offer a number of suggestions, below.

Many institutions already have guidance policies or are currently working on them. Further education colleges tend to be at a more advanced stage than HEIs because their funding currently requires that guidance be placed explicitly at the centre of their work. HEIs seeking to establish a guidance policy would find it useful to investigate existing policies (in both further and higher education) and the means by which they were formulated in order to avoid reinventing the wheel.

All staff should be involved in this process from the earliest stages if policy is to be more than a mere statement of intent. Common guidance principles and transferable definitions must be established before substance can be determined and a cooperative approach to these tasks would enhance the quality of the final statements. In addition, staff involvement in the formulation of the guidance policy should help raise awareness and increase commitment throughout the institution.

Networking inter-institutionally could help to clarify ideas. The ways in which institutions have responded collaboratively to the requirement to provide better access for students with a disability might provide a useful precedent, bearing in mind the lessons of this experience. Key among these, reported to us in interview, had been the importance of institutions being at the same stage of development when discussions took place.

The final policy should be reflected in institutional strategic plans and set out in publicity material and student charters. The discussion of the policy and individuals' responsibilities arising from it must be made a part of induction procedures for all new members of staff.

POLICY SUBSTANCE

What should be included in an institutional guidance policy? The Scottish Higher Education Funding Council (SHEFC) uses seven indicators of quality and HEQC (1995) offer more detailed guidelines on the content of policy that will provide a framework for institutions. We reiterate these here together with findings from our own research.

A key consideration must be whether HEIs should have separate guidance policies for adults. Our data seem to indicate that this would be inappropriate. Respondents viewed as undesirable a policy which 'labelled' people or forced them into categories. Adults were one sub-group only and a very diverse group, so it was felt that providing particular strategies for them would require particular strategies for innumerable other groups as well, resulting in a fragmented, divisory service. Far more attractive was a student-centred, flexible, sensitive service that would appeal to all who would benefit from it. Of course, student characteristics need to be taken into account and specialist resources might exist that people could access when and as they wished. Supply-side factors such as the culture of various disciplines and professions must also be considered. Policy should be consistent with the mission and overall objectives of the institution and consistent with key principles of guidance.

We should suggest that policies should include the following:

- student entitlements, both in terms of principles and services. The former should include entitlements to confidentiality, impartiality, and equality of access to guidance and support. The latter should include clear statements of what students may expect in more concrete terms: referral onwards to the most appropriate agency, for example, or careers guidance at any point of the course
- student responsibilities: these might include students making themselves aware of the guidance services that are available; being open about difficulties in time for help to be given; and following up referrals
- a clear description of the mechanisms by which guidance and support are delivered throughout the institution and details of how students can access these services
- clear statements of managerial roles and responsibilities for guidance, including the names of key individuals
- arrangements for monitoring and review of the impact of policy on practice, including named individuals responsible for it.

These five suggestions are intended as a minimum starting point only: in their discussions, HEIs will no doubt identify other important points within and beyond these. It would be interesting to see, if a collaborative approach was taken to policy development, how far final statements differ from institution to institution. Our belief is that general principles of effective guidance are transferable across not just institutions, but educational sectors as well.

In this chapter we hope that by focusing attention on one group of institutions' responses to adult learners' guidance needs that lessons can be learnt by all HEIs. The importance of guidance at all stages cannot be over-emphasized and it is clear that practice can be improved if institutions collaborate and network together.

BIBLIOGRAPHY

Blair, A., McPake, J. and Munn, P. (1993) *Facing Goliath: Adults' Experiences of Participation, Guidance and Progression*, Edinburgh, The Scottish Council for Research in Education.

Blair, A., McPake, J. and Munn, P. (1995) 'A new conceptualisation of adult participation in education', *British Educational Research Journal*, 21(5), pp. 621–44.

Blencowe, L., Denning, P. and Tett, L. (1996) *Adult Education Guidance in Higher Education: a story of three institutes*, Edinburgh, Moray House Institute of Education.

Bown, L. (1988) 'Implications of wider access for the higher education curriculum', *Scottish Journal of Adult Education*, 8(4), pp. 25–35.

CNAA (1989) *Access Courses: Documentation*, London, CNAA.

Cross, K.P. (1986) *Adults as Learners: Increasing Participation and Facilitating Learning*, San Francisco, Jossey-Bass.

Crozier, W.R. and Garbet-Jones, A. (1996) *Finding a Voice*, Leicester, NIACE.

Gallagher, J. and Wallis, W. (1993) *The Performance of Students with Non-traditional Qualifications in Higher Education*, Centre for Continuing Education, Glasgow Caledonian University.

HEQC (1994) *Guidance and Counselling in Higher Education*, London, Higher Education Quality Council.

HEQC (1995) *A Quality Assurance Framework for Guidance and Learner Support in Higher Education: the guidelines*, London, Higher Education Quality Control.

Howieson, C. (1992) *The Guidance Project*, Edinburgh, The University of Edinburgh.

Huxham, C. (1996) 'Collaboration and collaborative advantage' in Huxham, C. (ed.) *Creating Collaborative Advantage*, London, Sage Publications Ltd.

Imeson, R. and Edwards, R. (1990) 'Embedding educational guidance in access to higher education', *Journal of Access Studies*, 5(1), pp. 60–71.

Kelly, P. (1989) 'Older students in education', *Adults Learning,* September 1(1), pp. 10–13.

Lowden, K. and Powney, J. (1993) *Where Do We Go From Here? Adult Educational Guidance in Scotland*, Edinburgh, SCRE.

Metcalfe, H. (1993) *Non-Traditional Students' Experience of Higher Education*, Committee of Vice-Chancellors and Principals.

Morstain, B.R. and Smart, J.C. (1974) 'Reasons for participation in adult education courses: a multivariate analysis of group differences', *Adult Education*, 24, pp. 83–98.

Munn, P., MacDonald, C. and Lowden, K. (1992) *Helping Adult Students Cope: mature students on science, mathematics and engineering courses*. Edinburgh, SCRE.

NIACE (1986) *The Challenge of Change. Developing Educational Guidance for Adults,* Leicester, NIACE.

Norris, C. (1985) 'Towards a theory of participation in adult education', *Adult Education,* 58(2), pp. 122–6.

SOEID: Scottish Office Education and Industry Department (1996) *Adult Guidance in Scotland: Strategy Proposals,* Edinburgh, HMSO.

Chapter 13

A whole-school approach to guidance

Chris Watkins

In this chapter I aim to emphasise key characteristics of any whole-school approach, and do not aim to propose a single model of school guidance. This is for two reasons. First, a variety of forms is possible and indeed present in the school system. Within this variety different schools may operate different models equally effectively. To believe that there is a single effective model is to treat the school like a machine. We often do this, thinking of inputs and outputs, with all the machinery well oiled. It leads to the view that a 'good' organisation is an efficient organisation. This is ingrained in everyday conceptions of organisation and order, particularly in the minds of policy makers. However, it is by no means the whole picture: high quality is related to a wider range of considerations than just the organisational structure of guidance (Watkins, 1997). Second, the particular model of guidance which a school operates should properly reflect local conditions of the organisation and its environment. This gives recognition to the school as an organism, living and developing. It helps us to highlight how the various parts of the organism relate and connect, their needs for growth and development. It may also highlight the importance of beliefs which prevail in the school, including those about guidance.

I will take the term guidance to mean any planned process which helps students learn more about themselves, about life opportunities and their optimisation. In school-based guidance, the need has always been to develop an approach which is:

- comprehensive in its clientele
- developmental in its mission
- distributed in its mode of operation.

When these characteristics are in evidence, it can be called a whole-school approach, whatever its organisational form.

COMPREHENSIVE

A comprehensive approach emphasises guidance for all. It sees the need for guidance as normal rather than pathological, so that all students will need planned occasions to learn about themselves and their opportunities. It may state that all students have a right to guidance, and may try to develop clear statements of this entitlement. Rather than wait for difficulties to arise, a comprehensive approach aims to be proactive towards all students, and thereby prevent difficulties.

This approach contrasts with one which emphasises a range of marginal categories such as the 'deprived', 'disadvantaged', 'deviant', 'disturbed', and so on. Although such special groups are attractive to those who think guidance will rescue them, we must not over-estimate the power of school or of school-based guidance in ameliorating such difficulties. Services set up on these lines may be dealing with the difficulties which attract most attention rather than those which carry most need. Further, we must recognise the disadvantages of creating special client groups when many adolescent difficulties may be both transient and widespread. In almost any organisation, the helping services can all too easily set themselves up to deal with the difficulties, but in so doing they may be seen as omnipotent, or as an antidote to the rest of the organisation, or as a cosy corner. This is largely what happened to school counsellors trained in England and Wales during the 1970s – they became marginalised, burned out and excluded from school change (Aubrey, 1985).

A comprehensive approach has logistical implications as responsibility is shared across the school. It requires a move away from a sole focus on students working individually with a guidance professional, toward other aspects of guidance which are more embedded in the daily life of the organisation and the core activities of school. In this way other aspects of guidance are brought into focus:

- Personal tutoring. Here students meet with a teacher who has ongoing personal contact with them, and who knows the profile of their overall performance. The tutoring may sometimes be on a one-to-one basis, and include reviewing achievement, considering progress, devising strategies on a range of issues.
- Group guidance. This includes group tutoring and specially focused guidance lessons, but also all lessons. We need to consider teaching and the extent to which its process and content relate to guidance principles: learning about self, about life opportunities and their optimisation.
- Wider experience outside the classroom. Residential experience, work experience, access to information resources and computer-based guidance would be included. This opportunity structure of experiences is less directly controlled by the school staff, but can be very important

in extending the student's experience and may be linked to direct guidance at some other time.

Figure 13.1 attempts to display some of the elements which need to be considered in a comprehensive approach to guidance, listing direct and indirect elements which are available to all. It also emphasises the point that such provision needs to be planned and evaluated, in order that the evidence of 'guidance for all' is available and the phrase does not degenerate into an empty slogan.

This is not a new idea: essentially it updates the idea of the school as a guidance community (Rowe, 1971). Nor is it peculiar to the UK: research in Canada (Levi and Ziegler, 1991) has shown that 'good guidance is total school guidance', meaning that it receives strong support, contributes to the atmosphere, permeates the curriculum, and includes a proactive developmental programme, collaboratively planned and delivered. In Hong Kong, efforts are being made to move away from crisis-orientation in highly

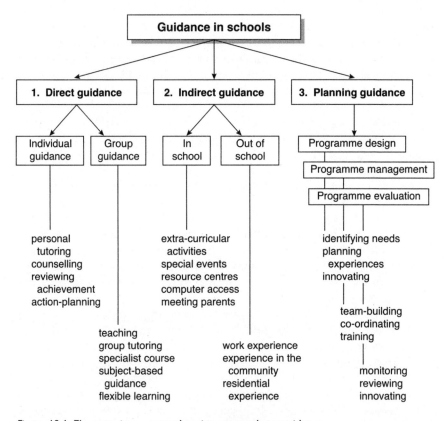

Figure 13.1 Elements in a comprehensive approach to guidance

pressurised schools, towards a 'whole school approach to guidance' (Hong Kong Education Department, 1990) which emphasises the holistic growth of pupils (Hui, 1994). In the USA, a number of states have also been adopting and developing comprehensive programmes and moving away from a counsellor-clinical services approach (Gysbers, 1990; Gysbers and Henderson, 1994). In Scotland, guidance has been identified as an aspect contributing to the effectiveness of the whole school (HMI/SED, 1988), and policy statements have defined guidance as a whole-school responsibility, clarifying both the role of first line guidance teachers and of promoted posts in guidance (HMI/SOEID, 1996; Scottish Central Committee on Guidance, 1986).

DEVELOPMENTAL

Guidance which has a developmental mission is best suited to the context of an educational organisation. To make the best connections with the overall goals of the school, guidance needs to describe its mission as contributing to students' development and learning. However, broad areas of guidance such as health education and careers education regularly find themselves driven by the latest panic, the latest set of published resources or political fashion. In this way specialist guidance programmes in some schools become what can be termed 'the sex and drugs and litter curriculum'. This highlights the way in which a guidance focus can be dominated by adult anxieties rather than young people's needs. Teachers' underlying motivation is to make a positive contribution to students' development at an important life stage, but they need support to achieve this and to avoid the pitfall of guidance provision being modelled on their views and assumptions.

A developmental approach needs a framework which makes interconnections between the various areas which guidance specialisms may have separated (health, careers and so on). This is more genuinely a whole-person view. It needs to describe developmental themes as suggested by the following framework of headings:

- bodily self
- sexual self
- social self
- vocational self
- moral/political self
- self as a learner
- self in the organisation.
        (Watkins, 1995)

This framework has the following benefits. The overall set of inter-connected headings creates a whole-student view rather than a fragmented view. The repeated use of the term 'self' can help teachers focus on the student perspective and needs in a more person-centred way. It can also help them recognise other influences in a student's development, including cultural and gender issues. For the school it helps develop a distributed approach (to be discussed below), in which the contribution of each planned element may be considered using these headings. Even teachers who are described as hostile to guidance readily explain how their subject teaching makes a contribution to student development under these headings.

The content of the framework is similar to the findings of surveys of adolescent needs (Gallagher, *et al.*, 1992; Poole and Evans, 1988). Probably the most creative use of the framework is to promote the identification of students' own guidance needs. This set of headings, suitably adapted in detail and language, can help students communicate the areas in which they would want to be more competent.

Currently, the heading 'self as a learner' is increasingly important. Given the rapid expansion in society's knowledge base, the increased focus on information access and handling, and the collapse of jobs for life in favour of jobs which add value through learning, people need to learn in an increasing range of contexts, not just the compulsory ones (Watkins, *et al.*, 1996). Thus school plays a role in helping young people understand and extend their learning repertoire, as a springboard for many different parts of their future lives.

A developmental and person-centred view has implications for the view of learning which is appropriate in guidance. Adolescents can adopt an experimental approach to their development, trying out new strategies in order to seek feedback, develop their understanding and become more competent. The activities used in guidance mirror this approach by using an action learning cycle as characterised in Figure 13.2.

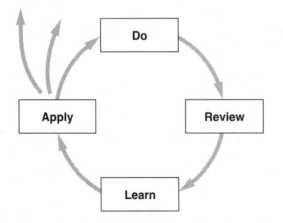

Figure 13.2 An action learning cycle

The 'Do' phase in the figure might be an activity in the classroom: a case study, a simulation, a learning activity, or it might be some experience outside the classroom. The 'Review' phase is a structured way of looking at the important points in the experience of that activity. The 'Learn' phase is where students learn from different experiences, identifying new strategies and effective approaches. They may also identify what more they wish to learn. The 'Apply' phase helps them to transfer their learning to situations they know, to plan some action and to set goals. The role of the teacher is to provide the necessary structures for students to progress through this process. Action learning at its best, whether with individuals or with groups, is a highly structured but still open-ended process.

DISTRIBUTED

A distributed approach to guidance recognises that a range of school-linked experiences contribute to the student's development of understanding and action. It is based on the view that guidance is the responsibility of all teachers, but that they do not all have exactly the same responsibility. It aims to clarify how various experiences and roles can best play a part in the whole picture. Thus it contrasts both with an approach which claims that only some people or some experiences are likely to help, and also with one which suggests that all experiences are useful but fails to specify in what way.

Using, for example, the broad elements of comprehensive guidance, a distributed approach will need to deal with contributions at three levels:

Organisational level

- the ethos and messages of the school
- the range of non-classroom opportunities offered.

Classroom level

- all subject lessons
- specialist guidance lessons
- group tutoring.

Individual level

- tutor guidance
- specialist staff guidance
- other adult guidance.

A coherent distributed view of guidance first needs a common language for describing the content of various contributions: the framework of the seven selves in the previous section is one. It then becomes possible to clarify which aspects of the overall learning offer should be addressed in each element. This approach might therefore clarify some of the similarities and differences between, for example, subject tutoring and personal tutoring (Watkins and Thacker, 1993).

For example, if we consider the tutorial occasion, distinctive features are that:

- the tutor's contact with members of the group is a cumulative one
- the tutor has a cross-subject view of the student
- the tutor group has a 'core' function amongst the various teaching groups
- the tutor has contact with parents and their view of the student.

Thus the following areas of guidance may be salient:

- social and group relations, and any other issues which arise from the tutor's close knowledge of the group (i.e. a *responsive* curriculum)
- overall achievement, recording a wide range of achievements, approaches to study, learning about learning across subjects
- how students are making best use of the school
- decisions where parents' views are influential (e.g. option choice, career choice).

Similarly, if we clarify some of the distinctive features of subject lessons, we see that:

- different subject lessons offer different approaches to learning
- students may perceive their own achievements in subject terms
- students are often motivated specifically through subjects.

The areas of guidance which may be salient include:

- the learning goals and processes in this particular subject
- reviewing strategies for achievement in the subject
- understanding how uses of this subject may inform life-styles and work-styles.

Thus we may develop what may be termed 'the classroom as a guidance community' (HMI, 1992) in which one of the characteristics of good practice in the context of the curriculum is that schemes of work contain references, as appropriate, to guidance.

Again, the specialist course, often labelled personal-social education (PSE), has a specific role to play in the overall picture. Its distinctive features include:

- it is planned and supported by a team including staff with specialist training in guidance
- it uses learning approaches which engage the personal-social dimension
- it addresses areas of priority which would not be sufficiently developed elsewhere.

For these reasons, some aspects of guidance are more effective through PSE than through subjects: for example preventive education on smoking (Eiser *et al.*, 1988) and alcohol education (Balding and Bish, 1992).

A distributed approach can reduce conflict and competition between different elements. Such contests oversimplify issues and do not exploit the different offering of each. It can also reduce the loading of some elements with inappropriate demands: 'something on AIDS – do it in the tutor group'. It also helps to bridge old divides such as that between the 'pastoral' and 'academic' (HMI, 1989). In a distributed approach, the specialists in guidance are key players in developing the practice of other staff. In that sense they become coordinators who are worthy of the title, with clear support from senior managers, a budget, and a key position in the overall structure (Whalley and Watkins, 1991). Their role is to inform support, review and evaluate the whole-school picture, rather than do it all themselves.

Note, however, that the main focus of a distributed approach is the planned work undertaken by teachers. An omission here is the increasing role played by students in school guidance. Provision such as peer counselling and peer tutoring is known, but not always practised, in most schools. Its development in recent years may be a reflection of increased pressure on teachers, but it has sometimes moved schools on from an over-paternalistic view of guidance. It conveys a very important message about young people's skills and the value of peer networks. When it is prevalent in schools, a distributed approach will need to accommodate pupils' contributions.

FORCES HELPING AND HINDERING A WHOLE-SCHOOL APPROACH

There are a range of features which will work for and against a comprehensive, developmental and distributed approach, some of which have been indicated already. The range is quite large since schools' practice is influenced from many angles. As a recent study of guidance practice in Scotland showed, in six 'illustrative' schools biased towards good practice, teachers were nonetheless hostile to their role in first-level guidance, despite a strong national policy context which favoured this position (Howieson and Semple, 1996). Whatever the policy statements say, key practices and perspectives inside the school can have major impact on whether the approaches described in this chapter are realised. Figure 13.3 outlines some of the forces which may help and hinder the development of these approaches.

In the mid 1990s in England, the marketisation reforms of education, including the National Curriculum, school performance tables, and the rhetoric of standards had a generally divisive impact on schools and a negative impact on guidance provision. The vast majority of secondary schools have crystallised even more strongly a subject-based view of the

Forces helping a whole-school approach	Forces hindering a whole-school approach
Wider context, including national policy schools are seen in context of wider systems and influences schools are seen as helping young people learn strong view of overall curriculum is put forward schools are encouraged to learn from each other	schools are seen as either scapegoat or saviour for public concerns schools are seen as helping young people perform curriculum is dominated by subjects and divisions schools are encouraged to compete with each other on performance
Aspects of the school school goals are broad and explicitly include guidance senior management and school policy support a whole-school view planning and review is done collaboratively posts of responsibility are for coordination, support to teams developmental framework is used and student needs are identified	school goals are narrowed to assessed outcomes guidance is managed as a low-status add-on planning is hierarchical, review is rare posts of responsibility are for casework or referral the major focus is on teacher provision
Teachers' points of view feel a responsibility to contribute to guidance feel supported and wish to contribute to overall student development teaching as supporting learning	guidance is the province of specialists to whom cases are referred feel isolated and don't want extra responsibility teaching as 'delivery'
Guidance specialists' point of view leader, coordinator and supporter of others' curriculum and casework	someone who is skilled at helping individual students in difficulty

Figure 13.3 Factors helping and hindering a whole-school approach

curriculum, careers education has been squeezed from the timetable and health education increasingly marginalised (Health Education Authority, 1993). Since the change of government in 1997, the overall picture has changed little and a new set of pressures regarding numeracy and literacy targets has emerged. Unless the negative impact of such forces is recognised, and a more modern view of the role and process of schools emerges, the implications for guidance are severe. In schools which are characterised by fragmentation and division, guidance not only becomes marginalised, it also can become biased towards teachers' needs for survival.

BIBLIOGRAPHY

Aubrey, R. (1985) 'A counselling perspective on the recent educational reform reports', *The School Counselor*, 33, pp. 91–9.

Balding, J. and Bish, D. (1992) *Alcohol Education in Schools*, Exeter, Schools Health Education Unit, University of Exeter.

Eiser, J.R., Morgan, M. and Gammage, P. (1988) 'Social education is good for health', *Educational Research*, 30(1), pp. 20–5.

Gallagher, M., Millar, R., Hargie, O. and Ellis, R. (1992) 'The personal and social worries of adolescents in Northern Ireland: results of a survey', *British Journal of Guidance and Counselling*, 20(3), pp. 274–90.

Gysbers, N.C. (1990) *Comprehensive Guidance Programmes That Work*, Ann Arbor, Michigan, ERIC Clearinghouse.

Gysbers, N.C. and Henderson, P. (1994) *Developing and Managing your School Guidance Programme*, Alexandria VA, American Association for Counseling and Development.

Health Education Authority (1993) *A Survey of Health Education Policies In Schools*, London, HEA.

HMI (1989) *Pastoral Care in Secondary Schools: an inspection of some aspects of pastoral care in 1987–8*, London, DES.

HMI (1992) *Survey of Guidance 13–19 in Schools and Sixth Form Colleges*, London, DES.

HMI/SED (1988) *Effective Secondary Schools*, Edinburgh, Scottish Education Department/HMSO.

HMI/SOEID (1996) *Guidance*, Edinburgh, Scottish Office Education and Industry Department/HMSO.

Hong Kong Education Department (1990) *Education Commission Report No 4*, Hong Kong, Government Printers.

Howieson, C. and Semple, S. (1996) *Guidance in Secondary Schools*, Edinburgh, University of Edinburgh Centre for Educational Sociology.

Hui, E.K. (1994) *Guidance and Counselling*, Hong Kong, Longman Hong Kong.

Levi, M. and Ziegler, S. (1991) *Making Connections: Guidance and Career Education in the Middle Years*, Ottawa, Ontario Ministry of Education.

Poole, M.E. and Evans, G.T. (1988) 'Life Skills: adolescents' perceptions of importance and competence', *British Journal of Guidance and Counselling*, 16(2), pp. 129–44.

Rowe, A. (1971) *The School as a Guidance Community*, Hull, Pearson.

Scottish Central Committee on Guidance (1986) *More than Feelings of Concern*, Edinburgh, Consultative Committee on the Curriculum.

Wagner, P. (1995) 'Schools and pupils: developing their responses to bereavement' in Best, R., Lang, P., Lodge, C. and Watkins, C. (eds) *Pastoral Care and Personal-Social Education: entitlement and provision*, London, Cassell.

Watkins, C. (1992) *Whole School Personal-Social Education: policy and practice,* Coventry, National Association for Pastoral Care in Education.

Watkins, C. (1995) 'Personal-social education and the whole curriculum' in Best, R., Lang, P., Lodge, C. and Watkins, C. (eds) *Pastoral Care and Personal-Social Education: entitlement and provision*, London, Cassell.

Watkins, C. (1997) *Quality Review in Pastoral Care*, Coventry, National Association for Pastoral Care in Education.

Watkins, C., Carnell, E., Lodge, C. and Whalley, C. (1996) *Effective Learning*, London, Institute of Education School Improvement Network (Research Matters series).

Watkins, C. and Thacker, J. (1993) *Tutoring: INSET resources for a whole-school approach*, Harlow, Longman.

Whalley, C. and Watkins, C. (1991) 'Managing the whole curriculum in the secondary school – a structure', *Management in Education*, 5(3), pp. 19–22.

Chapter 14

Guidance and retention of mature students in further and higher education

Veronica McGivney

BACKGROUND

This chapter is based on a study sponsored by the former Department of Employment in the UK and conducted in 1995. The aims were to examine the extent and causes of mature student withdrawal from further and higher education programmes, and to identify measures that might improve completion rates. The study involved a review of existing research; consultation with representatives from further and higher education, and a survey of a sample of higher and further education institutions in England and Wales.

Mature students were defined as people who had entered further and higher education after a gap of at least two years since completing compulsory full-time education.

The research suggested that too many students were failing to complete programmes of study because of inadequate prior information and preparation. Provision of good quality guidance at key stages in their contact with a learning provider, particularly at the pre-entry stage, might therefore significantly reduce withdrawal rates.

CONTEXT

The study was undertaken at a time when mature students (those aged over 21) had become the majority of learners in both further and higher education. In the past, university students were composed mainly of individuals who had come straight from school or sixth form colleges with the requisite A Level examination grades to enter the programme of their choice. Many students now enter through a vocational qualification route or specially designed 'Access' courses.

In the early 1990s, changes in the structure and funding of post-compulsory education had started to focus attention on retention and non-completion rates. Since the Further and Higher Education Act of 1992, further and higher education institutions have been required to collect and record more comprehensive student data than in the past and, specifically, to monitor completion rates and outcomes. In 1997, central funding was linked to student numbers, retention rates and outcomes. This means that institutions can lose a proportion of their core funding if students fail to complete programmes of study. The costs to students may also be considerable: they can incur financial penalties for leaving courses prematurely and some suffer from a sense of personal failure and inadequacy if they abandon a programme of study. Institutional and student funding models have traditionally been geared to full-time students following fixed, time-limited programmes of study whereas the learning pattern of mature students tends to be part-time and spasmodic for reasons usually related to employment, domestic responsibilities and health.

At the time the study was conducted it was widely believed that non-completion rates were increasing in both further and higher education although opinions differed on the actual number of withdrawals. Since the number of mature students had grown dramatically in both sectors, it seemed timely to conduct a study looking particularly at their record of completion and non-completion.

The first research task was therefore to obtain a reliable overall estimate of completion and non-completion rates. This proved difficult for a number of reasons: the national data base was still extremely inadequate and institutional arrangements for collecting the information required by the Further and Higher Education Funding Councils were not yet fully in place. The figures available usually applied only to full-time students and often lumped together different categories of non-completion such as student transfers, academic failure and interrupted learning. Different institutions defined and measured non-completion in different ways and their student tracking methods were sometimes uncoordinated and idiosyncratic. Moreover, concerns about funding and reputation had made student withdrawal rates a sensitive issue and some were reluctant to divulge any figures.

Although most of the sample institutions had started to establish data-collection systems to fulfil the new data requirements, some were encountering a number of problems: the management information systems (MIS) in place were not set up to record the kind of information required by the Quality Assurance and Funding bodies; it was difficult to track students who were not in conventional full-time modes of study and the measurement of completion rates was complicated by the increase in flexible learning patterns, modularised courses and transfers between learning modes, courses and institutions.

Central funding criteria and the terminology generally used for abandonment of a course of study imply that any non-completion is automatically a negative step. However many tutors object to the term 'drop-out' being applied to all students who fail to complete. They argue that students can leave programmes for positive as well as negative reasons: because they have achieved their learning goals, because they have been offered employment or because they wish to transfer to a more suitable course or institution. Moreover, it is frequently found that non-attending students intend to return to study when their personal circumstances allow. From an administrative point of view, however, they are deemed to have 'dropped out' if they fail to return within the cut-off periods specified by the funding councils.

NON-COMPLETION RATES

All the evidence indicates that non-completion rates vary significantly according to type and size of institution, the student cohort, the subject or discipline studied, the qualification sought and attendance mode. Student retention is generally higher in arts and humanities programmes than in science and technology. It is also generally high in vocational programmes linked closely to the labour market and where there is a strong sense of professional identity among students (as in courses leading to nursing qualifications). Women generally have a better staying-on rate than men and more full-time students complete their studies than those learning part-time.

At the time of the study, estimates of withdrawal rates in further education ranged from 13 per cent to 80 per cent on some courses, with 30 per cent being generally regarded as the norm. More recent Further Education Funding Council (FEFC) figures, however, suggest that about 18 per cent of full-time and 16 per cent of part-time students fail to complete. Such 'blanket' figures tend to disguise significant variations between institutions and subject areas.

In higher education, the official figure also hovers around 18 per cent for students on full-time and sandwich (courses in which students spend some time in work experience) first-degree courses. Again, the national figure camouflages very considerable differences between institutions and subject disciplines.

There was some evidence that mature students in higher education are slightly more likely than younger ones to leave full-time courses before completion (CVCP, 1995). Some individual institutions, however, had found mature learners less likely than younger students to leave prematurely.

REASONS FOR NON-COMPLETION

In all post-compulsory education sectors, some degree of student loss is inevitable. The fundamental question is why some leave and others do not. Given the diversity of students, institutions and courses, it is impossible to provide a definitive answer to that question and, as with all aspects of non completion, there is a dearth of reliable evidence. There are, however, a considerable number of what have been described as 'autopsy studies' (Kember, 1995). Most commonly these have involved postal surveys and interviews with samples of students who have withdrawn from programmes of study. However, such studies vary enormously in scope and scale. They involve diverse institutions, student cohorts and subject areas and are based on evidence from different sized samples ranging from under ten to over a thousand. Not surprisingly, their findings 'display a bewildering variety' (Woodley et al., 1987). Nevertheless they do provide a core of generally accepted evidence.

FACTORS ASSOCIATED WITH NON-COMPLETION

Students often abandon their course of study not for a single reason but for a mixture of causal factors related to:

- the course
- the institution
- individual circumstances and study environment
- negative self perceptions and doubts about learning ability
- changes in motivation (changes in goals or early achievement of goals).

(Woodley et al. 1987: 160)

These clusters of reasons recur in most non-completion studies, with many drawing a clear distinction between institution- and course-related factors and factors which are external to the institution. In Britain, there has ostensibly been an increase in both academic and non academic reasons for non-completion in recent years, although the evidence is not unanimous. The former is frequently attributed to the increased number of non-traditional students entering further and higher education and the latter to the severe financial hardship now faced by many students.

Follow-up studies generally reveal that mature students leave courses more for personal than for academic reasons and that those studying part-time experience particular pressures in trying to combine study with outside commitments. However, the stated reasons for withdrawal should not always be taken at face value. Former students often cite those reasons which are most immediate (the last straw) or which protect their self-esteem. Their responses can also be influenced by the way in which follow-up studies are conducted. It has been found, for example, that mature students tend to cite external 'life crises' reasons in follow-up questionnaires but are more likely to cite institution- and course-related factors during in-depth interviews. Thus reasons for leaving which are ostensibly unrelated to the institution or course may disguise academic problems and dissatisfaction with the learning experience which have neither been expressed by learners nor picked up by teaching staff.

EARLY ABANDONMENT OF A COURSE OF STUDY

Follow-up studies are unanimous in finding that withdrawal rates are highest among all student cohorts early in a programme of study and that the chances of successful completion rise significantly as students progress through a course. Common factors associated with early withdrawal are:

- inappropriate or rushed course choice
- unmet expectations (of course/institution)
- lack of preparedness for level of work
- greater than anticipated workload and time commitment
- insufficient background knowledge and grounding in a subject
- lack of academic skills such as essay-writing, note-taking
- difficulties in settling into the academic and social life of an institution
- entering higher education through Clearing (the process that brings together unfilled course places and students who have not achieved the A level grades they need to take up a provisional offer of a place on their preferred course).

Factors identified as having a bearing on withdrawal at a later stage include:

- early achievement of desired goals
- changes in personal circumstances*
- work-related factors (e.g. being offered employment)*
- financial problems and lack of financial support
- domestic commitments or problems*
- demotivation arising from long duration of programme of study*
- fear of not being able to catch up with work after a temporary absence
- fear of or lack of preparedness for examinations
  *applies particularly to mature and part-time students.

STRATEGIES FOR IMPROVING COMPLETION RATES

High non-completion rates imply that some students do not experience what they want or expect. This means that some have been ill-advised (or *not* advised at all) and have consequently made the wrong choice of course and/or institution. Some, however, may experience problems that are potentially solvable given the right kind of intervention and support. The project suggested that if students receive adequate and well-informed advice on choosing the most appropriate course; guidance and support throughout their studies and practical help with any academic or non-academic problems they face, staying-on rates might be significantly enhanced.

PRE-ENTRY GUIDANCE

Many of the factors associated with early withdrawal could be avoided if students were better informed about and prepared for the programmes and institutions they elect to join. However, the research literature indicates that a disturbing number in both further and higher education receive little or no substantial advice before starting an advanced course. One study (Webb *et al.*, 1994) found that Access and Alternative entry students (i.e. those who entered higher education through routes other than the standard A Level examination) frequently gained their education in an 'unplanned and haphazard' manner and entered higher education without any formal guidance. Another study (Booth, Layer and Moore, 1994) found that nearly 30 per cent of mature students had entered higher education without seeking advice from any source.

In further education, studies also commonly reveal that despite the Further Education Funding Council requirement that colleges provide all new students with initial guidance, many of those who abandon programmes entered them with very little knowledge of and preparation for what they would entail. This is particularly the case with part-time students, many of whom receive only limited information and advice at the time of enrolment.

A starting point for improving retention rates might therefore be closer relationships and liaison between education establishments, their 'feeder' institutions (the schools, colleges, etc., from which many of their students habitually come) and any local guidance services in the area. One further education college reduced its non-completion rate to four per cent mainly by maintaining good communication with feeder institutions and ensuring that students were well-informed and prepared (HMI, 1991).

The need for individual institutions to provide good pre-entry information and guidance to prospective and actual enrolees is paramount. A Scottish study of mature students revealed that early, face-to-face contact with a skilled and experienced staff member plays an essential role in preparing them for the nature and demands of a learning programme:

> The need for a good match between student and course seems self-evident and yet it is by no means easy for either college or student to achieve. . . . Face-to-face consultation with a skilled tutor allows more thorough exploration of options than even the best produced brochure or prospectus.
>
> (Munn, MacDonald and Lowden, 1992: 9)

Not all institutions provide this kind of facility, however, and there has been a tension between the UK government's requirement for the further and higher education sectors to expand and the need for institutions to provide impartial guidance on the best study options for individuals. At the time the study was conducted, further education colleges were required to achieve a growth target of 28 per cent (scaled down in 1996) in order to achieve full core funding. Higher education institutions were also required to expand and achieved growth so rapidly that student numbers were eventually consolidated and a maximum aggregate student number (MASN) set for each institution. Institutions which exceed or underachieve their MASN face financial penalties.

Many believe that student growth policies have undermined the provision of impartial guidance since they have led to: 'the temptation ... to hang onto a client rather than refer them to the most appropriate [education] service' (Booth, Layer and Moore, 1994: 152). To meet their targets, some institutions have been offering people financial incentives to enrol. These practices mean that individuals are being denied the honest and comprehensive advice they need to help them select the most appropriate course of study. This inevitably increases the risk of early withdrawal.

CONTENT OF PRE-ENTRY GUIDANCE

Those entering higher or further education often rely on the information given in prospectuses when they are selecting a course and institution. However, institutional literature cannot contain the kind of in-depth information that applicants require. Individuals need to have access to a guidance service which supplies, at the very least:

- practical details such as times, dates and costs
- content and depth of subject coverage
- discussion of the suitability of the course in relation to applicants' background, experience and goals
- details of entry qualifications or previous experience required
- background knowledge and skills required
- details of likely workload and discussion of how it will fit in with applicants' other commitments
- information on the type and frequency of assessments
- recommended reading lists
- details of outcomes and progression routes
- contact name(s) and phone number(s) for further information
- information about alternative programmes for those for whom the course is not suitable.

(Adapted from Munn, MacDonald and Lowden, 1992)

Other useful areas to cover would be: assessment of unaccredited prior learning and experience; finance and sources of financial help; information on childcare facilities, and, particularly for those who have been out of formal education for a considerable time, some preparation for the experience of student life.

PREPARATION FOR STUDENT LIFE

Many people who abandon their programmes of study have found that the realities of student life do not match their expectations. This is often the case for individuals who have come from a more intimate and supportive learning environment such as community education and Access programmes. The size and anonymity of formal education institutions can take students of all ages by surprise and this, together with poor academic and social facilities, often contributes to decisions to withdraw. It is imperative, therefore, that an accurate picture of institutional life be conveyed to prospective students *before* they make the decision to register or, at the very least, before they start their programme of study. Many institutions have recognised the importance of this, particularly to people returning to education after a considerable time gap. One university has produced a detailed video and information pack providing honest student testimony on the pitfalls as well as the pleasures of being a mature student. Some now run special workshops or residential courses to prepare Access students for university life. One organises a special Welcome Weekend to introduce new students, their families and friends, to campus life. Others train current students to liaise with prospective applicants, to welcome new students and facilitate their integration into the institution.

GUIDANCE AND SUPPORT FOR NEW STUDENTS

The first weeks in a new learning environment can be difficult and disorienting for all students, especially those who have done little formal learning since leaving school. The quality of initial help, guidance and support they receive at this stage is therefore of critical importance.

INDUCTION

Induction is an important form of initial guidance for new students. It has been argued that good induction strategies lead to lower absenteeism and drop-out levels, as well as to improved course work and examination results (Bourner and Barlow, 1991). Induction should include:

- familiarisation with institutional facilities such as teaching, private study and social areas; library; learning resource areas; advice, counselling and careers services
- introductions to course members and teaching staff
- clarification of what is expected of students in relation to their programmes of study
- introduction to study skills and work planning. (A number of institutions now provide short introductory or orientation courses to help students adapt to the challenges of study.)

Many educationalists argue that induction should be a continuing process rather than a single activity at the beginning of a student's experience.

FORMAL GUIDANCE SERVICES

At the beginning of (and throughout) their learning experience, students are likely to need information and advice on a wide range of issues to do with the programme studied, the institution and its facilities, accommodation and finance, progression routes and personal problems. Although most colleges and universities now have some form of formal guidance service, their size and quality vary enormously between sectors and institutions. The further education sector has recognised the importance of guidance and many colleges now have special units and specialist staff. Some have a 'front-line' service, located near the reception area, at which actual and prospective students can receive information and guidance on courses, qualifications, finance, accommodation, careers and progression routes.

By comparison, higher education has not been proactive in relation to guidance, despite the needs generated by the rapid expansion of the sector and the increase in 'non-traditional' students. As McNair (1993) has pointed out, the fact that higher education has become more accessible, more diverse in terms of student composition and more flexible in terms of learning modes, means that it now presents more opportunities for confusion, mistaken choices and wasted effort. Yet as Robertson (1994) and others have claimed, many universities still lack a strategic approach to guidance and attach low priority to its provision.

STAFF–STUDENT RELATIONS

Guidance can, however, take a number of forms, some of which can be complementary to a formal service. Since students are most likely to experience problems, both personal and academic, at the beginning of a programme of study, having a known person to turn to at this stage can help them adjust to the new situation. Accordingly, some institutions now have staff members with a particular responsibility for specific cohorts such as mature students or those from a minority ethnic community. For some students, informal contact and rapport with a tutor – not necessarily a personal tutor or guidance officer – can provide the reassurance and encouragement they need to continue on a learning programme. The key attributes of such a person are friendliness, availability and interest in the student.

The quality of tutors is of critical importance to part-time students since a common finding of research is that they receive far less guidance and support than those studying full-time. Even when guidance services are ostensibly open to all students, the times when these are available may not coincide with part-time learners' attendance at the institution. This means that they are effectively denied access to such facilities and rely wholly on their tutors for information and advice. According to one former further education manager who reported to the retention study:

> We can talk till the cows come home about the vital importance of guidance but we are seriously in error if we do not acknowledge the pivotal guidance role of the tutor for the part-timer. For many, the teacher *is* the guidance system.

Despite this assertion (with which many tutors would agree) relatively few teaching staff receive training in providing guidance – a gap that some argue should be remedied in staff development programmes (Munn, MacDonald and Lowden, 1992; Kember, 1995). Moreover the expansion of the sectors has meant that, in some institutions, the potential for staff–student contact has diminished rather than grown.

In higher education, the expansion of student numbers without an equivalent increase in resources has led, in many cases, to the loss of the tutorial system. A study at a new university typically found that about a third of students who had left the institution had good relations with less than 50 per cent of the staff with whom they came into contact (LJMU, 1995).

PEER SUPPORT GROUPS

Peer guidance can be provided by students themselves and, in some institutions, mentor schemes have been successfully introduced to support new students. In one university where second-year students were paid to run weekly sessions for new students, first year withdrawal rates were significantly reduced and end of year academic performance enhanced (HMI, 1993).

Many reports emphasise the importance of creating an early sense of group cohesion among learners, especially part-time students who tend to form weaker ties with an institution than those learning full-time. It has been found that mature and other 'non-standard' students and those engaged in open and distance learning are more likely to continue on a programme of study if they feel part of a supportive group (Metcalf, 1993; Kember, 1995). Some institutions therefore encourage and facilitate the formation of peer support and study groups.

CONTINUING GUIDANCE AND ACADEMIC SUPPORT

Changes in the composition of further and higher education mean that there are now wide differences in individual students' prior educational experience and 'preparedness' for study. The academic performance of those returning to study after a gap can depend heavily on the nature, extent and quality of learning support they receive.

As with guidance services, there are wide differences between institutions in the amount and quality of learning support they provide. Some have few facilities while others, particularly colleges and the 'new' universities (former polytechnics that became universities after the 1992 Further and Higher Education Act) offer a wide range of supports such as special workshops, open learning resources and 'drop-in' assistance for students needing help with study skills, English language, numeracy and computer skills, as well as special help for people with learning difficulties and disabilities. Part-time students, however, generally receive less academic support than full-time learners. A study of further education (NIACE, 1995) found that the extent to which on-course guidance, learning support, language support and study skills assistance were promoted to part-time students, especially those not based on main sites, varied considerably and that such students were often considered less of a priority. Some colleges which do have guidance and support facilities open to part-time learners have found that such students are often unaware of, or choose not to use them. One has introduced a telephone 'helpline' to assist learners who have limited contact with the main campus with any general or academic problems they may be experiencing.

In many of the 'old' universities, student support services are less well developed. According to a report on student support services in higher education, the best practice is to be found in institutions:

> where the needs of specific groups are identified and linked to the provision on offer; where there is good communication between departments and services and a determination to ensure adequate provision . . . where, although students may be experiencing personal difficulties, they know where to go for support and are pleased by the quality of support given. Staff are not isolated in their support work which is well coordinated.
>
> (HMI, 1993: 16)

The report identified the poorest practice in:

> institutions experiencing the most rapid change; where policy appeared overnight and staff were not consulted; where students were taken on an 'all comers' basis and the nature of support was for students to find a staff member who would listen to their difficulties.
>
> (HMI, 1993: 16–17)

Experience over the last decade has shown that academic and pastoral support facilities are often the first things to be cut at times of change and financial crisis despite the fact that any short-term financial savings may be cancelled out by an increase in student withdrawals. This has been the case in a number of universities. It is significant, for example, that although one would expect distance learners to receive *less* support and contact with staff than those in conventional study modes, a study of Open University students who had transferred to other higher education institutions, revealed that they experienced far less support than they were accustomed to at the Open University. Complaints centred, among other things, on slow turn-round of course work, lack of feedback, minimal face-to-face contact with staff, unsuitable accommodation and crowded and under-resourced libraries (Rickwood, 1993). For many students, such problems contribute to decisions to leave.

EXIT GUIDANCE

Whatever the quality of student support offered, there will always be some learners who want or are obliged to abandon a programme of study. It is disturbing therefore that, according to some institutional reports, a significant proportion leave without informing the institution or discussing their decision with a member of staff. Those who do announce their intention to leave are not always adequately advised on alternative courses, their entitlement to credit or the financial implications of withdrawing. Nor are they always referred to internal guidance systems (Moore, 1995). This suggests the need to develop institutional strategies to identify and advise students who are experiencing difficulties. High student withdrawal rates have prompted some further education colleges to establish 'retention services' with particular members of staff responsible for identifying, contacting and advising students at risk.

The evidence suggests that the best time to contact absent students is shortly after they have stopped attending. However, this requires staff to notice, or to be promptly notified of, their absence. Follow-up research indicates that it is all too easy for some students to drift from temporary into permanent withdrawal without anyone noticing. For such students, especially if they are part-time, contacting an unknown student counsellor may not be an easy option. Students need to have access to a person familiar to them before their problems become insuperable.

Fear of losing continuity and not being able to catch up with course-work can turn a temporary absence into a permanent one. Some colleges encourage tutors and fellow students to keep in contact with absentee students and send them notes on the sessions they have missed. One college contacts missing students by letter every three months offering support. It also circulates a newsletter to all actual and former students and encour-ages the formation of student networks.

CONCLUDING OBSERVATIONS

The retention study on which this chapter is based showed that individual motivation *together with* the quality of the guidance and support students receive have a greater impact on academic performance than age, outside commitments and qualifications on entry. Provision of guidance and support should therefore be of paramount concern, particularly at a time when insti-tutions are attracting large numbers of adult and other 'non traditional' learners, many with few qualifications and limited recent experience of education. However, although the former Higher Education Quality Council (1994) called for the expanded system of higher education to be under-pinned by comprehensive, effective and impartial guidance and learning support systems, the changes in student body have not been accompanied by any large-scale increases in these services. This is despite a view that is fast gaining currency that some institutions are accepting students who are neither ready nor equipped to undertake advanced courses. In part the contradiction is due to policies on student expansion. These have inevitably put pressure on institutions and subject departments to recruit the numbers required to obtain the maximum number of funding units, with implica-tions for marketing and admissions practices in some institutions. There has consequently been more concern with finding the right *number* of students than with finding the *right* students for the course and this has undermined the role of institutional guidance in encouraging individuals to enter the most appropriate programme of study.

Similarly, the fact that institutions are financially penalised when students withdraw has led some to be more concerned with their financial position than with the quality of student experience. Monitoring and student tracking tends to be quantitative and institution-based rather than qualitative and student-focused. This is counterproductive: attention to individual learning experience through regular staff–student contact and the provision of ongoing guidance and support, can improve academic performance and increase student retention rates.

The stress, within the current drive towards lifelong learning, on the desirability of encouraging people to become independent learners and the increasing use of new technology and open learning facilities in education and training, also underline the need for guidance. It is not enough to give individuals a learning package and tell them to get on with it: guidance on its use and expert feedback are essential to ensure a satisfactory learning outcome.

Nevertheless, there will always be some students who do not complete their programme of study and this should not invariably be perceived as failure either on the part of the individual or on the part of the institution. It is a fact of life that people's choices, aspirations and circumstances change. For many, leaving may be the right decision and guidance also has a role in helping them to move on.

The provision of guidance and counselling and different forms of student support is expensive and difficult to provide at a time when education institutions are experiencing acute problems with finance. However, if institutions do not or cannot offer such support, the loss of substantial numbers of students may, in the long run, prove far more costly.

BIBLIOGRAPHY

Booth, J., Layer, G. and Moore, R. (1994) 'Access, Credit and Guidance: the CNAA/UDACE Guidance in Higher Education Project' *Journal of Access Studies* 9 (1), 146–53.

Bourner, T. and Barlow, J. (1991) *The Student Induction Handbook: practical activities for institutions and new students*, London: Kogan Page Ltd.

Committee of Vice Chancellors and Principals (CVCP) (1995) *Survey of Student Financial Support*, London: CVCP.

Her Majesty's Inspectorate (HMI) (1991) *Student Completion Rates in Further Education*, HMI Report 26/91/NS, London: HMSO.

Her Majesty's Inspectorate (1993) *Student Support Services in Higher Education*, Education Observed Series, London: Department for Education.

Higher Education Quality Council (1994) *Guidance and Counselling in Higher Education*, London: HEQC.

Kember, D. (1995) *Open Learning Courses for Adults: a model of student progress*, New Jersey: Education Technology Publications.

Liverpool John Moores University (LJMU) (1995) *Report on the reasons given by students for withdrawing from LJMU award programmes*, Liverpool: LJMU.

McNair, S. (1993) *An Adult Higher Education: a vision*, a policy discussion paper, Leicester: The National Institution of Adult Continuing Education (NIACE).

Metcalf, H. (1993) *Non-Traditional Students' Experience of Higher Education: a review of the literature*, London: Committee of Vice Chancellors and Principals (CVCP).

Moore, R. (1995) *Retention Rates Research Project, Final Report*, Sheffield: Division of Access and Guidance, Sheffield Hallam University.

Munn, P., MacDonald, C. and Lowden, K. (1992) *Helping Adult Students Cope*, Edinburgh: The Scottish Council for Research in Education.

National Institute of Adult Continuing Education (1995) *Adult Learners in Further Education Colleges*, Leicester: NIACE.

Rickwood, P.W. (1993) *The Experience of Transfer: a study of a cohort of students who used Open University credits to transfer to other institutions of higher education*, Birmingham: The Open University, West Midlands Region.

Robertson, D. (1994) *Choosing to Change: extending access, choice and mobility in higher education*: The report of the HEQC CAT Development Project, Executive statement and summary, London: HEQC.

Webb, S., Davies, P., Green, P., Thompson, A. and Williams, J. with Weller, P., Lovell, T. and Shah, S. (1994) *Alternative Entry to Higher Education*, Summary Report, Leicester: NIACE.

Woodley, A., Wagner, L., Slowey, M., Hamilton, M. and Fulton, O. (1987) *Choosing to Learn: adults in education*, Buckingham: The Open University Press.

Chapter 15

The interpersonal relationship in the facilitation of learning

Carl Rogers

An edited version of 'The interpersonal in the facilitation of learning,' in *Freedom to Learn for the 80s*, Merril (1983).

This chapter is passionate and personal, as it endeavours to probe my relationship to the learning process and the attitudinal climate that promotes this process. I believe that it expresses some of my deepest convictions in regard to the process we call *education*.

I wish to begin with a statement that may seem surprising to some and perhaps offensive to others. It is simply this: Teaching, in my estimation, is a vastly over-rated function.

Having made such a statement, I scurry to the dictionary to see if I really mean what I say. *Teaching* means 'to instruct'. Personally, I am not much interested in instructing another in what she should know or think, though others seem to love to do this. 'To impart knowledge or skill.' My reaction is, why not be more efficient, using a book or programmed learning? 'To make to know.' Here my hackles rise. I have no wish to *make* anyone know something. 'To show, guide, direct.' As I see it, too many people have been shown, guided, directed. So I come to the conclusion that I *do* mean what I said. Teaching is, for me, a relatively unimportant and vastly overvalued activity.

But there is more in my attitude than this. I have a negative reaction to teaching. Why? I think it is because it raises all the wrong questions. As soon as we focus on teaching, the question arises, what shall we teach? What, from our superior vantage point, does the other person need to know? I wonder if, in this modern world, we are justified in the presumption that we are wise about the future and the young are foolish. Are we *really* sure as to what they should know? Then there is the ridiculous question of coverage. What shall the course cover? This notion of coverage is based on the assumption that what is taught is what is learned; what is presented is what is assimilated. I know of no assumption so obviously untrue. One does not need research to provide evidence that this is false. One needs only to talk with a few students.

We are, in my view, faced with an entirely new situation in education where the goal of education, if we are to survive, is the *facilitation of change and learning*. The only person who is educated is the one who has learned how to learn; the one who has learned how to adapt and change; the one who has realized that no knowledge is secure, that only the process of *seeking* knowledge gives a basis for security. Changingness, a reliance on *process* rather than upon static knowledge, is the only thing that makes any sense as a goal for education in the modern world.

So I turn to an activity, a purpose, which really warms me – the facilitation of learning. When I have been able to transform a group – and here I mean all the members of a group, myself included – into a community of *learners*, then the excitement has been almost beyond belief. To free curiosity; to permit individuals to go charging off in new directions dictated by their own interests; to unleash the sense of inquiry; to open everything to questioning and exploration; to recognize that everything is in process of change – here is an experience I can never forget. I cannot always achieve it in groups with which I am associated, but when it is partially or largely achieved, then it becomes a never-to-be-forgotten group experience. Out of such a context arise true students, real learners, creative scientists and scholars, and practitioners, the kind of individuals who can live in a delicate but ever-changing balance between what is presently known and the flowing, moving, altering problems and facts of the future.

Here then is a goal to which I can give myself wholeheartedly. I see *the facilitation of learning* as the *aim* of education, the way in which we might develop the learner, the way in which we can learn to live as individuals in process. I see the facilitation of learning as the function that may hold constructive, tentative, changing *process* answers to some of the deepest perplexities that beset humankind today.

But do we know how to achieve this new goal in education? My answer is that we possess a very considerable knowledge of the conditions that encourage self-initiated, significant, experiential, 'gut-level' learning by the whole person. We do not frequently see these conditions put into effect because they mean a real revolution in our approach to education and revolutions are not for the timid.

We know that the initiation of such learning rests not upon the teaching skills of the leader, not upon scholarly knowledge of the field, not upon curricular planning, not upon use of audiovisual aids, not upon the programmed learning used, not upon lectures and presentations, not upon an abundance of books, though each of these might at one time or another be utilized as an important resource. No, the facilitation of significant learning rests upon certain attitudinal qualities that exist in the personal *relationship* between the facilitator and the learner.

We came upon such findings first in the field of psychotherapy, but now there is evidence that shows these findings apply in the classroom as well. We find it easier to think that the intensive relationship between therapist and client might possess these qualities, but we are also finding that they *may* exist in the countless interpersonal interactions between the teacher and pupils.

QUALITIES THAT FACILITATE LEARNING

What are these qualities, these attitudes, that facilitate learning? Let me describe them very briefly, drawing illustrations from the teaching field.

Realness in the facilitator of learning

Perhaps the most basic of these essential attitudes is realness or genuineness. When the facilitator is a real person, being what she is, entering into a relationship with the learner without presenting a front or a facade, she is much more likely to be effective. This means that the feelings that she is experiencing are available to her, available to her awareness, that she is able to live these feelings, be them, and able to communicate them if appropriate. It means that she comes into a direct personal encounter with the learner, meeting her on a person-to-person basis. It means that she is *being* herself, not denying herself.

From this point of view it is suggested that the teacher can be a real person in her relationship with her students. She can be enthusiastic, can be bored, can be interested in students, can be angry, can be sensitive and sympathetic. Because she accepts these feelings as her own, she has no need to impose them on her students. She can like or dislike a student product without implying that it is objectively good or bad or that the student is good or bad. She is simply expressing a feeling for the product, a feeling that exists within herself. Thus, she is a person to her students, not a faceless embodiment of a curricular requirement.

It is obvious that this attitudinal set, found to be effective in psychotherapy, is sharply in contrast with the tendency of most teachers to show themselves to their pupils simply as roles. It is quite customary for teachers rather consciously to put on the mask, the role, the facade of being a teacher and to wear this facade all day removing it only when they have left the school at night.

But not all teachers are like this. Take Sylvia Ashton-Warner, who took resistant, supposedly slow-learning primary school Maori children in New Zealand, and let them develop their own reading vocabulary. Each child could request one word each day, and she would print it on a card and give it to him. Soon they were building sentences, which they could also keep. The children simply never forget these self-initiated learnings. But it is not my purpose to tell you of her methods. I want instead to give you a glimpse of her attitude, of her passionate realness that must have been as evident to her tiny pupils as to her readers. An editor asked her some questions, and she responded: 'A few cool facts you asked me for . . . I don't know that there's a cool fact in me, or anything else cool for that matter, on this particular subject. I've got only hot long facts on the matter of Creative Teaching, scorching both the page and me' (Ashton-Warner, 1963: 26).

Here is no sterile facade. Here is a vital *person*, with convictions, with feelings. It is her transparent realness that was, I am sure, one of the elements that made her an exciting facilitator of learning. She doesn't fit into some neat educational formula. She *is*, and students grow by being in contact with someone who really and openly *is*.

Take another very different person, Barbara Shiel. She had made art materials freely available, and students often used these in creative ways, but the room frequently looked like a picture of chaos. Here is her report of her feelings and what she did with them.

> I find it maddening to live with the mess – with a capital M! No one seems to care except me. Finally, one day I told the children . . . that I am a neat, orderly person by nature and that the mess was driving me to distraction. Did they have a solution? It was suggested there were some volunteers who could clean up . . . I said it didn't seem fair to me to have the same people clean up all the time for others – but it would solve it for me. 'Well, some people like to clean,' they replied. So that's the way it is.
>
> (Shiel, 1966).

In this instance, Miss Shiel is taking the risk of being transparent in her angry frustrations about the mess. And what happens? The same thing that, in my experience, nearly always happens. These young people accept and respect her feelings, take them into account, and work out a novel solution. Miss Shiel wisely comments, 'I used to get upset and feel guilty when I became angry. I finally realized the children could accept *my* feelings too. And it is important for them to know when they've "pushed me". I have my limits, too' (ibid).

I trust I am making it clear that to be real is not always easy, nor is it achieved all at once, but it is basic to the person who wants to become that revolutionary individual, a facilitator of learning.

Prizing, acceptance, trust

There is another attitude that stands out in those who are successful in facilitating learning. I think of it as prizing the learner, prizing her feelings, her opinions, her person. It is a caring for the learner, but a nonpossessive caring. It is an acceptance of this other individual as a separate person, having worth in her own right. It is a basic trust – a belief that this other person is somehow fundamentally trustworthy. Whether we call it prizing, acceptance, trust, or by some other term, it shows up in a variety of observable ways. The facilitator who has a considerable degree of this attitude can be fully acceptant of the fear and hesitation of the student as she approaches a new problem as well as acceptant of the pupil's satisfaction in achievement. Such a teacher can accept the student's occasional apathy, her erratic desires to explore byroads of knowledge, as well as her disciplined efforts to achieve major goals. She can accept personal feelings that both disturb and promote learning – rivalry with a sibling, hatred of authority, concern about personal adequacy. What we are describing is a prizing of the learner as an imperfect human being with many feelings, many potentialities. The facilitator's prizing or acceptance of the learner is an operational expression of her essential confidence and trust in the capacity of the human organism.

Let me indicate how this attitude of prizing, of accepting, of trusting appears to the student who is fortunate enough to experience it.

> Your way of being with us is a revelation to me. In your class I feel important, mature, and capable of doing things on my own. I want to think for myself and this need cannot be accomplished through text-books and lectures alone, but through living. I think you see me as a person with real feelings and needs, an individual. What I say and do are significant expressions from me, and you recognize this.
>
> (Appell, 1959)

College students in a class with Dr. Patricia Bull describe not only these prizing, trusting attitudes, but the effect these have had on their other interactions.

> I still feel close to you, as though there were some tacit understanding between us, almost a conspiracy. This adds to the in-class participation on my part because I feel that at least one person in the group will react, even when I am not sure of the others. It does not matter really whether your reaction is positive or negative, it just *IS*. Thank you.
>
> (Bull, 1966)

I am sure these examples show that the facilitator who cares, who prizes, who trusts the learner, creates a climate for learning so different from the ordinary classroom that any resemblance is purely coincidental

Empathic understanding

A further element that establishes a climate for self-initiated, experiential learning is empathic understanding. When the teacher has the ability to understand the student's reactions from the inside, has a sensitive aware-ness of the way the process of education and learning seems *to the student*, then again the likelihood of significant learning is increased.

This kind of understanding is sharply different from the usual evalua-tive understanding, which follows the pattern of 'I understand what is wrong with you.' When there is a sensitive empathy, however, the reaction in the learner follows something of this pattern, 'At last someone understands how it feels and seems to be *me* without wanting to analyze me or judge me. Now I can blossom and grow and learn.'

This attitude of standing in the other's shoes, of viewing the world through the student's eyes, is almost unheard of in the classroom. One could listen to thousands of ordinary classroom interactions without coming across one instance of clearly communicated, sensitively accurate, empathic understanding. But it has a tremendously releasing effect when it occurs.

Let me take an illustration from Virginia Axline, dealing with a second grade boy. Jay, age seven, has been aggressive, a trouble maker, slow of speech and learning. Because of his 'cussing,' he was taken to the principal, who paddled him, unknown to Miss Axline. During a free work period, Jay fashioned very carefully a man of clay down to a hat and handkerchief in his pocket. 'Who is that?' asked Miss Axline. 'Dunno,' replied Jay. 'Maybe it is the principal. He has a handkerchief in his pocket like that.' Jay glared at the clay figure. 'Yes,' he said. Then he began to tear the head off and looked up and smiled. Miss Axline said, 'You sometimes feel like twisting his head off, don't you? You get so mad at him.' Jay tore off one arm, another, then beat the figure to a pulp with his fists. Another boy, with the perception of the young, explained, 'Jay is mad at Mr. X because he licked him this noon.' 'Then you must feel lots better now,' Miss Axline commented. Jay grinned and began to rebuild Mr. X (Axline, 1944).

The other examples I have cited also indicate how deeply appreciative students feel when they are simply *understood* – not evaluated, not judged, simply understood from their *own* point of view, not the teacher's. If any teacher set herself the task of endeavouring to make one non-evaluative, acceptant, empathic response per day to a student's demonstrated or verbalized feeling, I believe she would discover the potency of this currently almost nonexistent kind of understanding.

WHAT ARE THE BASES OF FACILITATIVE ATTITUDES?

A 'puzzlement'

It is natural that we do not always have the attitudes I have been describing. Some teachers raise the question, 'But what if I am *not* feeling empathic, do *not*, at this moment, prize or accept or like my students. What then?' My response is that realness is the most important of the attitudes mentioned, and it is not accidental that this attitude was described first. So if one has little understanding of the student's inner world and a dislike for the students or their behaviour, it is almost certainly more constructive to be *real* than to be pseudoempathic or to put on a facade of caring.

But this is not nearly as simple as it sounds. To be genuine, or honest, or congruent, or real means to be this way about *oneself*. I cannot be real about another person because I do not *know* what is real for them. I can only tell, if I wish to be truly honest, what is going on in me.

Let me take an example. Early in this chapter I reported Miss Shiel's feelings about the 'mess' created by the art work. Essentially she said, 'I find it maddening to live with the mess! I'm neat and orderly and it is driving me to distraction.' But suppose her feelings had come out somewhat differently in the disguised way that is much more common in classrooms at all levels. She might have said, 'You are the messiest children I've ever seen! You don't take care about tidiness or cleanliness. You are just terrible!' This is most definitely *not* an example of genuineness or realness, in the sense in which I am using these terms. There is a profound distinction between the two statements, which I should like to spell out.

In the second statement she is telling nothing of herself, sharing none of her feelings. Doubtless the children will *sense* that she is angry, but because children are perceptively shrewd, they may be uncertain as to whether she is angry at them or has just come from an argument with the principal. It has none of the honesty of the first statement in which she tells of her *own* feeling of being driven to distraction.

Another aspect of the second statement is that it is all made up of judgements or evaluations, and like most judgements, they are all arguable. Are these children messy, or are they simply excited and involved in what they are doing? Are they *all* messy, or are some as disturbed by the chaos as she? If a group of visitors were coming, would their attitude be different? When we make judgements, they are almost never fully accurate and hence cause resentment and anger as well as guilt and apprehension. Had she used the second statement, the response of the class would have been entirely different.

I am going to some lengths to clarify this point because I have found from experience that to stress the value of being real, of *being* one's feelings, is taken by some as a licence to pass judgements on others, to project on others all the feelings that one should be 'owning'. Nothing could be further from my meaning.

Actually the achievement of realness is most difficult, and even when one wishes to be truly genuine, it occurs but rarely. Certainly it is not simply a matter of the *words* used, and if one is feeling judgemental, the use of a verbal formula that sounds like the sharing of feelings will not help. It is just another instance of a facade, of a lack of genuineness. Only slowly can we learn to be truly real. For first of all, one must be close to one's feelings, capable of being aware of them. Then one must be willing to take the risk of sharing them as they are, inside, not disguising them as judgements, or attributing them to other people. This is why I so admire Miss Shiel's sharing of her anger and frustration, without in any way disguising it.

A trust in the human organism

It would be most unlikely that one could hold the three attitudes I have described, or could commit herself to being a facilitator of learning unless she has come to have a profound trust in the human organism and its potentialities. If I distrust the human being, then I *must* cram her with information of my own choosing lest she go her own mistaken way. But if I trust the capacity of the human individual for developing her own potentiality, then I can provide her with many opportunities and permit her to choose her own way and her own direction in her learning.

Living the uncertainty of discovery

I believe it should be said that this basically confident view of the human being and the attitudes towards students that I have described do not appear suddenly, in some miraculous manner, in the facilitator of learning. Instead, they come about through taking risks, through *acting* on tentative hypotheses. I started my career with the firm view that individuals must be manipulated for their own good; I only came to the attitudes I have described and the trust in the individual that is implicit in them because I found that these attitudes were so much more potent in producing learning and constructive change. Hence, I believe that it is only by risking herself in these new ways that the teacher can *discover* for herself, whether or not they are effective, whether or not they are for her.

When a facilitator creates, even to a modest degree, a classroom climate characterized by all that she can achieve of realness, prizing, and empathy; when she trusts the constructive tendency of the individual and the group; then she discovers that she has inaugurated an educational revolution. Learning of a different quality, proceeding at a different pace, with a greater degree of pervasiveness, occurs. Feelings – positive, negative, confused – become a part of the classroom experience. Learning becomes life and a very vital life at that. The student is on the way, sometimes excitedly, sometimes reluctantly, to becoming a learning, changing being.

The evidence

The research evidence for the statements in the last paragraph is now very convincing indeed. It has been most interesting to watch that evidence accumulate to a point where it seems irrefutable.

First, in the 1960s, several studies in psychotherapy and in education led to some tentative conclusions. When clients in therapy perceived their therapists as rating high in genuineness, prizing and emphatic understanding, self-learning and therapeutic change were facilitated. The significance of these therapist attitudes was supported in a classic research by Barrett-Lennard (1962).

Another study focused on teachers. Some teachers see their urgent problems as 'Helping children think for themselves and be independent'; 'Getting students to participate'; etc. These teachers were regarded as the 'positively oriented' group. Other teachers saw their urgent problems as 'Getting students to listen'; 'Trying to teach children who don't even have the ability to learn'; etc. These were termed the negatively oriented group. It was found that their students perceived the first group as exhibiting far more of empathy, prizing, and realness than the second group. The first group showed a high degree of facilitative attitudes, the second did not (Emmerling, 1961).

An interesting study by Schmuck (1963; 1966) showed that when teachers are empathically understanding, their students tend to like each other better. In an understanding classroom climate, every student tends to feel liked by all the others, has a more positive attitude towards self, and a positive attitude towards school. This ripple aspect of the teacher's attitude is provocative and significant. To extend an empathic understanding to students has effects that go on and on.

The foregoing are samples of the many small studies that began to pile up. But it could still be asked, does the student actually *learn* more when these attitudes are present? David Aspy (1965) did a careful study of six classes of third-graders. He found that in the three classes where the teacher's facilitative attitudes were highest, the pupils showed a significantly greater gain in their reading achievement than in those classes with a lesser degree of these qualities.

Evidence from students

Certainly before the research evidence was in, students were making it clear by their reactions to student-centred or person-centred classrooms that an educational revolution was underway.

The most striking learnings of students exposed to such a climate are by no means restricted to greater achievement in the three Rs. The significant learnings are the more personal ones – independence, self-initiated and responsible learning, release of creativity, a tendency to become more of a person. I can only illustrate this by picking, almost at random, statements from students whose teachers have endeavoured to create a climate of trust, of prizing, of realness, of understanding, and above all, of freedom.

> In retrospect, I find that I have actually enjoyed this course, both as a class and as an experiment, although it had me quite unsettled at times. This, in itself, made the course worthwhile since the majority of my courses this semester merely had me bored with them and the whole process of 'higher education.' Quite aside from anything else, due mostly to this course, I found myself devoting more time to writing

poetry than to writing short stories, which temporarily interfered with my writing class.

(Moon, 1966)

This course is proving to be a vital and profound experience for me. . . . This unique learning situation is giving me a whole new conception of just what learning is. . . . I am experiencing a real growth in this atmosphere of constructive freedom . . . the whole experience is challenging.

(Bull, 1966)

I feel that the course had been of great value to me. . . . I'm glad to have had this experience because it has made me think. . . . I've never been so personally involved with a course before, especially *outside* the classroom. It has been frustrating, rewarding, enjoyable, and tiring!

(ibid)

I like this plan because there is a lot of freedom. I also learn more this way than the other way you don't have to wate [*sic*] for others you can go at your own speed rate it also takes a lot of responsibility.

(Shiel 1, 1966)

I have been thinking about what happened through this experience. The only conclusion I come to is that if I try to measure what is going on, or what I was at the beginning, I have got to know what I was when I started – and I don't . . . so many things I did and feel are just lost . . . scrambled up inside. . . . They don't seem to come out in a nice little pattern or organization I can say or write. . . . There are so many things left unsaid. I know I have only scratched the surface, I guess. I can feel so many things almost ready to come out . . . maybe that's enough. *It seems all kinds of things have so much more meaning now than ever before.* . . . This experience has had meaning, has done things to me and I am not sure how much or how far just yet. I think I am going to be a better me in the fall. *That's one thing I think I am sure of.*

(Appell, 1963)

I can't read these student statements – sixth grade, college, graduate level – without being deeply moved. Here are teachers, risking themselves, *being* themselves, *trusting* their students, adventuring into the existential unknown, taking the subjective leap. And what happens? Exciting, incredible *human* events. You can sense persons being created, learnings being initiated, future citizens rising to meet the challenge of unknown worlds.

THE EFFECT UPON THE INSTRUCTOR

Let me turn to another dimension that excites me. I have spoken of the effect upon the *student* of a climate that encourages significant, self-reliant, personal learning. But I have said nothing about the reciprocal effect upon the instructor. When she has been the agent for the release of such self-initiated learning, the faculty member finds herself changed as well as her students. One such says:

> To say that I am overwhelmed by what happened only faintly reflects my feelings. I have taught for may years but I have never experienced anything remotely resembling what occurred. I, for my part, never found in a classroom so much of the whole person coming forth, so deeply involved, so deeply stirred. Further, I question if in the traditional setup, with its emphasis on subject matter, examinations, grades, there is, or there can be a place for the 'becoming' person with his deep and manifold needs as he struggles to fulfill himself. But this is going far afield. I can only report to you what happened and to say that I am grateful and that I am also humbled by the experience. I would like you to know this for it has enriched my life and being.
>
> (Rogers, 1961)

TOO IDEALISTIC?

Some readers may feel that the whole approach of this chapter – the belief that teachers can relate as persons to their students – is hopelessly unrealistic and idealistic. They may see that in essence it is encouraging both teachers and students to be creative in their relationship to each other and in their relationship to subject matter, and feel that such a goal is quite impossible. They are not alone in this. I have heard scientists at leading schools of science and scholars in leading universities, arguing that it is absurd to try to encourage all students to be creative – we need hosts of mediocre technicians and workers, and if a few creative scientists and artists and leaders emerge, that will be enough. That may be enough for them. It may be enough to suit you. I want to go on record as saying it is *not* enough to suit me. When I realize the incredible potential in the ordinary student, I want to try to release it.

I'm sorry I can't be coolly scientific about this. The issue is too urgent. I can only be passionate in my statement that people count, that interpersonal relationships *are* important, that we know something about releasing human potential, that we could learn much more, and that unless we give strong positive attention to the human interpersonal side of our educational dilemma, our civilization is on its way down the drain. Better courses, better curricula, better coverage, better teaching machines will never resolve our dilemma in a basic way. Only persons acting like persons in their relationships with their students can even begin to make a dent on this most urgent problem of modern education.

SUMMARY

Let me try to state, somewhat more calmly and soberly, what I have said with such feeling and passion.

I have said that it is most unfortunate that educators and the public think about, and focus on, *teaching*. It leads them into a host of questions that are either irrelevant or absurd so far as real education is concerned.

I have said that if we focused on the facilitation of *learning* – how, why, and when the student learns, and how learning seems and feels from the inside – we might be on a much more profitable track.

I have said that we have some knowledge, and could gain more, about the conditions that facilitate learning, and that one of the most important of these conditions is the attitudinal quality of the interpersonal relationship between facilitator and learner.

Those attitudes that appear effective in promoting learning can be described. First of all is a transparent realness in the facilitator, a willingness to be a person, to be and live the feelings and thoughts of the moment. When this realness includes a prizing, a caring, a trust and respect for the learner, the climate for learning is enhanced. When it includes a sensitive and accurate empathic listening, then indeed a freeing climate, stimulative of self-initiated learning and growth, exists. The student is *trusted* to develop.

I have tried to make plain that individuals who hold such attitudes, and are bold enough to act on them, do not simply modify classroom methods – they revolutionize them. They perform almost none of the functions of teachers. It is no longer accurate to call them *teachers*. They are catalyzers, facilitators, giving freedom and life and the opportunity to learn, to students.

I have brought in the cumulating research evidence that suggests that individuals who hold such attitudes are regarded as effective in the classroom; that the problems that concern them have to do with the release of potential, not the deficiencies of their students; that they seem to create classroom situations in which there are not admired children and disliked children, but in which affection and liking are a part of the life of every child; that in classrooms approaching such a psychological climate, children learn more of the conventional subjects.

But I have intentionally gone beyond the empirical findings to try to take you into the inner life of the student – elementary, college, and graduate – who is fortunate enough to live and learn in such an interpersonal relationship with a facilitator, in order to let you see what learning feels like when it is free, self-initiated and spontaneous. I have tried to indicate how it even changes the student–student relationship – making it more aware, more caring, more sensitive, as well as increasing the self-related learning of significant material. I have spoken of the change it brings about in the faculty member.

Throughout, I have tried to indicate that if we are to have citizens who can live constructively in this kaleidoscopically changing world, we can *only* have them if we are willing for them to become self-starting, self-initiating learners. Finally, it has been my purpose to show that this kind of learner develops best, so far as we now know, in a growth-promoting, facilitative relationship with a *person*.

BIBLIOGRAPHY

Appell, Morey L. 'Selected Student Reactions to Student-centered Courses.' Unpublished manuscript, Indiana State University, 1959.

Appell, Morey L. 'Self-understanding for the Guidance Counselor.' *Personnel & Guidance Journal*, October 1963, pp. 143–8.

Ashton-Warner, Sylvia. *Teacher.* New York: Simon and Schuster, 1963.

Aspy, David N. 'A Study of Three Facilitative Conditions and Their Relationship to the Achievement of Third Grade Students.' Unpublished PhD dissertation, University of Kentucky, 1965.

Axline, Virginia M. 'Morale on the School Front.' *Journal of Educational Research*, 1944, 521–33.

Barrett-Lennard, G.T. 'Dimensions of Therapist Response as Causal Factors in Therapeutic Change.' *Psychological Monographs*, 76 (Whole No. 562), 1962.

Bull, Patricia. 'Student Reactions, Fall, 1965.' Unpublished manuscript, New York State University College, 1966.

Emmerling, F.C. 'A Study of the Relationships Between Personality Characteristics of Classroom Teachers and Pupil Perceptions.' Unpublished PhD dissertation, Auburn University, Auburn, Alabama 1961.

Moon, Samuel F. 'Teaching the Self.' *Improving College and University Teaching, 14* (Autumn 1966): 213–29.

Rogers, Carl R. *On Becoming a Person.* Boston: Houghton Mifflin, 1961: 313.

Schmuck, R. 'Some Aspects of Classroom Social Climate.' *Psychology in the Schools* 3 (1966): 59–65.

Schmuck, R. 'Some Relationships of Peer Liking Patterns in the Classroom to Pupil Attitudes and Achievements.' *The School Review* 71 (1963): 337–59.

Shiel, Barbara J. 'Evaluation: A Self-directed Curriculum, 1965.' Unpublished manuscript, n.p. 1966.

Chapter 16

Putting problems in context
The family and the school

Graham Upton

An edited version of 'Putting problems in context – the family and the school', in *Counselling in Schools: a Reader,* Chapter 6, London: David Fulton (1993).

In schools there is a tendency to conceptualise difficulties in behaviour and learning in ways whereby the pupil is seen as being, or having, the problem. For the teacher concerned with establishing an effective learning environment for a whole class of children or young people, the pupil who does not participate easily in classroom activities, the pupil who disrupts those activities and the pupil who fails to earn from them is a pupil without whom life would clearly be easier and more rewarding. Working from the assumption that education in general, and schools in particular, are positively good features of our society, historical attempts to understand and intervene with problems such as these have traditionally focused on the individual in isolation from the immediate context of the classroom and school and the broader context of family and society.

Children and young people have been variously labelled as educationally sub-normal and maladjusted or as having learning difficulties and emotional and behavioural problems. Intervention has ranged from temporary withdrawal from their ordinary class for counselling and remedial teaching to more permanent placement in a special class, unit or school. The objective of specialist help has invariably been the remediation of the pupils' difficulties so that they will be able to respond more appropriately to the requirements of classroom life. Thus 'the counsellor is concerned with the understanding and prevention of alienation and the production of attitudes which allow pupils to avail themselves of the resources of the school' (Hamblin, 1978).

The individual ascription of blame and an individualised approach to intervention is understandable, but it ignores much of what we know about the nature of behaviour and learning problems in schools and fails to address the limitations of such an approach to intervention.

WHY SHOULD PROBLEMS BE VIEWED IN THEIR CONTEXT?

There are several reasons why we need to look at both behaviour and learning problems in a broad context.

1   Schools and individual teachers vary enormously in what they regard as acceptable behaviour. Whether pupils are seen as having behaviour problems depends as much on the school in which they are pupils and on the particular teachers with whom they are in contact as it does on the actual behaviour which the pupils exhibit. Thus, a pupil who fails to wear school uniform may be seen as presenting a more serious challenge to the values and attitudes of the school if, for example, that school was a grant maintained school striving to improve its image amongst parents, rather than an eleven to sixteen comprehensive faced with problems of severe social deprivation where such an issue may be seen as inconsequential. In other words it is not the behaviour *per se* which is problematic but where it occurs and how it is perceived in that situation. Any attempt to intervene in that situation should logically address the context as well as the behaviour.

2   Behaviour in schools is frequently situation-specific and it is common for pupils to behave very differently from one class to the next, and from one teacher to the next. This applies equally to learning difficulties where marked differences in achievement between subject areas frequently characterise the performance of pupils. It is possible to see this as being determined solely by the pupil but more accurately it must be seen as reflecting different sets of interactions between the pupil and the teachers involved, and the different ways in which whole groups of pupils behave in different situations. Equally, it is important to understand that not all teachers find it easy to establish positive relationships with 'difficult' pupils. Thus, it is important to consider where behaviour and learning problems occur and to identify the different roles played by the individual, the peer group and teachers who are involved in their occurrence.

3   Behaviour at home is frequently very different from that at school. This is in line with the situation-specific nature of behaviour referred to above but also frequently reflects differences between parents and teachers in their attitudes towards what constitutes good and bad behaviour. Aggressive or violent behaviour, for example, might be considered unacceptable by teachers and society at large but may well constitute a norm in the family and within the family's social network. Failure to see the 'problem' in context could be counter-productive to any attempt to modify a pupil's behaviour in school and could create an even greater divide between the family and the school.

4   Behaviour problems in school often reflect underlying emotional diffi-
    culties whereby pupils can be seen to be acting out severe emotional
    difficulties, the origins of which lie within the disturbing experiences
    of their family life. The importance of this has been highlighted in
    relation to problems of sexual and physical abuse (Hall, 1992) but the
    concept has long provided a rationale for the placement of children and
    young people in residential special schools. While such problems can
    be responded to as individual difficulties they can only be fully under-
    stood in the context of the interpersonal dynamics of the family where
    they originate.

5   The study of school differences has suggested that teachers and schools
    too must be seen as potential causative factors in the occurrence of
    behaviour and learning problems (Rutter *et al.*, 1979; Reynolds, 1976,
    1984). Until recently there has been an imbalance in the understanding
    of educational problems which has emphasised matters of individual
    and family pathology and environmental deprivation and ignored the
    differences which clearly exist between schools and teachers in creating
    effective learning environments. Yet it is abundantly clear to parents,
    for example, that some schools are 'better' than others and it would be
    professionally dishonest to suggest that all teachers possessed an equally
    high level of teaching competence. If this is accepted then it is inap-
    propriate to focus all our attention on the individual pupil when trying
    to understand the difficulties that pupil is experiencing in school. We
    need to recognise the role which the school's academic and manage-
    ment systems might be playing in the generation of a learning or
    behaviour problem and to acknowledge the necessity to focus inter-
    vention sometimes on the teacher rather than the pupil.

THINKING IN TERMS OF SYSTEMS

Support for the argument that pupils' behaviour needs to be considered
in terms of its context has been provided by the development of theories
and practices of psychotherapy and counselling which emphasise the
interactional nature of behavioural patterns. Psychodynamic theorists and
practitioners (e.g. Brown and Pedder, 1979) and behaviourally oriented
writers (e.g. Wheldall and Glynn, 1989) have long emphasised the importance of interactions in the generation of emotional and behavioural
difficulties, as have humanistically oriented psychotherapists such as Rogers
(1951) who have been so influential in the development of counselling both
in schools and with adults.

   In spite of their recognition of the importance of interactions in the
development of problems the orientation of most of the traditional schools
of psychotherapy and counselling has primarily been with the individual.

However, in recent years alternative approaches have been developed which have a more direct focus on the systems of which the individual is part. This type of thinking has had a significant influence on the work of the educational psychologist (Campion, 1985) but the growth of family therapy represents a more complete application of systemic thinking and there now exists a substantive body of literature and research which demonstrates the efficacy of systemic approaches in the treatment of a wide range of psychiatric disorders and emotional and behavioural difficulties (see Burnham, 1986).

However, the application of these ideas in British schools in general, and in relation to school counselling in particular, has been slow. While American workers (Amatea, 1989; Molnar and Lindquist, 1989) have provided substantive evidence of their value in dealing with a wide range of school-based behaviour problems their use in Britain has been more limited. Nonetheless, good examples of their potential do exist. Family therapists working with educationalists (Dowling and Osborne, 1985) have illustrated the ways in which behaviour and learning difficulties in schools can be symptomatic of dysfunctions in the family system, the school system and in the family–school relationship system, and have provided good case study material to support the effectiveness of intervention based on systemic principles.

THE ECOSYSTEMIC APPROACH

A framework for the application of systemic thinking to the understanding and treatment of behaviour problems in schools has been provided by the development of what has come to be termed the ecosystemic approach. The principles of this approach have been enunciated by Upton and Cooper (1990) and Cooper and Upton (1990a), and its relevance to pastoral care and school counselling by Cooper and Upton (1990b), but its key components can be summarised as follows:

1   Problem behaviour in the classroom does not originate from within the individual who displays the behaviour, but from within the interaction between that individual and other individuals.
2   Interactional patterns may be conceptualised in simple or complex ways. A simple analysis is confined to here-and-now situations, and will define a student's negative behaviour in terms of the interactions in the classroom which immediately surround the behaviour. A complex analysis will take into account factors in the wider ecosystem and explore purposes which the here-and-now behaviour might serve in other, related ecosystems. Such an analysis may relate oppositional behaviour in the classroom to interactional patterns in the student's family or include broader considerations within the school.

3   The cause of any instance of problem behaviour is part of a cyclical chain of actions and reactions between participants. Each event in an interactional chain can be seen as both a cause of ensuing events and the effect of preceding events depending where we choose to 'punctuate' the chain. Furthermore, student classroom behaviour which is defined as 'problematic' is always goal directed and, from the student's viewpoint, it is understandable, rational and, above all, necessary. What appears problematic to the teacher may well be the solution to a problem for the student, for a subsystem in the classroom or school, or the student's family.

4   Intervention strategies must be based on a recognition of the contribution made to a problem situation by all participating parties in the interaction surrounding the problem. Thus, in a classroom the teacher and the other children in the class must be seen to contribute to the generation of the particular behaviour problem as much as the child or children concerned. Each is equally involved and each may thus be the focus of intervention.

The central focus of the approach is on understanding behaviour problems in schools in terms of the interactions of the persons involved, either within the school situation or in related contexts.

PUTTING THE ECOSYSTEMIC APPROACH INTO PRACTICE

For most teachers and in most schools thinking in terms of systems is not common primarily because it rejects the tendency to ascribe blame to individual pupils and puts in its place a model which necessitates a more balanced evaluation of the contributions made by all the people who 'contribute' to its occurrence. It is in keeping with the wealth of research evidence which illustrates the ways in which schools, individual teachers and families influence the behaviour and learning of pupils. But, clearly, such an approach can be threatening to teachers and parents in that it requires them to recognise that their influence on the pupil may be negative. This is something which neither teachers nor parents find easy. Great sensitivity is needed in introducing such a contextually oriented approach.

WORKING WITH COLLEAGUES

An ecosystemic analysis of conflict within schools invariably reveals individuals or groups pursuing different goals and ignoring, denying or opposing the validity of others' goals, with the results that opposition leads to entrenchment and continually escalating conflict. The ecosystemic solution to such conflict is to look for explanations which do not apportion blame or guilt and which lead to the development of cooperative relationships between the individuals concerned. Teachers, thus, need to be encouraged to develop an empathic understanding of pupils with whom they come into conflict, as a means of gaining a critical insight into their own behaviour. Empathy itself becomes a form of cooperation which, at once, is both disarming to a potential opponent as well as providing encouragement for an open and harmonious relationship. Equality and cooperation, however, do not always characterise relationships within schools or between schools and parents, and care needs to be taken when working with colleagues to avoid the approach as being seen as a threat to their status as teachers.

There are many specific ways in which such an approach can be applied in schools but a technique described by Molnar and Lindquist (1989) as 'reframing' illustrates clearly how such principles can be put into practice. This technique is based on four propositions which, in combination, can help colleagues move towards a balanced understanding of conflict in the classroom and the broader context of the school. These are:

1   In a conflict situation we behave in accordance with our interpretation of that situation.
2   There are often many different but equally valid interpretations of any given situation.
3   If we change our interpretation we can change our behaviour.
4   Change in our behaviour will influence the perceptions and behaviours of others, particularly if we break out of a pattern of behaviour which has become predictable.

To illustrate these ideas they use the example of a child repeatedly calling out answers in class. In this situation a common reaction of teachers is to consider the behaviour as inappropriate attention-seeking and to ignore it. The pupil's view can offer a very different perspective and it is conceivable, for example, as Molnar and Lindquist suggest, that children may call out because they believe that the teacher tends to ignore them. Such differing perceptions can lead to children and teachers becoming locked in a vicious circle of calling out and ignoring. In this type of situation reframing can be a simple and effective means of breaking the vicious circle that has developed. This would require the teacher to see the situation differently and on the basis of this perception to change his or her behaviour accordingly. Thus, if the teacher could be helped to re-interpret the student's calling out positively as reflecting involvement and interest, or perhaps as anxiety to please the teacher, rather than negative attention-seeking then the teacher may be able to evolve other ways of responding to the child than ignoring. Such a positive interpretation frees the teacher to initiate changes in the situation by behaving differently, which will, in due course, necessitate a change in the child's behaviour.

Such a strategy will not, of course, produce instant results. It will also need to be given time to work. The pupil will have to be convinced of the genuineness of the teacher's reframing, and be confident that this is not an example of teacher sarcasm or 'kidology'. Achieving this will require a willingness on the teacher's part to persevere beyond the initial trial of the method. It will also require a good understanding of the strategy and its underlying rationale and it will be necessary to consider specialist training for staff if such strategies are to be used effectively. It will in addition be necessary for at least one member of staff to have sufficient knowledge of the approach to act as consultant to other members of staff; a person who is highly skilled in ecosystemic analysis and who can function on a 'meta' level as consultant to both teachers and pupils. Consideration might also profitably be given to the development of a staff support group. Such a group can help facilitate alternative interpretations of problematic situations, especially those where the teacher is a key participant, and to provide help with determining intervention strategies as well as a source of encouragement for the continued exploration of the use of the approach.

If the approach is successful there can be far reaching consequences for the quality of the teacher–pupil relationships in a school, and these may evolve into a new found spirit of cooperation, with concomitantly positive effects on the quality of classroom relationships generally (see Molnar and Lindquist, 1989). Another important outcome is the influence such an approach has on the development of a reflective approach by teachers to their classroom practice. It is suggested that the type of self monitoring advocated here is as important as the pupil monitoring common in behavioural approaches to classroom disruption.

WORKING WITH PARENTS

The principles outlined above in relation to the use of the ecosystemic approach within schools can be readily transferred for use with parents and families. However, if attempts are to be made to work systemically with parents the general climate which exists in the school in relation to home–school relationships is vitally important. Since the Plowden Report recommended that all primary schools should have a programme for contact with children's homes the need for good parent–teacher relationships has been established in education. In special education the concept of 'parents as partners' was introduced in the Warnock Report, and more recently parents have been given significant rights in regard to their children's education under the 1991 Education Act and 1988 Education Reform Act. In practice, however, the rhetoric and reality are often far apart. While some schools operate an 'open door' policy and work hard to encourage parental interest and involvement others seem covertly (if not overtly) hostile to parents, especially with regards to parents whose children present learning and behavioural difficulties. The experience of this student teacher is unfortunately all too familiar:

> The teachers in her primary school used to gather at the staffroom window every morning, watching parents bring their children to school. They would make cutting remarks about how parents treated their children or how they dressed. They were particularly scathing about the parents of those who gave them the most trouble, those with learning or behaviour difficulties.
>
> (Sewell, 1986)

To engage in 'therapeutic' interaction with parents in this situation would clearly be extremely difficult. The task is not made any easier by a tendency, even in schools where more positive attitudes towards parents exist, for school/parent contact to be uni-directional (from school to parents) and primarily concerned with imparting information to parents rather than working with them in any real sense of partnership. At the same time, and in fairness to schools and teachers, it must also be acknowledged that it is often difficult for schools to make more than token contacts with parents because of the limited time which staff can realistically devote to this aspect of their work and the fact that, even in situations where an open door policy operates, contact with parents frequently focuses on the parents of the more able and the highly motivated, because the parents whom teachers really want to see simply don't respond to initiatives to involve them. Not all parents are willing (and able) to cooperate readily with the school. This is probably particularly true in relation to behavioural problems where the problem presented by the pupil in school may originate from family difficulties or differences in attitudes and values between the home and school.

The role of the consultant

When faced with problems where the family is seen as having a major responsibility for the generation and maintenance of a problem, either because of the existence of serious family conflict or where there is a strong element of parental–school conflict, it is advisable to utilise the skills of an expert consultant with teachers and school very much in the role of client. An example of the effective use of a consultant is provided by Power and Bartholomew (1985), who present a case study involving a student with learning and behaviour difficulties and in which parent–school enmity was a significant issue. After a period of sustained conflict between the school and family, a family therapist was brought in as a consultant. The therapist was able to develop an interpretation of the situation which the involvement of the teachers would have made it almost impossible for them to do.

In brief this 'meta' analysis suggested that while the teachers were concerned to overcome the pupil's learning difficulties, his parents appeared to be using their son's difficulties as a diversion from their marital problems. In their concern for their son's problems the parents were able to unite with one another and this helped to prevent marital break-up. As a result the parents had a vested interest in maintaining their son's difficulties and did so by opposing the school's efforts to solve their son's problems through, for instance, over-protectiveness and encouraging him not to complete homework assignments. Teachers at the school responded to what they saw as family collusion by being unsympathetic towards the student and making further demands upon him.

The family therapist saw this pattern of school–family interaction as being characterised by a pattern of symmetrical interaction, 'that is, one in which each party responds to what the other is doing in a similar way' whereby the parents and teachers were locked in constant competition for the dominant position. Thus, the teachers' suggestion that the student's school problems were related to family circumstances would be met by the counterclaim that the teachers were not working effectively. It is the nature of such relationships to escalate, leading to deeper entrenchment on both sides, with each party undermining the efforts made by the other to help the student. Ironically, the chief loser was, of course, the student.

Without assistance from an outsider a solution to the student's difficulties would seem unlikely to emerge from such a conflict. The consultant, however, was able to propose an intervention which sought to convert this symmetrical relationship into a more positive complementary relationship characterised by non-competitive interaction. The strategy which was devised was subtle and simple. To begin with the consultant persuaded the school staff to resist argument and to be compliant with the parents' views at the next meeting. When, during the meeting, the parents became hostile towards the school staff, the consultant took up the parental position and presented it in exaggerated form, suggesting that their son should be relieved of all pressure in class. Paradoxically, the parents resisted this and responded to it in a contradictory manner arguing that 'the teacher did have the right to place some expectations on the students in her class'. This was the point at which the staff and parents were in agreement for the first time. The deadlock was broken and an opportunity to develop a collaborative relationship was established.

The eventual outcome of the case was that the parents and the school staff agreed to recognise the primacy of each other in their respective domains. The teachers agreed not to pressure the student in class and, instead of setting specific homework tasks in addition to classwork, they agreed to allow him to take uncompleted classwork home. Further, it was agreed that whether he completed the tasks at home was a matter for the parents to decide and the school would simply award the appropriate grade without placing any pressure on the student. By allowing the student to take classwork home, the school was enabling the parents to control the pressure which was placed on their son. This newly collaborative relationship between the school and the family also led to their accepting advice from a psychologist on aiding their son with stress management. Thus, the student's therapeutic needs were met, as were the parents' needs for a collaborative activity with one another (i.e. as a diversion from their marital difficulties) and the school's position was also validated.

To some extent the reason why consultants can be effective in situations such as this is partly explained by the opportunity which their position as outsider provides for them to obtain a meta–perspective of the situation. But it also clearly depends on their therapeutic skill and there are clearly dangers for schools in embarking on such work with parents without appropriate support.

Teachers working independently

For the most part, learning and behaviour problems do not involve a high degree of family pathology and there are many situations in schools when teachers can work within a systemic framework with parents supported either by a specially trained member of staff or within the context of a peer support group.

There are many features of practice in schools which involve interaction between teachers and parents and it is possible to utilise these to devise practicable ways in which teachers can work therapeutically with parents.

1   In responding to learning and behavioural difficulties schools commonly invite parents to come to the school to discuss problems but such contact can be initiated by the parents. Often the session is conducted solely by a single member of staff but the involvement of teachers and staff external to the school, such as social workers and educational psychologists, is common. The value of this approach is that it requires limited resources, it can be initiated quickly by parents or school staff, it brings the parents into the school and can facilitate the school and parents working together in quite intensive ways. It does, however, have disadvantages. Parents can feel unequal on school territory and feel that they have been victimised/singled out for special treatment. Often, too, only the mother can come during school hours and travelling to school can create problems for some parents.

2   In some schools staff take on part of the traditional role of the social worker and visit children's homes to work with parents. This is

sometimes formalised with the appointment of a teacher-social worker. The advantages of this are that the interaction takes place on the parents' territory and can result in them feeling more at ease and more willing to enter into meaningful dialogue. It also allows the teacher to see something of the child's behaviour at home and gain some direct insight into actual home conditions, which knowledge can be used to facilitate the development of programmes to use at home based on advice from the school. On the negative side it is not always practical in terms of the demands it makes on school staffing and the special skills which staff should have to undertake this work.

3 A variation on the idea of school staff visiting the homes of individual children is for groups of parents who live close to one another to meet with school staff on a regular basis as a discussion group. Issues of general concern can be dealt with effectively in this way and if a positive group atmosphere is generated specific issues related to individual children and families can also be addressed. The fact that the interaction takes place on the parents' territory is a positive feature of this way of work, but more important perhaps is the way in which it fosters the sharing of problems between parents. Some parents can gain enormous confidence from working in a group and can establish a more equal relationship with school staff than they might otherwise be able to do. Such groups can also foster relationships between parents and generate an ethos of self-help and the shared solution of problems. Unsocial hours for school staff can be a problem and parents may easily opt out while careful leadership is needed to ensure that sessions do not degenerate into aimless chat sessions.

4 Teaching/learning workshops for parents can be organised to focus on specific issues such as behavioural management, reading, or play activities. There are many ways in which workshops can be organised but commonly parents come to school for a pre-determined number of sessions in which they participate in a structured teaching programme. These are usually conducted out of school hours but if conducted in school time have the added advantage of involvement of the children. Ideally staff participate alongside the parents to ensure home and school are working in the same direction. A particular benefit of these activities is that they provide parents with advice and guidance. The didactic nature of the activities and the fact that they involve group activity can also foster feelings of security and paradoxically allow parents to share problems more directly than they might be willing to do when that is a more explicit expectation of the group.

5 A Home/School diary which travels with the child from home to school has been found by many schools to provide a valuable means of communication between parents and teachers. In this way teachers and parents can cooperate on specific activities, teachers can keep parents informed

of progress in school, and parents can keep school informed of events at home.

6   Formal events such as open days and parent evenings are intended to provide an opportunity to keep parents informed of academic and behavioural progress of their children and do not provide extended opportunities for in-depth dialogue. However, they can be used to raise and share issues of concern, in a situation where parents do not feel singled out for special attention. Similarly, parent–teacher organisations provide a non-threatening arena in which problems can be aired. Many teachers are already aware of the therapeutic potential of the relatively informal parental contact which these situations provide but therapeutic gain does not occur by chance and if such situations are to be fully exploited careful thought and planning must go into the way in which issues are broached and care taken to present a balanced view of the issues involved.

The child's involvement

Children can easily come to suspect some sort of conspiracy if parents and teachers are seen to be working closely without permitting the child any involvement in meetings that take place. Within a systemic framework the child's involvement is highly desirable if not essential and careful thought must be given, whatever model for working with parents is adopted, to the feelings and possible involvement of the child in that process.

CONCLUSION

In advocating the importance of an approach which conceptualises school-based problems in terms of their context it is important not to underestimate the challenge which this presents to current thinking and practice. Systemic approaches involve a fundamentally different understanding of behaviour problems in schools which deny schools and teachers the possibility of locating problems in behaviour and learning entirely within the individual pupil. While recognising the role which the context of the home may play in the generation of problematic behaviour may not be too difficult for schools, to accept the need to recognise the role which teachers can play in the generation and maintenance of behaviour problems, and the need to face the possibility that intervention must focus sometimes on the teacher rather than the pupil, may be more unpalatable.

Any attempt to view behaviour or learning problems in context requires teachers to be analytic of their own behaviour and to recognise the perceptions of those with whom they might be in conflict. In this sense approaches such as the ecosystemic approach have, as Tyler (1992) argues, much in common with humanistic approaches to education and counselling which stress the need for teachers to exercise qualities of empathy and foster the development of self-esteem, autonomy and self-direction in their pupils. Such approaches are, thus, far more than strategies for responding to problematic behaviour or under-achievement in that they enrich the teachers' understanding of their interactions with pupils, parents and colleagues which form the core of educational experience. Equally, the emphasis which must be placed on multiple perceptions of events when trying to understand them in their context has important effects for school management structures in that it underlines the value of cooperation among staff and the support that staff can provide for one another in coping with the demands of teaching.

If schools can be encouraged to view problems more in terms of their context, there would seem to be great potential benefit not only in terms of the management and amelioration of behaviour and learning difficulties but also in the development of a more generally cooperative and supportive climate within schools and between the schools and parents. Such approaches have the potential to provide teachers and schools with an armoury of techniques with which to respond to a wide range of problems and help make schools more effective for all.

BIBLIOGRAPHY

Amatea, E.S. (1989) *Brief Strategic Intervention for School Behaviour Problems*. San Francisco: Jossey-Bass.

Brown, D. and Pedder, J. (1979) *Introduction to Psychotherapy*. London: Tavistock.

Burnham, J.B. (1986) *Family Therapy: First Steps Towards a Systemic Approach*. London: Tavistock.

Campion, J. (1985) *The Child in Context: Family Systems Theory in Educational Psychology*. London: Methuen.

Cooper, P. and Upton, G. (1990a) 'An ecosystemic approach to emotion and behaviour in schools'. *Educational Psychology*, 10, 4, pp. 301–23.

Cooper, P. and Upton, G. (1990b) 'Turning conflict into co-operation: an ecosystemic approach to interpersonal conflict and its relevance to pastoral care in schools'. *Pastoral Care in Education*, 8, 4, pp. 10–15.

Dowling, E. and Osborne, D. (1985) *The Family and the School: A Joint Systems Approach to Problems with Children*. London: Routledge.

Hall, N. (1992) 'Psychological and Health Related Problems', in R. Gulliford and G. Upton (eds) *Special Educational Needs*. London: Routledge.

Hamblin, D. (1978) *The Teacher and Counselling*. Oxford: Basil Blackwell.

Molnar, A. and Lindquist, B. (1989) *Changing Problem Behaviour in Schools*. New York: Jossey-Bass.

Power, T. and Bartholomew, K. (1985) 'Getting uncaught in the middle: a case study in family–school system consultation'. *School Psychology Review*, 14, 2, pp. 222–9.

Reynolds, D. (1976) 'The delinquent school', in M. Hammersley and P. Woods (eds) *The Process of Schooling*. Milton Keynes: The Open University.

Reynolds, D. (1984) 'The school for vandals: a sociological portrait of the disaffection prone school', in N. Frude and H. Gault (eds) *Disruptive Behaviour in Schools*. Chichester: Wiley.

Rogers, C. (1951) *Client Centred Therapy*, Boston: Houghton Mifflin.

Rutter, M., Maugham, B., Mortimore, P. and Ouston, J. (1979) *Fifteen Thousand Hours: Secondary Schools and their Effects on Children*. London: Open Books.

Sewell, G. (1986) *Coping with Special Needs*. London: Croom Helm.

Tyler, K. (1992) 'The Development of the Ecosystemic Approach as a Humanistic Education Psychology'. *Educational Psychology*, 12, 1, pp. 15–24.

Upton, G. and Cooper, P. (1990) 'A new perspective on behaviour problems in schools: the ecosystemic approach'. *Maladjustment and Therapeutic Education*, 8, 1, pp. 3–18.

Wheldall, K. and Glynn, T. (1989) *Effective Classroom Learning*. London: Blackwell.

Chapter 17

Impartiality in adult guidance

A Scottish study

Graham Connelly

INTRODUCTION

An important aim of adult guidance practitioners is to provide guidance
that is impartial and not unduly influenced by the needs of any particular
provider to recruit students or trainees. Neutrality of guidance has emerged
as a strong theme in identifying characteristics of professionalism amongst
workers in a relatively new discipline. This chapter explores the complex
nature of impartiality in the practice of adult guidance, with reference to
an empirical study of the work of practitioners in Scotland in the mid
1990s (Connelly *et al.*, 1996).

IMPARTIALITY AS A PRINCIPLE IN ADULT GUIDANCE

The words 'impartial' and 'impartiality' – meaning 'unprejudiced' or 'fair'
or 'equal treatment' – appear in a number of important policy documents
and research reports. The Institute of Careers Guidance and the National
Association for Educational Guidance for Adults published a joint statement known as A *Guidance Entitlement for Adults*, in which they said that
guidance should 'be independent of the interests of any supporting agency
or institution', and 'be delivered by trained advisers whose competence and
impartiality can be proven' (ICG/NAEGA, 1992). The National Advisory
Council for Careers and Educational Guidance includes impartiality in its
'code of principles' and says providers should 'declare factors which might
limit the impartiality of the guidance offered to the individual' (NACCEG,
1996). The impression given by these statements is of impartiality in guidance regarded as synonymous with 'client-centred' behaviour.

Guidance professionals highlight impartiality as a basic principle
governing their practice. The importance of workers giving clients impartial guidance, not influenced by recruitment targets for courses, is stressed
in practitioners' statements of good practice. The value base of these codes

tends to be strongly 'person-centred'. Guidance and learning support services have progressed in recent years and changes have been happening against a background of increasing competition between course providers and sophisticated marketing in the post-school sector. This has raised concerns about loss of impartiality. The political climate of Scotland in the mid 1990s, with incorporated colleges, the reorganisation of local government into smaller authorities and threats to community education funding, created great uncertainties within the organisational structures of guidance, unsettling the professional ethos of workers, who feared the loss, potential or otherwise, of impartiality.

Guidance workers are concerned that collaborative work supporting impartial guidance, might in future be more difficult to maintain as a result of market pressures. For example, college guidance staff experience conflicts between their advisory and recruitment functions. Munn *et al.* (1993) found evidence of adults being recruited to inappropriate courses in colleges, apparently unduly influenced by course managers' concerns to attract funding. They concluded that: 'The diversity of opportunities can bewilder and confuse adult students so it is important that nationally and regionally co-ordinated services offering impartial guidance are available' (p. 5).

The professional culture of workers has changed significantly. College managers discuss how guidance responsibilities should be shared between lecturers and specialist counsellors. Careers officers, typically styled as independent, 'honest brokers', have been recruited to work in colleges and assigned to Local Enterprise Company (LEC) projects where their impartiality is less clear. Community education workers have found a wider role supporting adults in their first tentative steps in education and need to give detailed impartial advice about progression opportunities.

There is support for the view that impartiality is a principle that guidance providers aspire to, but which may be compromised by the political, economic and institutional culture within which services operate, as well as by poorly developed networks and inadequately trained staff. The research project upon which this chapter is based was concerned with the way impartiality is perceived by practitioners, including the influences on workers attempting to provide an impartial service to clients.

EXPLORING THE COMPLEXITIES OF IMPARTIAL PRACTICE

The meanings which practitioners place upon their day to day experiences with adults in guidance are of great interest, as are the constraints and opportunities affecting impartial behaviour within different agencies, and those which derive from personal-professional belief systems and exposure to professional training. During 1995 a research team from the

University of Strathclyde and The Open University conducted an exploratory seminar on impartiality with experienced adult guidance practitioners in Scotland. The seminar highlighted issues – such as the blurred distinction between guidance and selection – which were then followed up in lengthy interviews with twelve experienced workers representing different practice settings. The key issues emerging from a review of these interviews are now discussed from the different perspectives of workers, providers and clients.

The workers' perspective

Most interviewees, asked about their understanding of impartiality, referred to ideals commonly listed in guidance charters and mission statements. Examples include helping people to reach informed decisions about their future, based on gathering together information about a range of options and giving unbiased information not linked to the needs of one provider or the worker's own livelihood. A careers officer described her work as 'trying to guide a client through all the aspects and avenues'. She aimed to 'try and raise the questions for them in the sense of helping themselves look at issues, all brought together by helping that person make their own decision without ourselves colouring it.'

The perceived meaning of impartiality changes according to the different contexts in which guidance is offered. Careers officers, for example, tend to hold a view of impartiality as determined by three characteristics inherent in their service. First, they are not direct providers of courses or jobs and therefore have no recruitment targets to meet. Second, they have access to comprehensive sources of information about occupations and educational opportunities. And third, they have typically experienced training grounded in the person-centred approach in working with clients. In practice there are complicating factors affecting this rather neat view of impartiality in guidance. Despite having access to extensive information, careers officers know more about some opportunities than others, or have formed favourable views from their relationships with one provider compared to another.

Community education staff and workers in voluntary adult education and guidance projects tend to speak about impartiality in terms of 'empowering' adults to evaluate information from a range of different sources. Often this is a gradual process, developing out of an educational experience itself. 'You are working with them so that they are enabled to make the choices or come to the decisions that will suit them for their future direction.' Workers typically describe the satisfaction which comes from ideas about progression or the suitability of particular courses of action arising naturally as a result of participation – guidance embedded within a programme, rather than a 'bolt-on' extra. They worry about not being able to provide adequate information and being extremely limited in the amount of time they can give to individual participants.

Guidance staff in FE colleges encounter factors limiting their ability to give impartial guidance, such as pressure to fill courses: 'We are selling our courses, that's the dilemma'. The distinction between *internal* and *external* impartiality is another important consideration in the college setting. Staff striving for good practice in guidance could guarantee to give factual information about competing courses *within* their college, and to treat all students with the same degree of respect. Loyalty to the employing institution makes it difficult, or unreasonable, to expect guidance staff to recommend competitors' courses or to encourage potential students to consider other options – at least at the pre-entry stage. Payne and Edwards (1996), in a study of impartiality in guidance in three London colleges, noted concerns among workers which went beyond the usual worries about the quality of interpersonal transactions. The researchers identified three areas of tension – access, process and outcomes – exemplified in the following questions.

- do all the students and potential students coming to a college have fair access to guidance?
- are initial guidance interviews conducted in such a way as to ensure impartiality?
- can impartiality be demonstrated in the outcomes of initial guidance interviews?

(Payne and Edwards, 1996: 19)

The work shows that the answers to these questions are rather complex.

In each case they place question marks around the centrality of impartiality as feasible in current guidance practice in colleges. More importantly, they also raise questions about the desirability of impartiality as a universal principle in the provision of guidance.

(Payne and Edwards, 1996: 19)

There are two situations, however, when it appears to be easier for college staff to be impartial by giving information about opportunities available elsewhere. First, if it emerges that an enquirer is seeking a course not available in the guidance worker's own college, then other options could be legitimately raised. Second, at the pre-exit stage a range of progression opportunities could be discussed. However, even then, the increasing tendency to provide higher level courses in further education means colleges understandably wish to develop an internal market and encourage students to remain within their current institution.

Workers in different work settings tend to have different professional identities. Careers officers see themselves as 'honest brokers' who can more easily 'put the client first'. This is true, to a lesser extent, of community education staff, proud of their role in general confidence-building and awareness-raising with adults returning to education. College staff are seen as the villains of the piece, apparently interested mainly, in steering enquirers to their own courses, even if a more suitable alternative is available elsewhere.

Marketing activities by colleges may be more influential with prospective students than the careful ministrations of trained guidance workers, because the information is accessible and immediate. The research uncovered cases of adult clients talked into unsuitable courses and of FE staff who were not guidance specialists (e.g. heads of subject departments) vigorously recruiting students into their own programmes. FE guidance staff could relate experiences of their own attempts to offer an impartial service being frustrated by colleagues' overriding concern with recruitment. Interviewees told 'horror stories' of the partial advice of others, motivated apparently by self-interest. Practitioners seem to define their own practices in relation to the perceived partiality of guidance provided elsewhere. This suggests a possible lack of critical reflectivity in relation to their own practices.

Joint training of workers suggests that no single group can justifiably claim the moral high ground in relation to impartiality. As one of our interviewees said 'you might have very laudable ethics . . . but it's only as impartial as the information you have, so you might just have a very incomplete picture and be offering it impartially.' Only by acknowledging their limitations can guidance workers provide a more honest service.

Stresses occur where guidance workers reconcile two apparently contradictory sets of beliefs, for example, where there is a professional obligation to be 'client-centred' while working in an organisation with different motivations. A careers officer in the information centre of an FE college felt obliged to direct enquirers to the best available educational provision, yet she was aware that her employers assumed her function was to entice students into the most appropriate course *within that college*. While this did not always represent a conflict, it did so sufficiently often to cause considerable negative feelings about the college and about her situation.

Experienced careers officers who move to employment in FE colleges are likely to retain their external professional links and remain active in professional associations. These links are likely to be particularly important in providing support where there are tensions between adult guidance staff and department-based selectors. Similar support can come from formal guidance networks.

The experience of conflict is affected by the guidance worker's position within either the formal or informal power structure of the organisation. Where guidance workers are relatively junior members of staff, or where they have few allies in more powerful positions, they appear likely to experience more difficulties in operating impartially. Conversely, the support of senior management is important in maintaining good guidance practice.

The providers' perspective

Guidance agencies may fall short of their obligations to behave impartially towards clients due to deliberate action (protectionism), practical constraints (e.g. inadequate time and resources), and lack of awareness or limited knowledge (e.g. failure to refer). There may be nothing wrong with college managers expecting guidance staff to provide information solely about courses in their own colleges. Community education workers or staff of training organisations may feel under pressure to meet targets or fulfil quotas by encouraging clients towards their own provision. The research uncovered a climate of concern within FE colleges about the effect of student recruitment on staffing. Interviewees were acutely aware that a good guidance service could give a prospective student a favourable impression of the institution.

While there is no simple relationship between resources and impartial guidance, a guidance worker pressed for time may find this a restriction in providing a complete service. These demands are felt most by lecturers and community education workers for whom guidance is one aspect of a multiplicity of roles. They are concerned about being partial in the sense that they provide guidance 'on the hoof', rather than in a more considered, planned fashion.

It is unrealistic to expect guidance staff employed by one education or training provider to have comprehensive information or to be personally as well informed about the courses of competitor organisations. This is not to say that a full knowledge base is a sufficient condition for impartial guidance. While it helps to know something about opportunities elsewhere, that wider knowledge cannot guarantee impartiality or client-centredness in the absence of an organisational agreement about the importance of sharing information with the client. Networking has an important part to play and referral is rightly identified as a key professional competence of guidance staff. Referral is much more likely to occur in situations where guidance workers know that their own organisation has nothing to offer the client.

All the interviewees in our study were trained in adult guidance, and most were either undertaking or had completed advanced training. They provided accounts of poor or incomplete guidance by other workers lacking specialist training. It is simplistic to suggest that partial guidance is related, in whole or part, to a lack of training. Trained workers regard impartiality as an important principle. However, that belief in itself cannot protect against students being recruited onto courses without being encouraged to consider alternatives. There is a persuasive argument that FE colleges will give impartial guidance where it is in their interests to do so, for example, to meet the requirements of external audit of guidance or to reduce drop-out.

The research suggested agencies not providing education or training opportunities seem to perceive fewer conflicts in relation to giving impartial guidance. There are operational differences between different sectors where guidance staff work affecting how impartiality is perceived and defined. The extent to which impartiality is seen as problematic also varies between sectors. Careers officers feel that, almost by definition, their practice is impartial. This confidence can be related to professional training and occupational socialisation, but also to more tangible factors such as a generous supply of information and the fact that careers officers are not usually themselves providers of education or training.

In reality careers officers quite properly 'filter' or 'select' the information they offer to clients and this selection process is based on judgements both about opportunities and about clients. This raises questions about the basis of assessment and selection and the importance of making explicit the criteria used in that process.

A voluntary agency worker told us that she recommended courses in a particular college because she had received good feedback from past clients and furthermore she had invested time in developing close professional relationships with college staff. She was aware that preferment ran counter to values she considered important – and indeed differed from the general advice given to prospective students to 'shop around' and evaluate a range of possibilities – but rationalised this tension on the basis that adult learners benefited from her good relations with the college. Many such preferential arrangements exist, where it is almost understood that adult learners completing a community-based course and wishing to progress will enrol on courses in the local college. Further, it is only in the larger urban areas that there is any real choice of provider for many adults who need to study close to their domestic commitments.

The clients' perspective

Guidance that is clinically impartial, objective and free from opinion, may not always be perceived by clients as being in their best interests, and, indeed, adults may expect a more judgemental approach from professional advisers. Several interviewees argued that impartial guidance was not necessarily what the client expected or wanted. If clients choose to visit an FE college for information and guidance about courses of study, they are unlikely to expect to be given details of courses on offer at another college. According to this viewpoint, supplying 'impartial' guidance has the potential for both puzzling and irritating the enquirer.

The equation of 'impartiality' with 'client-centredness' is not unproblematic. Providing the most beneficial service to the client may well involve being 'partial', based on the guidance practitioner's experience and understanding of the relative strengths and weaknesses of different service providers. A worker in an FE college described a situation involving his own son who had obtained an HND place in a college; the young person consulted a careers officer, who told him he should cancel the place and take time out to think more deeply about his future. The parent was grateful, aware that his son was uncertain about his choice. The worker was certainly directive, probably partial, but arguably client-centred. In other words the neutrality implied by a non-directive approach to adult guidance is often the method of choice, but there is a danger of the client being placed at a disadvantage against clever marketing and lack of clarity about personal interests and motivations.

Clients for pre-entry guidance often arrive for appointments having previously gained highly subjective, partial information from personal contacts. Our fieldwork suggests workers rarely meet clients totally devoid of any preconceptions about the opportunities open to them. The encounter with a guidance worker commonly takes place a reasonable distance along a path which may have begun with vague feelings that life has more to offer, has progressed through discussions with family and friends, and may have involved earlier encounters with other agencies. In these circumstances it is unlikely that guidance workers will give equal weight to every option. Rather they may encourage clients to consider alternatives to those already identified, in order to ensure that decisions are taken thoughtfully and based on adequate information. In other words, they are partial in their guidance as a counterbalance to the partial information previously offered to the client.

It is dangerous for adult guidance workers to assume that information from family, friends, the media and press is necessarily partial and possibly prejudiced, while their own approach is totally impartial. The bind is friends and family may have a better prospect of knowing the advice-seeker well. Careers officers and pre-entry guidance staff in colleges are disadvantaged by not knowing the client, and being dependent on information given at interview. Careers officers routinely follow up interviews with written summaries, including suggestions and information based on further consideration or research. Community education workers and other on-programme guidance staff can develop relationships with students, which is helpful in tailoring guidance to individual needs.

Workers speak of concerns about 'leading' or unduly influencing clients in a particular direction. Their unease seems to be consistent with a desire to operate in a client-centred way, by first building a relationship and undertaking subsequent guidance activities within the context of better understanding of the client's needs and interests. Community education workers and FE lecturers advising students they teach, speak of the satisfaction that this deeper knowledge of the person can bring to their guidance work. Careers officers can feel under pressure to come to some conclusions within the time constraints of an interview, particularly as they work to targets expressed in terms of the number of clients seen.

Unequal power relationships between guidance worker and client may militate against impartial behaviour. A degree of equality in the contractual relationship between lecturer/worker and adult learner is necessary to offer a good guidance service. One view of impartiality is that it involves objectivity achieved by attention to the facts available from a client's referral documentation and by interview, and also the possible use of psychometric tests. This view of the worker seems to put the professional in a position of power, directing the transaction by requesting personal information, issuing forms to be completed, structuring the interview and defining the guidance process. Concerns about inequality between worker and client are expressed by community education workers, who see guidance as an integral part of the tutorial relationship and not 'tagged-on'. Guidance, in this sense, becomes an educational process.

Considerable experience in providing guidance for adults in vocational and educational aspects of their lives, combined with access to extensive resources and local information and contacts, is an important characteristic of professional competence. Perhaps it is too simplistic to say that adult clients approach guidance relationships meekly, but rather they expect professionals to be considerably more knowledgeable than themselves. As one worker put it: 'If they have poor decision-making skills, then they really want you to narrow the options for them.' What is clearly important is the client's confidence in their own aspirations, the ability to express these clearly and to guard against being 'nudged' in a particular direction due to the limited range of opportunities being suggested.

One important aspect of impartiality concerns the perceived obligation to be impartial between clients – not to discriminate between them in the delivery of the guidance service. An interviewee, working for an organisation employing large numbers of volunteer advice workers, said that a major part of induction training for volunteers was concerned with the need to overcome prejudices and to attempt to provide equal treatment for all clients. If the job of the guidance worker is seen as 'matching' clients with opportunities and vice versa, then impartiality between clients is as important as impartiality between providers. Workers should approach both clients and opportunities without prejudice. It's not about treating people the same. People don't need to be treated the same; they don't want to be treated the same. To provide fair and equal guidance may involve treating people differently to take account of issues such as class, gender, race and ability.

IMPLICATIONS OF THE ISSUES FOR ADULT GUIDANCE PRACTICE

The research uncovered considerable fears about the supposedly deleterious impact of marketing approaches within further education following 'incorporation' of FE colleges. These fears were expressed by college guidance practitioners concerned that their ability to remain relatively independent of funding and recruitment considerations might be threatened. Fears were also expressed by careers officers and community education staff, highly critical of colleges for putting recruitment before individual needs. Subsequent discussions indicate that this is a very complex issue. One effect of a market approach in FE management is that colleges tailor their courses to match demand. In one sense this is liberating – and also exactly what community educators say they do – meeting expressed local needs. On the other hand, courses have to be cost-effective and this may have the effect of narrowing the choice of provision, limiting the extent to which a full range of local needs can be met. This might be a smaller problem in urban areas where competitor colleges can agree a certain amount of specialisation, though this would reduce any advantages for potential students in having a choice of provider.

FE colleges now control their own finances, but are also responsible to their employees and to the wider community to remain viable. In terms of provision of a service to students there have been both gains and losses. Educationists often speak of marketing pejoratively, but some of our contacts have commented that reaching out more effectively to students through advertising, paying careful attention to the design of course information and providing permanently staffed drop-in advice centres can help to make colleges more 'client-centred', one definition of impartial guidance.

Adult guidance workers face similar difficulties where they are aware of differences in quality between providers. A common response is to brief the client on how to interrogate the education/training provider. One interviewee said he might use this form of words 'All I can suggest to you is that you go and ask some searching questions, like, What am I getting for my money? What happened to the last batch of trainees that went through that process? Can you name one organisation that respects the bit of paper you get at the end of the course?' It is doubtful whether the experience of conflicts between workers' responsibilities to clients and loyalty to their employers is an entirely new situation.

Impartiality is given prominence in guidance charters; it is clearly important to workers, but is it important to clients? It seems to depend on the circumstances. Impartiality as a crucial principle of adult guidance is sustained by workers being able to point to its absence in the practice of other agencies. This cannot be an entirely satisfactory justification. The notion of impartiality as client-centredness is seen in its most positive expression where community workers engage in a partnership with clients to explore options. However, the call for FE colleges to provide this kind of impartial service in their advice centres may be both unrealistic and misplaced in its assumption of client vulnerability. It is surely unlikely that clients walking into a college expect to receive information about courses elsewhere. Impartiality in particular settings may therefore work against the clients' expectations and interests. The Guidance Council, an independent body set up in 1994 to advise professionals and employers working in adult guidance, has drawn attention to the need for providers to declare factors which can limit the impartiality of the guidance offered to clients. This principle is an important element in the council's quality standards which were being piloted at the time of writing (Hawthorn 1995; NACCEG, 1996).

Course providers have an arguable right to expect that information about courses in different institutions are given equal prominence, leaving potential students to weigh up the advantages and disadvantages attached to each option. Some projects develop preferential relationships with a particular provider, giving considerable advantages to adult learners, but also limiting choice and denying potential students to other institutions. In reality, however, these monopolies often occur where there is only one local provider and travel to another would be impractical for most clients.

CONCLUSION

Adult guidance practitioners are concerned about their obligations to give impartial guidance. Some have given careful thought to both the importance of impartiality and to its practical applications. These practitioners are aware that being impartial in respect of the different options available could bring them into conflict with other parts of their organisations, or other aspects of their roles. Being 'client-centred' and being 'impartial' are not necessarily the same thing. Clients may come for guidance with their own prejudices, which will require to be addressed. Impartial guidance does not simply consist in supplying clients with as much information as possible.

Being impartial can have more to do with the nature of the worker–client interaction than with the supply of information available. Impartial guidance might involve equipping clients with *questions* to ask opportunity providers. Rather than engage in a fluitless pursuit of 'perfect impartiality', perhaps guidance practitioners should content themselves with a commitment to declare openly the limitations of their ability to provide a completely full and impartial service, a kind of guidance 'health warning'. The assumption that because workers feel impartiality in guidance is a good thing it will happen cannot be sustained. 'Perfect impartiality' is often unattainable for good practical reasons. Feelings amongst practitioners about the importance of impartiality in adult guidance are sustained by the view that others behave partially; this view is unfair because it is based on rather simplistic assumptions about transactions between clients and workers. The view that impartiality is compromised simply by the arrival of new market principles in post-school education is also not entirely supported.

BIBLIOGRAPHY

Blair, A., McPake, J. and Munn, P. (1993) *Facing Goliath: Adults' Experiences of Participation, Guidance and Progression in Education*. Edinburgh: SCRE.

Connelly, G., Milburn, T., Thomson, S. and Edwards, R. (1996) *Impartiality in Adult Guidance: A Scottish Study*. Milton Keynes: The Open University.

Edwards, R. (1990) *Understanding Guidance Practices: Some Critical Thoughts*, Occasional Paper No 16. Wolverhampton: NAEGS.

Hawthorn, R. (1995) *First Steps – a Quality Standards framework for Guidance across all sectors*. London: The Guidance Council/NACCEG/RSA.

ICG/NAEGA (1992) *A Guidance Entitlement for Adults*. Institute of Careers Guidance/National Association for Educational Guidance for Adults.

Lowden, K. and Powney, J. (1993) *Where Do We Go From Here? Adult Educational Guidance in Scotland*. Edinburgh: SCRE.

Munn, P., Tett, L. and Arney, N. (1993) *Negotiating the Labyrinth: Progression Opportunities for Adult Learners*. Edinburgh: SCRE.

NACCEG (1996) *Guidance Code of Principles*. London: NACCEG/RSA.

Payne, J. and Edwards, R. (1996) *Impartiality and the Self in Guidance: A Report on Three London Colleges*. Milton Keynes: The Open University/The National Association for Educational Guidance for Adults.

SOED (1992) *Staying on Course: Student Guidance in Scottish Further Education Colleges*. Edinburgh: The Scottish Office.

SOEID (1995) *Circular No: (FE) 21/95*. Edinburgh: The Scottish Office.

SOEID (1997) *Lifelong Learning: Summary of Responses to Public Consultation*. Edinburgh: The Scottish Office.

UDACE (1986) *The Challenge of Change: Developing Educational Guidance for Adults*. Leicester: National Institute of Adult Continuing Education.

Watts, A.G., Dartois, C. and Plant, P. (1988) *Educational and Vocational Guidance Services for 14–25 age group in the European Community*. Brussels: Commission of the European Communities.

Chapter 18

Guidance in the workplace

Principles under pressure

Roger Harrison

INTRODUCTION

In the UK, and in many other countries, the 1990s have seen dramatic changes both in the significance attached to adult learning, and in the diversity of contexts in which learning is recognised. Learning has become an essential means of survival in a 'learning society' where individuals are expected to act as self-reliant subjects, taking responsibility for the management of their own learning and development. Nowhere has this been more evident than in the workplace, as changes in the organisation of work and production are held to demand an ever increasing mobilisation of the cognitive and affective resources of workers and work-seekers. The workplace itself has become a powerful learning environment, informed by the concept of the 'learning organisation', in which employers, educators and workers engage in new forms of relationship, exemplified by the growth of Employee Development Programmes (EDPs). The position of guidance as a 'neutral' process, and the role of the guidance practitioner as an 'impartial' intermediary, become problematic in this new context, as a more diverse range of interests and loyalties come into play.

This chapter will draw on research undertaken by the author into one particular EDP (Harrison, 1997) to examine some of the tensions and ambiguities which emerge when the practices of guidance are displaced from the formal educational context in which they were developed, and introduced into an EDP. The fieldwork for this study took place during the summer of 1996, focusing on a large industrial employer which had been running an EDP for three years. The employer is not identified by name, and will be referred to as 'the Company'. The programme was organised from within the Company by an office which provided advice and guidance, as well as procuring learning opportunities in the form of computer-based self instructional packages, and tutor-led courses. This office is referred to as 'the Centre'. The research consisted of analysis of documentary material provided by the Company, together with semi-structured, recorded interviews with Centre staff, employee-participants, and one member of the Steering Group who was external to the Company.

The chapter will first contextualise EDPs, locating them within a wider discourse of lifelong learning; briefly describe the programme which provides the subject for this study, and then draw on material from the research to illustrate how current notions of guidance come under pressure when operating within this context.

EMPLOYEE DEVELOPMENT PROGRAMMES

Over the past decade there has been a growing interest in the concept of work-based EDPs, especially among large employers in both the public and private sectors. Their broad aims have been defined as:

> to encourage a wider learning culture within organisations, a culture which goes well beyond the provision of job-related training and the training plans for companies.
>
> (Corney, 1995: 1)

They have been associated with a human resource management approach which views employees as an investment rather than a cost. The development of a learning culture within the organisation then becomes part of a business strategy, linked with greater productivity and profitability.

> These initiatives (EDPs) are not simply benevolent gestures but sound business strategies to help to develop a workforce able and willing to respond to change, and capable of adapting and learning, rather than being limited by the boundaries of existing skills.
>
> (Metcalf, 1992: Introduction)

EDPs are presented as a deliberate move away from a traditional approach to training, characterised as narrowly instrumental and management-led, towards a more broadly-based, negotiated and person-centred approach, with the aim of promoting individual personal development as part of company culture (Metcalf, 1992; Forrester et al., 1995; Payne, 1996). They sit comfortably within the rhetoric of the 'learning organisation', in which individual learning is presented as a key strategy for managing change in a market economy where change is characterised as rapid and unpredictable (Argyris and Schon, 1978; Pedler et al., 1991; Dixon, 1994). The notion of training is displaced by the notion of learning, conceived as an activity initiated by individual workers which becomes the means by which the organisation 'continuously transforms itself' (Pedler et al., 1991: 2). Within this discourse new roles and subject positions are established, with individual workers being constituted as autonomous, enterprising learners, responsible for seeking out education and training opportunities. For instance, the Confederation of British Industry (CBI), representing mainly large industrial employers, described its ideal workforce in these terms, 'The CBI's vision is of individuals who are motivated to learn through life and who take responsibility for their own development' (CBI, 1994: 27).

This particular vision of a 'learning society' proposes a population of flexible, adaptable, individuals making rational choices within a marketplace of learning opportunities, available across a range of formal and informal settings over the course of a lifespan. Guidance occupies a central place in this vision, enabling learners to plan their individual choices, furthering their own personal development at the same time as contributing to the efficiency of the organisation and the economy. As Killeen (1996: 18) has observed, 'Lifelong flexibility and lifelong education and training are creating the conditions for lifelong guidance'.

THE SUBJECT OF STUDY

The EDP which forms the subject of the research operates from a Centre which provides a guidance service and procures a range of open learning packages and tutor led courses. It is independently funded and separate from mainstream Company training. Its origins lie with the 'Gateways to Learning' programme introduced by the then Employment Department in 1992, aiming to,

> introduce the concept of careers guidance into the workplace and to raise the awareness of both employers and employees of the benefits of information, advice and guidance.
>
> (DfEE, 1996)

In order to gain matching funding for its first year of operation the EDP had to conform to the specification of a 'Gateways' service as defined by the Employment Department, which specified, among other things, that it should:

- provide impartial and realistic advice and guidance
- provide full and up to date information about education, training and work
- be responsive to individual needs.
  (Employment Department, 1991)

The number and range of learning opportunities available through the EDP has grown rapidly; in 1996, there were 150 tutor-led and open learning courses provided on-site. Participation is measured in hours of learning per month. In 1993 this figure stood at 200 hours. In October 1995, it had increased to 2000 hours, with approximately half spent on open learning and half on tutor-led courses.

The range of courses available on-site is biased towards work-related training, though some courses such as languages, literacy and computer skills can also be related to personal development objectives. Employees gain access to courses through a guidance interview at the Centre, during which they will review their own work histories, interests, prior experience of education and training, strengths and weaknesses and aspirations for future development. At the end of the interview they will complete a personal Action Plan. The aim of the interview is to achieve a match between an employee and one of the existing courses provided on-site. If this is not possible, individuals can be referred on to an outside guidance service, or a college, or they can consult the Training Access Point – a computer-based directory of educational and training courses – housed within the Centre.

Tuition fees are paid by the Company, but participants must bear the initial cost, only gaining a refund on successful completion of the course. In order to qualify for a refund the course must be approved by the Centre, and employees must gain approval from their departmental manager. Participation, both in the initial guidance interview and the learning opportunities, is entirely voluntary.

The Centre reports to a Steering Group chaired by the Director of Personnel, with a membership including representatives from a Trade Union, from the local Training and Enterprise Council and from local Guidance Services.

DISCUSSION

A number of factors come together in making the study of guidance practices in the workplace particularly significant at this time: the spread of adult learning, and therefore guidance, beyond the traditional institutional boundaries into the workplace; the perceived economic imperative for a flexible workforce; and the growing body of managerial and ethical codes of practice governing the activities of guidance workers. Taken together they represent a challenge to guidance professionals – how are they to operate within this new context? – and to the clients of guidance services – how should they behave in response to the offer of advice and guidance? The discussion will examine some of the tensions and ambiguities which emerge for each of these groups, focusing on the principles of client-centredness and impartiality, which have become central to certain understandings of guidance work. Impartiality emphasises the importance of prioritising the learning needs of the user over the interests of the provider; client centredness focuses on the quality of the guidance interaction in which clients are helped to discover, clarify, assess and understand their learning needs. They are principles which were encoded in the report 'The Challenge of Change' (UDACE, 1986), and have been repeated, and adapted, in a variety of more recent formulations (e.g. Rivis and Sadler, 1991; HEQC 1995).

The Centre acknowledges the ideal of client centredness in its publicity, and the guidance interviews follow a process of self assessment and action planning which appears to place the client at the centre. However, the aims and organisation of the scheme create tensions at the interface between the interests of the individual and the interests of the Company. This tension in turn impacts upon the guidance interview which, whilst striving to be an interactive and exploratory process, is under pressure to fulfil certain instrumental purposes.

The publicity leaflet, distributed to all members of staff, contains a 'Statement of Service' which illustrates this tension. Whilst it appears to put an emphasis on employee choice and personal development, suggesting a client-centred and impartial approach, it also signals that those opportunities most readily available to employees are in fact constrained, and that the individual needs which can be most readily accommodated are those which align with the company's commercial interests. It reads:

The service will help you:

- to become aware of what you would like to do and what you would be suited to do within the company
- to increase your knowledge of opportunities for learning and development which are available
- to be better able to plan and make realistic decisions about your future
- to prepare a plan to meet your needs and have an agreed record of the interview completed with the individual, which states educational or training opportunities to meet identified needs.

The first statement describes an apparently open-ended approach to self assessment and self awareness familiar in the educational or careers guidance fields, but then comes a significant constraint: 'within the company'. The boundaries around what is likely to be discussed at the guidance interview are immediately drawn. This constraint also influences how the second statement, dealing with opportunity awareness, is likely to be understood. While apparently suggesting a very wide catchment of opportunities for learning, the words 'which are available' takes on the meaning 'which are being made available by the company'. The planning and decision-making processes referred to in the third statement are again familiar aspects of educational and careers guidance, but the word 'realistic' raises questions such as 'realistic in what sense?' and 'realistic in whose terms?'. The final statement switches from describing outcomes for clients to outcomes for managers of the scheme, rather undermining the client-centred message. It specifies that the learning opportunities agreed on should be 'suitable'; begging the question 'suitable from whose point of view?'

Evidence from interviews with worker-participants and manager-providers confirms that choices of education and training opportunities are understood to be constrained by work-related priorities. One of the Centre staff summed the position up, 'They (the Company) see their investment in the workforce ultimately to the benefit of the company. That individuals can also benefit is a bonus for them.' The programme coordinator was clear about the main criteria for including courses in the programme, 'It has to reach the requirements of (the Company), it can't be basketweaving or anything like that, it has to be work-specific.'

The interests of the Company appear to dominate and displace the normative values and principles of guidance, as expressed in codes of practice, and in the Gateways criteria. Centre staff, whilst committed to the principles of client-centredness and impartiality, were acutely aware that the dominant criteria for success were the programme's ability to enhance productivity and profitability. Their primary aim was to place clients on one of the courses approved and funded by the Company, rather than conduct a wider examination of individual learning needs.

The ambiguity of the guidance practitioner's position rests on the tension between loyalty to the Company, which is paying their salary and funding the programme, and loyalty to the client, whose interests they are ethically bound to serve. This kind of tension is by no means unique to this context. For instance, research on the use of guidance in the Training For Work programme for unemployed adults in the UK in the mid 1990s noted the strength of the link between independence of funding, and impartiality of advice (Taylor and Killeen, 1995). Similarly, the tensions inherent in working within a further education institution which is competing for students, and providing impartial advice on the basis of client need, has been indicated by a number of studies (Chapman 1990; Connelly et al., 1996; Payne and Edwards, 1996).

Employees themselves were well aware of the organisational culture they were operating in, and their understandings had a significant effect on how they approached the guidance interview. The programme coordinator noted that general diagnostic questions about strengths and weaknesses, skills and abilities, tended to be interpreted as pertaining to work, 'I think because we're work oriented people tend to go straight into that. For example, I had a Team Leader this afternoon who said "I'm a good communicator, I've got good organisational skills", obviously building on the fact that he was a Team Leader'. Shared understandings about the aims of the programme and its location within the Company meant that participants sometimes felt the need 'to engage simultaneously in impression management and self disclosure', a phrase used by Kidd (1996: 147) to describe an effect of career interventions in the workplace. In other words, what the client is prepared to discuss in this situation is conditioned by an understanding that impartiality and client-centredness cannot be guaranteed.

Centre staff actively encouraged employees to draw on a wider range of experience, but given the shared understanding of available outcomes it is perhaps not surprising that this was not always taken up. Whilst this had the effect of restricting the potential of the guidance interview, it did streamline the process, with would-be participants having already decided what they wanted to do:

> When we first started people were very unsure about why the company was doing this . . . Now, those that come are motivated to learn already, and are aware of what (the scheme) is trying to do. They've heard about a course so the action planning process is quite straight forward. They know what they want to do, we've got the course, so its just a case of match these two together and off you go.
>
> (Centre Coordinator)

Most participants valued the guidance interview, not for the guidance itself but as a necessary step in gaining access to a desired course. The understanding which had developed was of a scheme which provided courses, not one which provided guidance.

A further indication of the tensions and ambiguities surrounding the aims of the scheme is the attention given to containing expectations at the initial interview. As one member of Centre staff saw it, the function of the interview was to introduce a note of 'realism' into employee expectations:

> What we provide is not specific to their job and it will not necessarily gain them a promotion or help them in that way. We need to get away from that at the start so that they don't get any false hopes.

However, this message is tempered by the admission that participation in the programme: 'is a sign of commitment, and if they (participants) were to go for an internal vacancy, its something that is worth mentioning in their application.'

Several employees had indeed gained promotions and linked them specifically to the learning they had done through the Centre. A production line worker of 16 years, who had been promoted to Supervisor the same week as the interview, commented:

> With the NEBS course there was no sense that if I do this course I've got a chance of becoming a Supervisor, although that did turn out to be the case. I suppose that was in the back of my mind that it might help at some time to give me a step up the ladder.

Dealing with ambiguities surrounding the aims of the programme and establishing 'realistic' expectations had become the most important function of the guidance interview. The possibilities for a more client-centred exploration of learning needs and developmental possibilities had been marginalised, if not entirely excluded.

Employees had their own adaptive strategies, using the programme for their own individual purposes. Most described a mixture of personal and career related motives for studying. Courses in computer skills and languages lent themselves particularly well to this dual purpose. When asked whether she was studying for work related or personal reasons a participant on a computer course stated, 'The two sort of linked together, because I do a lot of computer work so I was interested in something which would help me at work, but would also be good for me if I ever leave and go elsewhere.' Some were more interested in greater job flexibility which would allow them to continue working, either for the Company or outside it. A forklift truck driver had this sort of progression in mind, 'They use computers in the office now, so if ever I was to get pregnant they could move me into there. My brother's got a business as well so I could help him out doing that.' Others were able to turn what were essentially work-related courses to their own purposes. A shop floor worker who did not use a computer as part of his work defined his interest in the course in purely personal terms, 'It's for myself, it's not for the Certificate. I've got young children and it's not long before they'll want their own computers, so it may help me not to look so stupid.'

In most cases employees accepted the scheme for what it was: a limited menu of learning opportunities geared to the needs of the Company, but offering the potential for personal development. Their reasons for involvement were modest and pragmatic, contrasting with the more visionary rhetoric of lifelong learning (CBI, 1994; DfEE, 1995; RSA, 1995) which has been incorporated into the rationale for EDPs.

An important question for guidance practitioners in assessing their own roles is 'whose interests does guidance serve?' a question identified by Hawthorn as crucial in the definition of standards in guidance work.

> much education-based guidance is carried out within institutions which may have some form of a vested interest in the outcomes of the client's decision. This question of who benefits from the outcomes is a key one in the definition of standards.
>
> (Hawthorn, 1995: 35)

The literature of the 'learning organisation' and the 'learning society' suggests mutual benefit; an ideal arrangement in which there are only winners. Certainly within this programme, outcomes for some participating employees were impressive, with evidence of entry and progression by individuals who had little or no experience of education and training since leaving school.

> Well I've always been quite good at learning, its just that being away from school for such a long time I thought that perhaps it wouldn't come as quickly, and as you get older you think 'I can't do it'. But I feel with this as though I'll carry on.

> I just want to learn now. I didn't want to learn at school but I want to learn now . . . its a bit late, but you know.

For these people, often constrained by work and family commitments, the programme represented their only opportunity to engage in learning, 'I've got (the Company) to thank because there's no other way I could go to university with three kids. They're paying me a good wage for sending me through university so I can't complain.'

Outcomes for the Company included a training programme benefiting from substantial public funding, which directly contributed towards a more highly skilled and motivated workforce, taking place in employees' own time. As a member of the Centre staff commented, this represented extremely cheap training. By blurring the boundary between technical, work-related training, and learning for personal development the Company had been able to gain the benefits of both. Some of the responsibility for work-related training and development had been devolved to employees, encouraging them to make their own learning choices and set aside their own time to pursue them. This is consistent with those constructions of the worker as autonomous and self-reliant contained in the literature on lifelong learning. But as Keep (1997) points out, it is ultimately the company which will decide which skills it will choose to deploy, and it is unlikely that employees will be able to anticipate company policy, which will itself be subject to fluctuations in local and global markets. In conditions of economic insecurity, shifting the responsibility for decisions about skills training can be represented as a management strategy, a non-repressive form of power, a 'normalising' device designed to manufacture consent by gaining the commitment and loyalty of workers to particular conditions and labour processes (Sakolosky, 1992). Benefits to the Company might then be seen as far more than the accumulation of relevant skills in the workforce, as the processes of guidance and learning become intertwined with the processes of management and employees learn self-management and self-regulation.

CONCLUSIONS

Universal principles of guidance can act as a useful yardstick with which to assess and locate particular examples of practice, but are less useful when attempts are made to simply 'apply' them to any situation where guidance is taking place. For guidance practitioners, ethical practice becomes increasingly problematic as the contexts in which they work become more diverse, involving a more complex interplay between the interests of a range of stakeholders. The case study presented here is illustrative of the difficulties of practicing as an impartial intermediary when the practitioners themselves are enmeshed in the web of stakeholder interests. It also serves to question some of the assumptions often made about the expectations of the users of guidance services. Participants in the programme could not be characterised as those autonomous individuals making free choices across the whole range of education and training opportunities envisaged by either UDACE or the CBI. They were not presenting themselves as subjects for the idealised practice of guidance. They were operating pragmatically and opportunistically, aware of the possibilities and limitations of the programme, and of the guidance being offered.

Practising ethically in these circumstances becomes more complex and nuanced than lists of activities or codes of practice might suggest. Client-centredness might be interpreted here as greater transparency, and perhaps modesty, about the services which are on offer; an openness about the constraints on principles such as impartiality and confidentiality, and an understanding of how the practices of guidance can be implicated in the exercise of power. This process of 'working through' (Carroll, 1996: 152) the implications of ethical codes in particular contexts, of maintaining a reflexive awareness of the operation of values (their own and others), of balancing competing stakeholder interests, become ever more central and more challenging tasks for guidance practitioners as the circumstances in which they operate become more complex and diverse.

BIBLIOGRAPHY

Argyris, C. and Schon, D. (1978) *Organisational Learning: A Theory of Action Perspective*, Reading, Mass.: Addison Wesley.

Carroll, M. (1996) *Workplace Counselling*, London: Sage.

Chapman, L. (1990) 'Role conflict and role diffusion: The counsellor in further education', in Corbett, J. (ed.) *Uneasy Transitions,* London: Falmer Press.

Confederation of British Industry (1994) *Flexible Labour Markets: Who Pays for Training?* London: CBI.

Connelly, G., Milburn, T. and Thomson, S. (1996) *Impartiality in Guidance Provision for Adults: A Scottish Study*, Milton Keynes: University of Strathclyde/The Open University.

Corney, M. (1995) *Employee Development Programmes. Current Practice and New Directions.* London. National Commission on Education Briefing, New Series 2.

Department for Education and Employment (1995) *Lifetime Learning: a Consultation Document*, London: HMSO.

Department for Education and Employment (1996) *Adult Guidance and Major Employers. The Gateways to Learning Projects*, London: DfEE.

Dixon, N. (1994) *The Organisational Learning Cycle*, London: McGraw-Hill.

Employment Department (1991) *Gateways to Learning*, Sheffield: Employment Department.

Forrester, K., Payne, J. and Ward, K. (1995) *Workplace Learning: Perspectives on education, training and work*, Aldershot: Avebury.

Harrison, R. (1997) *Guidance in Context: the role of guidance in an Employee Development Programme*, Milton Keynes: The Open University.

Hawthorn, R. (1995) *First Steps: A Quality Standards Framework for guidance across all sectors,* London: RSA.

Higher Education Quality Council (1995) *A quality assurance framework for guidance and learner support in higher education: the guidelines,* London: HEQC.

Keep, E. (1997) ' "There's no such thing as society . . .": some problems with an individual approach to creating a Learning Society' in *Journal of Educational Policy*, Vol 12, No 6, 457–71.

Kidd, J. (1996) 'Career planning within work organisations', in Watts, A., Law, B., Killeen, J., Kidd, J. and Hawthorn, R. *Rethinking Careers Education and Guidance: Theory, Policy and Practice*, London: Routledge.

Killeen, J. (1996) 'The social context of guidance', in Watts, A., Law, B., Kidd, J., Killeen, J. and Hawthorn, R. *Rethinking Careers Education and Guidance: Theory, Policy and Practice.* London: Routledge.

Metcalf, H. (1992) *Releasing Potential: Company Initiatives to Develop People at Work. Vol 1: The Main Report*, London: Policy Studies Institute.

Payne, J. (1996) 'Who really benefits from employee development schemes?' in Raggatt, P., Edwards, R. and Small, N. (eds) *The Learning Society: challenges and trends*, London: Routledge.

Payne, J. and Edwards, R. (1996) *Impartiality and the Self in Guidance: A Report on Three London Colleges*, Milton Keynes: NAEGA/CEPAM, The Open University.

Pedler, M., Burgoyne, J. and Boydell, T. (1991) *The Learning Company: A Strategy for Sustainable Development*, London: McGraw-Hill.

Rivis, V. and Sadler, J. (1991) *The Quest for Quality in Educational Guidance for Adults*, Leicester: NIACE.

Royal Society of Arts (1995) *Tomorrow's Company*, London: RSA.

Sakolosky, R. (1992) 'Disciplinary Power and the Labour Process' in Sturdy, A., Knights, D. and Willmott, H. (eds) *Skills and Consent: Studies in the Labour Process*, London: Routledge.

Taylor, P. and Killeen, J. (1995) *Assessment and Guidance in Training for Work: Evaluation of Initial Assessment and Guidance on Entry*, London: Policy Studies Institute.

Unit for the Development of Adult and Continuing Education (1986) *The Challenge of Change: Developing Educational Guidance for Adults*, Leicester: NIACE.

Author index

Subject index